One Teacher in 10

One Teacher in 10

LGBT Educators Share Their Stories

Second Edition

Edited by
Kevin Jennings

alyson books
los angeles

MANUFACTURED IN THE UNITED STATES OF AMERICA.

THIS TRADE PAPERBACK IS PUBLISHED BY ALYSON PUBLICATIONS,
P.O. BOX 4371, LOS ANGELES, CALIFORNIA 90078-4371.
DISTRIBUTION IN THE UNITED KINGDOM BY TURNAROUND PUBLISHER SERVICES LTD.,
UNIT 3, OLYMPIA TRADING ESTATE, COBURG ROAD, WOOD GREEN,
LONDON N22 6TZ ENGLAND.

FIRST EDITION: MAY 1983
SECOND EDITION: MARCH 2005

05 06 07 08 09 a 10 9 8 7 6 5 4 3 2 1

ISBN 1-55583-869-3

LIBRARY OF CONGRESS CATALOGING-IN-PUBLICATION DATA
ONE TEACHER IN 10 : LGBT EDUCATORS SHARE THEIR STORIES / EDITED BY KEVIN JENNINGS.—2ND ED.
    ISBN 1-55583-869-3
      1. GAY TEACHERS—UNITED STATES—BIOGRAPHY. 2. LESBIAN TEACHERS—UNITED STATES—BIOGRAPHY.
I. TITLE: ONE TEACHER IN TEN. II. JENNINGS, KEVIN, 1963–
LB2844.1.G39O64 2005
371.1'0086'64—DC22   2004062685

CREDITS
COVER PHOTOGRAPHY BY ANDY SACKS/PHOTOGRAPHER'S CHOICE/GETTY IMAGES.
COVER DESIGN BY MATT SAMS.

For Jeff,
who has been there every step of the way
for the past 10 years

Contents

Part Two
Lessons Taught...and Learned

Part Three
May–September

Part Four
Change Agent

Acknowledgments

I'd first like to thank Angela Brown of Alyson Publications, who reached out to me with the idea of doing a new collection of stories by LGBT educators on the 10th anniversary of the publication of *One Teacher in 10* by Alyson in 1994. It has been fascinating to see how times have changed, and I thank Angela and Alyson for giving me the opportunity to do this work again.

Numerous individuals and organizations helped with outreach for this collection, but one deserves special thanks: Jamison Green, through his personal arm-twisting, made sure that this anthology included the voices of transgender educators. For the second book in a row, Jamison, you have come through. Thank you!

More than anyone else, my assistant Tim Pappalardo deserves the credit for this book seeing the light of day. He has stayed on top of innumerable details, tracking the progress of the various edits of the different stories, proofing my illegible handwriting and incomprehensible two-finger typing, and generally just cheering me on when I felt like this would never get done. Thanks, Tim, you are a star.

In many ways, the changes documented in this collection are due at least in part to the work of GLSEN, the Gay, Lesbian, and Straight Education Network. I have been privileged to work with an extraordinarily dedicated group of staff, Board members, and volunteers at GLSEN for the past decade: I could never, ever say thank you enough to them for all of they have done, nor could I ever adequately express my gratitude to the extraordinarily generous individuals whose financial support has made this work possible. I want to specially thank our board president, Christie Vianson, for her leadership and support, and my deputy executive director, Eliza Byard, for whom I give thanks every day. I could not have two finer partners in leading this organization. I hope everyone associated with GLSEN is as proud as I am of what we have accomplished together.

Finally, I want to thank those who contributed their stories to this collection, especially to Judee King, who lost her battle with breast cancer shortly after submitting her story in 2004. I could never thank them enough for their bravery, their patience with the editing process, and most of all their willingness to put themselves on the firing line in defense of their students and the ideals of "liberty and justice for all" that we make students pledge allegiance to every day in our schools. We're not finished, but we're getting there.

Preface

What a difference a decade makes.

When I edited *One Teacher in 10* in 1994 it was a profoundly different time. Only two states (Massachusetts and Wisconsin) banned discrimination and harassment based on sexual orientation in their schools. There were probably fewer than 50 gay-straight student alliance clubs in the nation. Educational organizations generally wouldn't acknowledge the existence of lesbian, gay, bisexual, and transgender (LGBT) people or their concerns in schools, and LGBT organizations didn't make schools or young people much of a priority.

In this climate, most LGBT teachers adhered to the "don't ask, don't tell" policy, which governed our professional lives long before Clinton proposed it for the military. Finding enough teachers to fill a collection was a challenge. Many chose to use pseudonyms as they were too afraid to be known as LGBT in their schools or communities. While many stories in *One Teacher* did have "happy endings," those were often won at the price of considerable struggle.

Ten years later, the world has changed. A movement to make sure our schools are safe and effective educational environments for all students, staff, and families—regardless of sexual orientation or gender identity—has grown explosively throughout the United States. Today eight states (California, Connecticut, Massachusetts, Minnesota, New Jersey, Vermont, Washington, and Wisconsin) ban discrimination and harassment based on sexual orientation or gender identity in their schools. Over 2,000 gay-straight student alliance clubs are now registered with GLSEN, with at least one in every state in the nation.

Not that everything in 2004 is "all better." The 2003–2004 GLSEN National School Climate Survey found that four out of five LGBT high school students routinely experiences verbal, physical, or sexual harassment at school. But the education world is increasingly aware of this fact and more and more willing to take responsibility for doing something about it.

It is thus unsurprising that this second edition should be a very different book than the first edition was. First off, there was no problem in finding enough submissions this time: Over 100 people submitted stories, and the selection process was extraordinarily difficult due to the high quality of the submissions. The diversity of this collection is also far greater than its predecessor; there are many more voices from people of color and transgender educators.

But most of all, it is the tone of the stories that marks the greatest change. It is still not easy to be an LGBT educator, but a general sense of hope pervades the stories of this book. There are certainly still tales of struggle, but on the whole more LGBT teachers are able to be open and honest about their identities in the same way that non-LGBT teachers routinely are. There are many more "happy endings" this time around.

When I reflect on the reason for this change, one jumps out at me: the attitudes of the students themselves. While editing the collection I was struck by the number of stories in which students themselves were pushing LGBT educators to do more, in which LGBT educators were surprised to find how accepting their students were, in which the "gay thing" turned out to be much less of a big deal than the teachers had expected.

With such a diverse array of stories, it's a challenge to organize them in a way that makes sense. In an effort to help the reader navigate the many stories included herein, I have divided the stories into four major groupings:

Come Out, Come Out, Wherever You Are. While "coming out" is a feature of many of these stories, in this section it's the central theme. A diversity of individuals and settings are represented so that the reader can readily contrast educator experiences with this rite of passage.

Lessons Taught...and Learned. Many educators found themselves both teaching profound lessons to their students and, in many cases, learning such lessons from them. The stories in this section document these journeys.

May to September. Contributors were in all different stages of their careers, from rookies to retirees. The contrasting perspectives of "newbies" versus "old hands" makes for interesting reading!

Change Agents. Oftentimes contributors found themselves in leadership roles where they were leading a process of change in their schools, communities, or districts. How they found themselves in these roles and what they experienced is enlightening.

The level of dedication and professionalism among these contributors is stunning. Their commitment to the education and the lives of the students they serve shines through every story like a beacon.

No one goes into teaching for the money. In 2001 the average first-year teacher earned a salary of just under $29,000. This placed them well below the typical 2001 college graduate, who earned a first-year salary of $42,712—nearly 50% more than a first-year teacher. Add on to the low pay the struggle any LGBT person faces in a profession where homophobia is still pervasive, and you have a sense of the sacrifices the contributors to this book make daily to serve the needs of their students. In the end, people go into teaching because they want to help young people. And the contributors in *One Teacher in 10* are some of the most outstanding examples of that kind of dedication I have ever seen in our profession. Their students are lucky to have them, and it has been my privilege to work with them on this collection.

—Kevin Jennings, founder and executive director of the
Gay, Lesbian, and Straight Education Network

Prologue

CONVERSATIONS WITH JESUS
Steve Trujillo
English teacher
Skyline High School
Oakland, California

"Porque es usted un joto, Señor Trujillo?"

The words caused me a moment of discomfort, moving me from frenetic first-period preparations to freeze-frame. But only for a moment. This time. How many times would I have to deal with this question?

Jesus wanted absolution. He absolutely had to know why I was a fag. As the teacher of his U.S. history class, I was a history-making event in his eyes.

"I never had a gay teacher before."

The classroom was still mostly empty, and there were a few more minutes left before the opening of another day in 1988 at Alisal High School in Salinas, California. Before me stood Jesus, one of 35 juniors with a strong desire to learn about his newly adopted home and those people of significance in it.

Another Jesus was with me. This one I consulted daily. I was in conference with him now, while I stood with my student Jesus, formulating an answer that was both honest and measured within the school district policy.

"Jesus, I know that you have many questions about why I am the way I am," I began.

As I spoke, I thought of the day I came out to my coworkers at a faculty meeting. Our administrators had decided to do a day of sensitivity training at our campus, and they'd invited a team of people to our all-day in-service to help improve faculty-administrator-student-parent relationships. Each one of us was asked to take a risk and share something personal with the staff at lunch. *OK,* I thought. *Be brave.* It was 1978, and voters had recently defeated the Briggs initiative, which would have banned gays from teaching in California. Surely Salinas was not the *most* redneck rodeo town west of the Sierras, was it? Surely we had moved forward since the John Steinbeck era...

"Jesus, I know this is confusing for you. You were raised as a good Catholic boy, like me. I knew I was gay in high school, but I couldn't talk to anybody about it. Now I can be myself, and I can talk to students who are not sure what they are or who want to know why I am the way I am. I didn't choose this way—it chose me. If you trust me as your teacher, then you know I'm the same person you knew me to be before you knew I was gay."

Which Jesus was I talking to? Maybe both.

I was the one seeking absolution this time. I remembered the day I told my coworkers my big secret. I was hoping that Jesus was listening that day as well. I needed him to hear me.

"I've wanted to share this with you for some time," I began. "I have worked here for a few years now, and most of you know who I am and what I do here. Many of you have encouraged me, and some of you have noted that I attend all evening school functions alone. You don't see any family pictures on my desk. The reason for all that would make for a rather long movie, so I will give you just the part that might appear in the trailer of coming attractions: I am gay."

I never imagined that school cafeteria could get that quiet with more than 100 live bodies in it. It appeared much like the farmworker mural on the wall: Suspended animation. Suspension of disbelief. Suspense of anticipation.

Then, one by one, each of the staff slowly stood up and applauded. I felt as if I was being held up by an invisible presence. I felt hot, dry-mouthed, and dizzy.

Was Jesus speaking to me? Any Jesus?

After that watershed day, I knew I could talk with Jesus, Jose, Maria, or any of my students about who I am. I knew that I had moral support from different places. Maybe even places I had never seen. Places I had only heard about in Sunday school as a kid.

I was able to get my student Jesus to allow me to continue our conversation at lunch that day. Without getting graphic, or too personal, I was able to help him understand why I was a "*joto*." But I made sure windows and doors were open, for all to see and hear. My welcome mat, so to speak, was always out. Just like me.

Jesus later joined our MECHA club (which stands for Movimiento Estudiantil Chicano de Aztlan). He told me he felt at ease with me.

I hope beyond hope that any and all Jesuses will always feel the same.

Part One

Come Out, Come Out,
Wherever You Are

A GOOD DAY

Joel M. Freedman
English language arts and dramatic arts teacher
King/Drew Magnet High School of Medicine and Science
South Central Los Angeles, California

This being as good a day as any to die, the little man in my head is already on heightened alert. But first there is the phone call.

"Hey, Joel." It's Judd, the former tax auditor turned teacher. It's 7:30. I only just got in the door.

"Yeah, Judd?"

"D'you get a load of what's goin' on outside?"

I had seen dense L.A. traffic coming in, a dead dog in the dirt, the brownish dinge in the sky. "No, Judd. What're you talking about?"

"There's all these parents leafleting."

"Huh? Why?" There are no pedestrians outside our school or the state-of-the-art trauma and gunshot wound wards of the King/Drew Medical Center.

"I got one of their flyers right here. They're sayin' there's an emergency meeting tonight."

"There's no emergency. It's the regular Parent Advisory Council (PAC) meeting."

He sends the flyer down to my room. Sure enough: "Emergency meeting tonight." "Our children's future is at stake." "Our sons' and daughters' education is in jeopardy." Among other assorted cryptic nonsense.

My banana from breakfast begins its own leafleting of my stomach.

Just yesterday, I'd been e-requested by our Parent Advisory Council president to address the parents at tonight's monthly meeting. I wasn't informed why. It was just last month, dusty September, when I gave my annual spiel. This is dusty October.

I have the distinction of holding the position of Title IX Coordinator. Title IX, of course, is concerned with equity for men and women in schools. Being a magnet high school without a ball field of any sort, presumably, students—actually, their parents—elect to attend our school in pursuit of science, math, and our school-to-work program with the hospital. Our staff is five-to-one women to men; gender equity is not our major diversity issue. I, therefore, deem my responsibility to provide dignity and safety for all students, sexual minorities included, and their right to a hate-free, intimidation-free, harassment-free, and a free-access-to-relevant-information education.

A former actor who maintains his propensity for drama, I take my titular roles seriously. Recently, I had broadcast throughout the school the approaching Models of Pride event, a daylong conference for gay, lesbian, bisexual, transgender, and questioning youth held at Occidental College. "See Mr. Freedman for details." There's usually one parent who expresses the desire that his or her child not have to hear of such goings-on.

Homo announcements? Irate leafleting parents? Calls to arms? Coincidence? I don't think so. Neither does my principal. This is not simply a disconcerted parent on the phone. And there's only one day—a full schedule of classes and three hours, to be exact—to circle the wagons and get the cavalry in.

I start by recruiting all the colleagues I can to attend tonight's meeting and be a visible show of support. I'm asking a lot. "Stay in school till 6 o'clock for the meeting. Then stay longer."

As per instructions from the PAC president, I will be addressing the parents at this meeting. I still have no idea what I am expected to say, and I'm afraid to ask.

If we've got trouble, I shouldn't be surprised. My principal shouldn't be miffed. I'm an out gay teacher, the only one in our school (the only one out, that is); so I must be looking for trouble. Looking or not, it looks like trouble found me.

The decision to return to education at the age of 45 was made while standing on the porch of a thatched-roofed hut on stilts extended out over the South China Sea, facing Venus and the dawn sun. I simply did not want to return to L.A. and work the equivalent of three jobs for miserable pay just so I could continue to slave at my art. I was fed up. I figured I'd do something relatively easy, enjoyable, and rewarding, a job with normal work hours and appropriate pay. I'd go back to teach. That would fix everything.
What a jerk.
The overwhelming challenges of teaching notwithstanding, I knew what I was doing. I had taught all my life: swimming; reading; camp counseloring; student teaching in college; substitute teaching upon graduating with a lifetime teaching certification in Massachusetts; landing a permanent sub position, even; speakers bureau for the AIDS Coalition to Unleash Power (ACT UP); discussing anti-AIDS activism with college students and community groups.
However, at age 22, it was a breeze walking away from education to pursue theater. It was Boston, 1975, and I parted easily from a bureaucracy where the school librarian informed me that a library is not a classroom. I was witness to the frequent police activity that facilitated the busing of students from their local neighborhoods to distant places to satisfy Supreme Court demands for racial integration of public schools. The people needed armed military protection from one another, and I had to maintain tallies of how many students in each class were white, black, white Latino, black Latino, and "other."
"Tyrone Jones."
"Here." He sees I'm counting. "I'm black."
And the little man in my head is screaming, "Are you sure? How

do I know you're telling me the truth and not simply saying what you think I want to hear? How mortifying *is* this?"

I walked away before I figured out how I was going to manage being gay and a teacher. I migrated home to New York City to pursue a career in theater.

Fast-forward 23 years, and my husband of 13 years and I are returning home to L.A. from a half-year trip around the globe so that I might reenter the world of academia.

What is remarkable about my coming out in our high school is that it was unremarkable. After my first year of teaching, endeavoring to make myself indispensable, I approached my principal and told him that I was a gay teacher who considered personal disclosure an educational option. (Don't ask me how long I rehearsed that one.)

I gaped, amazed, as my principal acknowledged he had worked with many homosexual people in education. I feigned flabbergast to find that we probably have a number of students who might be gay. But what did I plan to do? Announce it to the whole school?

I honestly had no idea how I would inform students of my sexual orientation. Truthfully, it didn't seem appropriate. Certainly it has nothing to do with my job…except that, closeted, I'm working in an atmosphere much less dignified than that of my straight colleagues. Except that, without my husband and a life outside of school, I am bloodless flesh and bone to my students. Except that, if I'm closeted, my gay students have no role model, no validation of their very existence or recognition of shared experience, no adult to talk to when they have boy or girl troubles or problems at home, no place to go where they are certain they won't be negatively judged. Except that gay and lesbian family members and friends of my students are otherwise not represented or appreciated in the microcosm that is the public school.

Being out has nothing to do with my work except that, were I to be outed as gay, my prior silence would be interpreted as shame, fear, or both.

Until this discussion with my principal, I had lied to my students by omission. "No, I am not single." "I have family in San Francisco." "I'm not playing in the student-teacher basketball game due to a condition."

I'm not a very good liar. I write that not from pride; it's not due to any lack of trying. I write that because my authority in the classroom was being undermined by my vagaries. I needed to come up with a good truth, and soon.

To my principal's credit, he agreed. Dr. Ernie Roy also gave me what I think he believed to be Herculean tasks to perform first. One, come out to colleagues. Done; like, from the first day; after all, I'm from New York, I'm an atheist Jew, a leftish theatrical type, kinetic, opinionated, *and* verbose, you do the math. Two, get to know useful people in the district. An ongoing process since Day 1. Three, ingratiate myself with the parents and volunteers of the PAC. Already happening. And, four, do an in-service with teachers and staff on campus.

As a developing instructor going up before my coteachers, I set out to gather the blandest speakers I could find and sacrifice them in the least creative, least stimulating format: the one-hour panel discussion. The little man in my head was hollering, "What is wrong with you? I never agreed to a suicide pact."

Expertly proffering vital information, first-hand tales of challenges, victories, and loss, were representatives of Lambda Legal Defense; Parents, Families, and Friends of Lesbians and Gays; and the director of intergroup relations for the Los Angeles Unified School District (LAUSD). My normally comatose-at-in-services colleagues were conscious and kind to our guests. Dr. Roy even cracked a smile when I gave vent to the little man in my head by finding justification to speak the words "Damn you, Ernie."

I began coming out to students with a lesson on the impact of words, particularly epithets, created by Beverly Hills teacher Marla Weiss and published in a book of lesson plans I purchased through GLSEN-L.A. One student, daughter to the PAC vice president, stormed out of my class. Our newly appointed principal, J. Michelle Woods (a young former VP and protégé to Dr. Roy, who groomed her for the job knowing he was losing his life to cancer), requested that I inform parents in advance of such "controversial" lessons. I wasn't happy about it, but I decided I could do that and suffer that small indignity. I also suffered a one-hour-plus phone conversation with the PAC VP mom of the storming student. Her Christian beliefs permitted her—despite herself—to allow for our differences and to recognize that, by some fluke of nature, politics, and TV programming, I had sound ethics, political correctness, law, and *Will & Grace* on my side. The daughter has since graduated, but the mom still e-mails me and greets me like an old friend.

Other results of my coming out: My husband's photo sits prominently on my desk; it seems that every one of my school's 1,643 students knows me; now and then a student will peer into my room and flee without a word; despite my being in-your-face confrontational, I still hear "shut up," "nigga," "stupid," and profanity in our classroom, but never "faggot," "dyke," or "that's so gay"; a student—or two, on occasion—will demonstrably, physically distance himself from me as if I were contagious; a sub was immediately removed from a class and banned from our school after publicly addressing one of our gay students with "What, are you gay or something?"; a parent joined me for a performance of my husband's improv and sketch comedy group, *The Gay Mafia*; books from my classroom library, many with titles that reference gay themes or information, fly from the shelves; students talk to me, some come out to me; teachers talk to me, some come out to me; my room is constantly filled with children. These are all opportunities—those elusive, enriching "teachable moments."

It gets tiresome confronting everything. On good days I respond with patience, understanding, and clarity. On less-than-good days I go Bronx on their heads. I teach in a school with a near total minority student body. Our students usually know firsthand the isolation due to stereotyping and the dehumanizing effects of discrimination. They understand when they are dignified with respect and a response.

I don't say it's been easy. When asked, I recommend to closeted teachers they cease considering coming out. From my experience, I'm going broke on antacids and aspirin. But, if the horror stories I've heard are any indication, I've been extremely lucky—until today.

Today, all day long, I teach on autopilot. "Yes, whatever I just said."

Teachers, if you prepare well for class and have a little man (or woman) in your head, you don't have to think about what you're doing or what you're saying. You can conduct your lesson while simultaneously planning for your retirement, figuring out the meaning of life, or rehearsing what you are going to say to the villagers when they arrive at the schoolhouse door waving pitchforks and flaming torches.

Immediately upon classes ending, I meet with my principal and a vice principal. We strategize how we will handle the vitriolic tirades of homophobic parents. We are basically on our own. The director of intergroup relations for our school district was appropriately sympathetic, though regrettably unavailable to attend our meeting; he cried audibly to me at his inability to reschedule the detailing of his SUV. My contact at LAUSD's celebrated Project 10, also unable to attend, fortified me by insisting I had legal might and moral right on my side, then promised to light a candle on my behalf.

And so…into the meeting.

The PAC monthly meeting, traditionally lightly attended, has managed on this night to pack the lecture hall. There is a cadre of more than one dozen of my colleagues present. My informant, Judd, the former tax auditor turned teacher, is not one of them. He's comfortable being the harbinger of bad news but doesn't have the guts to stick it out.

Some people stand up, move around, say things. None of it registers with me. The little man in my head is howling, "Get me out of here."

And, then, "Mr. Freedman, if you please." *That* I hear just as the little man in my head clams up.

I rise. My upper lip's the size of a walnut. With the sharpest canines in all humanity, I had repeatedly chomped down on it during lunch. I still don't know what I'm expected to say. I'd been looking for a sign all day to no avail.

I mechanically go into my spiel, the same one I gave a month ago. "We here at King/Drew are committed...blah, blah, blah...regardless of race, religion, ethnicity, gender, sexual orientation, abilities either physical or mental, real or perceived...blah, blah, blah...blah, blah, blah, blah, blah...any questions?"

A hand goes up. Here it comes. The little man in my head is howling, "No-o-o."

"Yes?"

"How do we go about getting rid of a teacher?" And, of course, she's looking straight at me. The little whimpering man in my head quakes as he attempts to hide.

Huh? Uh. I don't know. Catch me in a sting operation? Offer me any job with respectable pay and reasonable hours? Explain to me the Amway Opportunity? Tell me "Shoo, go away"?

"There is a certain protocol..." This is my principal Mrs. Woods stepping in.

But the lady's not done. "He's failing my daughter. He's throwing chairs in the classroom. How does he do his grading? I really don't know."

Intrepid Mrs. Woods again: "This is a matter for private discussion. We have a rule whereby we don't speak of individual concerns in this public forum..."

Wait a second. This isn't about me.

"No, you hold on," someone else pipes in, "we've been trying to get rid of this guy for two years—"

Another lady has found her courage, "He's ruined my child's chances of going to a decent college."

There is cacophony of voices concurring and personalizing their concerns.

This is not about me. This is about Judd—the former tax auditor turned teacher.

"Joel. Get over here," mentor teacher Yvonne is hissing at me. "Sit your fool ass down."

I make like a Slinky going down stairs by pouring myself into my chair as all hell breaks loose. I leave Mrs. Woods to the lions. I am gloriously uninvolved.

Uninvolved, yet I get to continue to introduce students to the work of some of my gay and lesbian brothers and sisters: Sor Juana Inés de la Cruz, Walt Whitman, Emily Dickinson, Claude McKay, Langston Hughes, Countee Cullen, Hart Crane, Thornton Wilder, Aaron Copland, Samuel Barber, Willa Cather, W.H. Auden, Tennessee Williams, James Baldwin, Adrienne Rich, Anne Sexton, Lorraine Hansberry, Edward Albee, Audre Lorde, Alice Walker, Samuel Delaney, Robert Patrick, Richard Rodriguez, Jacqueline Woodson, Essex Hemphill, to name a few. I hesitate, at times, to mention their sexual orientation in class ("You say that about everybody, Mr. Freedman,") and sometimes I don't, for fear of appearing biased.

Five years teaching some of the finest and funniest youngsters in the nation. Five years learning from some of the most talented educators in the country. Fifty years of age. Eighteen years in love. Extraordinary good fortune and good health—I'd say it's a good day to be gay.

IF ELLEN CAN DO IT, SO CAN I

Patricia A. Nicolari
Health and PE teacher, administrator for alternative education
Ansonia High School
Ansonia, Connecticut

It was April of 1997 when Ellen DeGeneres came out on TV. There I was, at a New Haven restaurant, surrounded by other like-minded individuals who were equally thrilled about watching Ellen's brave step, when a photographer from the *New Haven Register* announced her presence. She was covering the *Ellen* episode and would be taking pictures; she would respect our wishes, however, if we didn't want to be photographed. One by one people stepped forward in fear, pleading to her to remember their face and not take their picture. These people included doctors, lawyers, and teachers. I sat back and silently observed.

After 15 years of teaching at Ansonia High School, the high school I had also attended as a student in the 1970s, I was exhausted by the energy it took to hide my sexual orientation. I was tired of pretending to be someone else, tired of dodging cameras, tired of not answering uncomfortable questions from teachers and students, and tired of losing respect for myself. So I decided to come out. I wasn't sure how or when this would happen, but I knew I was ready to let go of the fear and energy it took to hide. I saw the fear in those people the night of the *Ellen* episode and I knew I could not continue my teaching career in fear. I just wanted to teach.

In September of 1996 I requested a fireside chat with my

boss. Although it was her first year as principal, I needed to share with her that I was gay. I wasn't asking her permission to come out—I was simply wondering if I had her support, and it turned out I did. Like many others she suspected I was gay but had never hinted at such.

It felt reassuring to know the principal was in my corner. Of course I didn't know at that time how I would come out, but I knew if it felt right, I was ready.

In hindsight, I knew I was getting my ducks in a row and testing the waters. How safe was my school environment? Who would be my support system? When the topic of homosexuality came up in my classroom, I stopped discouraging discussion. If a student called someone a fag or a dyke, I addressed it—something I'd been afraid to do when I was in the classroom closet.

For 15 years as an "in" teacher, I lived in fear of being "found out." I lived with this silent, "less than" feeling. Occasionally situations would occur that would magnify this feeling. One afternoon I had a student after school serving a detention—and detentions always turned into a "what's going on in your life" discussion. He told me he had real problems at home. When I asked if he was comfortable enough to share them with me, he responded with disgust: "I have a mother who is lesbian, Ms. Nic, a *lesbian!*" He was so distraught. As a lesbian trying to conceal my own identity, I could only muster up an "It could always be worse" response. To this day I wonder the difference it would have made in his life if I could have had the strength to say, "Well, Tommy, I too am a lesbian. I know you respect me as your teacher; let's talk."

I had another student stop by my room many times after school; she was struggling to understand her sexual orientation yet appeared quite confident in doing so. As much as I wanted to be a support for her, she raised my anxiety level with her strong sense of self. Consequently, I always pretended to be busy, shuffling papers and avoiding her eyes. The reality that I couldn't be a support system for *all* of my students—especially the LGBTQ students—was taking its toll on me. My own homophobia was a self-imposed barrier that I didn't know how to break.

Unfortunately, students seem to have the power when a teacher has something to hide. I now know that I gave them that power. When I was on stage in front of the entire school hosting the school-wide talent show, I was anxious that a student might shout, "Get off the stage, you dyke!" After the show I would ask another colleague, who is also a lesbian, if she heard anyone say anything about me being gay.

As I entered my freshman health class in September of 1986, I found a note on my desk. The note said "We, the freshman class, want to know if it is true that you are gay?" While 28 students sat quietly observing me as I read this anonymous note, I listened to the inner dialogue. *Please, face, don't turn red, or for sure you will look like you are gay. Just relax, be calm, and pretend it is a joke. Should I address it or ignore it?* I decided to pretend it was a joke. "Who wrote this note?" I asked. "Oh, come on now, there are always rumors about teachers. Let's now turn to page 125." I had extreme difficulty focusing on any health lessons that day.

At the end of school one winter day, I walked out to my car to check out the work that the boys from shop had completed. As I approached the car I saw LES scratched into the entire side door panel. My heart raced, my head pounded, and I thought, "How could I drive this car around?"

When I brought it up to the shop teacher, he looked at me with this shocked expression and asked why the kids would do that. So I let it go. It took too much energy to pursue; along with the risk of exposing too much of myself, it wasn't worth it.

Another day, I unfortunately intercepted a note from another student in a health class. The note said, "No wonder she likes teaching PE; this way she can check out all the girls in the locker room." Honestly, I felt my character was being defamed in the eyes of my students because of my sexual orientation. How could I ever let them know that being gay has nothing to do with one's character? I felt so alone, and so alone in this harassment.

Faculty rooms didn't offer me much respite either. One day

during lunch, a veteran teacher of 32 years walked in, saying, "Hey, how about that three-dollar bill we had presenting at yesterday's professional development workshop? If he said he was gay one more time I was going to leave." Some other teachers laughed along with him. I am embarrassed to admit this, but I may have even smiled along with the joke.

Another teacher would joke with his students about wearing green on Thursdays. "Don't you know, if you wear green on Thursdays, you must be gay?" As innocent as he thought this statement was, he didn't know that on Thursdays I would make sure not to wear green. I felt so incredibly unsafe.

Feeling brave one day, I did bring my struggle up to the principal at that time. She seemed extremely uncomfortable when I told her about the harassment and could offer no direction other than, "Just try to ignore it and don't let it get to you…" and "Why would they be saying that?" Of course I could not say: Because it is true.

I began to question whether or not I could keep teaching. Would I always face this harassment? All this was happening without my students knowing for sure that I am gay. What would I face if I actually came out? What support systems did I have? There were other gay teachers in my building, but they were just as persecuted as I was. I began to feel hopeless.

So when a position for a K–3 "self-esteem teacher" was created, it seemed just for me. My six years of hearing myself attempting to impress upon my high school students the value of feeling good about "who you are" finally caught up with me: If I wasn't feeling good about who I was because I was hiding a part of my identity, how could I expect my students to feel good about who they were? I just wasn't practicing what I was preaching.

Upon my return to teaching at the high school—six years later, in 1996—I felt more confident. But I was still paranoid about my sexual orientation when I was at school. I wanted to let go of this extra negative energy, but how?

That April 1997 night provided the answer. It must have been fate that landed me on the front page of the morning newspaper. I hadn't dodged the camera like so many others had that evening. When the photographer perched herself in front of me, finally, I was ready for some controversy. And now I had it: There I was, smack in the middle of the group cheering away as we watched the events unfold. The headline read, "Ellen's Out, Gays Hail Historic Night."

Since my father was the former superintendent of schools in Ansonia, and my mom was in real estate there as well, I wanted to tell them about this before people approached them with the news. So at 6 A.M. we had a conversation about how my day might unfold. My parents and three sisters were fearful of what I might encounter in a homophobic world. They warned me that if I had a negative experience, I couldn't change my mind and say I was only kidding. My youngest sister said that I should tell people I'd just been out with some gay people, that I was not gay.

Throughout the years people always warned me not to disclose my sexual orientation, especially in a town like Ansonia, which many felt was not very progressive. So in all honesty, I did fleetingly consider using my 162 accumulated sick days. In the end, however, I decided I'd already spent far too much of my professional life in fear.

On the way to work I saw every newspaper box with my picture in it. My heart was racing. As I entered the main office, I could sense that the secretaries, along with the teachers present, did not know how to handle this awkward situation. I was sure they wondered if Ms. Nic had gotten "caught" and been outed in the paper? As their eyes looked elsewhere, anywhere but at me, I sensed their silence was out of respect. So I took the bull by the horn and said, "Hey, did anyone see this morning's paper? Ellen is out and so is Ms. Nic, and it feels great!" A few came up and hugged me, asked me a few questions, and we laughed; and it did feel great. Just then the principal, who had not yet seen the morning paper, said, "Why is everyone so gay this morning?" As our laughs grew even louder, I responded, "I don't know about the others being gay, but this teacher is." Then I left to continue on my new journey as an out teacher.

The first student to address the photo said, "Hey, Ms. Nic, was that your picture on the front of this morning's paper?" With 10 other students listening as they filed into an English class I said, "Yes, it is, Christy." With her thumbs up, she responded with the ubiquitous high school phrase, "Cool." I walked away with tears in my eyes, wondering where Christy found the strength to give me her approval in front of her peers. Later that day Christy told me her aunt is gay, something I had not known.

Upon entering the media center, I noticed the newspapers were not in the usual place, out on the counter. When I asked the media specialist where that day's *New Haven Register* was, she said, "Oh, are you sure you want them out?" Confidently I responded, "Yes, I have waited 15 years for this day, *please* put them out." As we continued our discussion, she hugged me, as did another teacher who was privy to the conversation.

One boy, upon entering our health issues class, stopped to quietly warn me that this class was going to be tough on me. He said the discussion about my sexual orientation in the previous class had some students in it who were going to give me a hard time. He also said, "Ms. Nic, did you know my mother is gay?" I was surprised by his admission, especially considering the vulnerable environment my classroom was about to become. He continued, "Well, she thinks you are very cute and wants to know if you are single." I told him to tell his mother that I was flattered but that I was already in a relationship. Another student stood in the hallway telling me—loud enough for all to hear—that his sister is a lesbian and she lives with her life partner in Florida, and if anybody gives me a hard time to let him know about it. He was a popular football player, and his allegiance to his sister, and his teacher, was admirable.

Once the bell rang and class began, I knew I had to be strong, not only for myself but for the student who had to remain silent about his own mother being a lesbian. The football player felt he could talk openly about his sister, but many others have not yet reached that level of empowerment to share about a gay relative. The more confidently I handled this situation, the better they might feel about themselves. I knew that my coming out broke the barriers and gave people permission to—whether privately or in public—share with me about their gay relatives or themselves. The school was feeling safer for me, and I'm sure it was for others as well.

Former students stopped by school that day to say congratulations. The superintendent called to offer her support and to ask how I was holding up. The president of the board of education came to my class to inquire about my well-being and offered her support as well. I came out to each class that day, and more students came out to me about their relatives who are gay. Some teachers approached me and quietly disclosed that they suspected their child might be gay and wished they came to this school so they could have me for a teacher. Other colleagues shared about their gay relatives. My buddy in the gym, Gennaro, a strong Italian with conservative views, hugged me and offered to cover my classes if I was having a difficult time.

This all happened in a six-hour school day. It was such an emotional high yet totally draining. All the fear I had bottled up for 15 years was now being released. If I had known the support would be so overwhelming, I would never have wasted so much time.

That day I went home in tears—tears of relief. When I called my dad and shared my stories, I could hear his tears of relief as well. I also contacted the reporter at the *New Haven Register* to let him know that I appreciated his story of the *Ellen* event, and that I thought the photo was in good taste. My appreciation was especially personal, I told him, because I'd come out today at my high school as a result of his work. There was silence at the other end. He was amazed that, as a teacher, I'd allowed myself to be photographed. In his quick reporter mode, he asked if I would be willing to let them do a follow-up story. I told him I needed time to think about that.

After asking the opinion of family, friends, and colleagues—who all advised me against it—I called back and said yes. I had learned to let my own intuition be my guide. I felt that a picture of the high school substance-abuse teacher at a bar surrounded by people with beer bottles didn't best represent me. This was an opportunity to attach a story to my picture, and I did.

With an entire page dedicated to "Today's Woman," my coming out of the classroom closet story was beautifully captured in the *New Haven Register*. The title of the article read, "Thanks to Ellen, Ms. Nic found the courage to come out the same night DeGeneres did."

The weeks that followed, I had received phone calls from radio stations wanting to do interviews, letters from teachers all around Connecticut telling me they wished they could come out at their school, a call from Robin Roberts from *20/20* interested in doing a segment, and public TV wanting an interview. It was hard to comprehend that all this was happening simply because I said I am gay. I quietly thought, *It will be nice when it is not newsworthy simply because a teacher is gay.*

After coming out in 1997 I became a GLSEN Connecticut member when I stumbled upon their booth at a conference. Shortly thereafter, I became a board member, then cochair. (Those involved with GLSEN know how quickly this transition occurs.) I was now developing and presenting teacher training seminars on creating safe school environments for all students regardless of sexual orientation or gender identity/expression throughout schools in Connecticut.

I also developed workshops for LGBT educators titled "Educator's Empowerment." I have presented this workshop for GLSEN National at the Teaching Respect for All conferences as well as at the Boston and Connecticut conferences. Hearing concerns and questions and sharing fears about coming out from teachers and administrators in Atlanta, Los Angeles, Boston, Chicago, and Connecticut is powerful stuff. No workshop ever ended without tears. Often I would get an e-mail from a teacher after these workshops telling me they came out on the Monday morning after their return to school, and they were elated.

Teachers who come out usually feel like a more complete human being. Being more complete impacts our teaching, which in turn impacts students. It is a powerful ripple effect that changes the school climate.

Coming out is a powerful transition. It allows you to be in control by taking the power away from others. I can now confidently handle any situation that comes my way regarding LGBT issues. Every September with a new freshman class is another opportunity for "teachable moments." When a student asked me during freshman homeroom what I did with my boyfriend this weekend, I calmly stated, "I don't have a boyfriend, but I went to the movies with my girlfriend." The class was speechless. I asked how many were shocked by that information; not one student raised their hand. Unassumingly one girl said, "I already knew you were gay; I was just shocked you said it." Then the student who had asked about my boyfriend confessed that he'd known I was gay, he just wanted to see my reaction.

We now have a GSA (gay-straight alliance) at our high school. Our first project was the Day of Silence, with 107 students out of 650 and 10 teachers out of 45 participating. No longer do teachers make inappropriate comments about being gay. No longer will I remain silent if they do.

I am now part of a support system for all students, including LGBT students or those with a gay relative. As an out teacher I have released my fears; I will be fine. I was even selected for Teacher of the Year for the 2004 school year and hired in March as the administrator for the alternative education program. It is my hope that someday all teachers and students feel comfortable coming out. It is my hope that one day GLSEN will not need to exist because its mission will have been accomplished.

THE MARRIAGE QUESTION

Brian Davis
Seventh and eighth grade language arts and social studies teacher
Claire Lilienthal School
San Francisco, California

"Mr. Davis, are you married?" asked the saucy eighth grader, eyeing my bear fetish ring on the telltale finger.

"No," I replied, unthinkingly giving the correct legal answer.

Thus suddenly arrived and rapidly departed the first opportunity to come out to my students at my new school. My resolve to not miss any chance to reveal my sexual orientation was momentarily derailed due to my confusion about how to answer this unexpected and, for me, complex question.

I had been prepared to answer the "Are you gay?" question with a calm and confident "Yes," but somehow I had never prepared to answer the marriage question. Throughout my previous four years, during the late 1990s at three tough inner-city middle schools in the San Francisco Unified School District, I had never had a student ask about my marriage status.

I had occasionally faced the "Are you gay?" question from some class disrupter who wanted to embarrass me. Always on those occasions I had stuck with the standard party line recommended to me by every teacher, counselor, or administrator, gay or straight: "That's a personal question. Personal questions are inappropriate…" The equivalent, if I were to judge by the students' faces, of: "Yes, I am gay, but I don't want you to know about it. So I'm avoiding the question."

I was cautious partly because, as a long-term substitute teacher for my first three years, I could theoretically be fired on a moment's notice for any reason. ("Long-term substitute" was a designation formerly used by my district to keep the "dime a dozen"—as one administrator interviewer once referred to us—fully credentialed language arts and social studies teachers from gaining any job security, despite our regular classroom status.)

Now, I know what you're thinking: *He was teaching in San Francisco, the land wrapped up in the rainbow, and he was afraid of being fired for being gay?*

What you have to realize is that many of the students and parents at these schools were anything but supportive of LGBT issues. But if I made an issue out of this, given my tenuous employment status, I was afraid I might rile up enough parents that the principal would find some excuse other than my sexuality to get rid of me just to avoid the hassle. I was also reluctant to be open because these students were often difficult to control under the best of circumstances, and I didn't want to do anything that could potentially make things worse.

However, when I became a probationary teacher at the start of my fourth year, which was also my first chance to teach at the same school for a second year in a row, I began to seriously consider opening up to my students. That year I had the misfortune of being assigned an extremely difficult group of seventh graders. I was not alone in this regard. Teachers who had been there for 30 years said that student behavior was the worst they had ever seen. Students frequently made both thinly veiled and completely unveiled insinuating comments. MR. DAVIS IS GAY appeared on the side of a desk and on the blackboard on two separate occasions.

I addressed the issue, of course, discussing the Matthew Shepard murder, doing antislur activities, but I continued to stick to the party line regarding my own sexuality, despite the knowing look in their eyes.

When I consulted a trusted colleague, asking if I should come out, she felt that I should consider what my motivations were—was I wanting to do it for myself or for my students? At the time I wasn't sure how to answer that. I knew that I felt dishonest, and that I could not expect students to open up to me if I concealed such an important part of my identity. For some reason I was not able to recognize the real reason I needed to come out—so that I could be a positive role model for LGBT students. Perhaps this was because I wasn't sure whether they were capable of seeing me in a positive light at this point. At any rate, I decided to finish the year unrevealed. But I did finish the year, which I considered quite an accomplishment, under the circumstances.

Feeling burned out, I decided to take a year's leave to look into other career options. During this time, I spent much of my time volunteering on a campaign to legalize same-sex marriage in California, which reaffirmed my commitment to teach the public that those of us in the queer community are ordinary people deserving of equal rights and respect. The slogan I wrote, which the organization adopted—"Marriage: Anything Less Is Less Than Equal"—sums up my perspective on this issue.

I decided that I would return to the district only if I could find a job in a less challenging environment. As much as I wanted to work with the kids who needed the most help, I knew that I couldn't survive in that kind of school any longer. Fortunately I found work at a K–8 "alternative" school with a more manageable student population. I knew that I had come to a different place when, during a discussion about racial discrimination related to a story we were reading early on in my seventh-grade language arts class, I asked whether they could describe other kinds of discrimination, and a pair of students spoke about gay friends of their parents in a positive way. I also loved my new principal, had good relations with other staff members and parents, and I had finally gained tenure, so it seemed that the time and the place were finally right for my students to find out that they had a gay teacher.

I decided that I didn't want to make a big deal out of coming out because I wanted the message to be that my being gay was a totally normal everyday thing, rather than some kind of terrible secret that needed to be couched in an air of dramatic revelation. I have since come to a different conclusion, as I will discuss later, but at the time I felt that this particular school in San Francisco in the new millennium was ready for this kind of casual approach.

I had hoped that I would one day make an offhand comment to the students along the lines of "My partner and I went to a movie the other day…" but somehow the words wouldn't leave my lips. Next I decided that I would wait for the inevitable "Are you gay?" question, but I had not counted on the less-predatory nature of my new students. The question never came.

After the aforementioned eighth grader caught me off guard with the marriage question, I considered how I would answer if given another opportunity. "No" was not a truthful answer since my partner, Ted, and I had been together longer than these students had been alive and were married in every way but legally. "Yes" was also untrue, as we did not have a marriage license. Eventually I came up with an answer that I thought would do the trick.

My opportunity finally arrived. During a semiprivate moment on a field trip, a seventh-grade girl (the product of a racially mixed marriage) inquired, "Are you married, Mr. Davis?"

"In a way," I replied cagily.

After looking at me curiously for a moment, she followed up with "What are you, then?"

"I'm domestic partnered."

"Oh. What's his name?"

"Ted."

"How old is he?"

"Thirty-one."

This seemed to satisfy her curiosity. Just as I'd hoped, it had been very relaxed. An ordinary conversation.

Word spread quickly at our small school. The next day two students came up to me independently and asked if I was gay. When I said yes they nodded and smiled. One exclaimed, "Cool!"

Only one student sought to taunt me with this new information:

a sixth-grade girl, whom I knew to be a troublemaker, waited in ambush for me in the schoolyard at the end of the day. Just as I was about to exit the yard on my bicycle I caught her out of the corner of my eye as she shouted: "Are you gay?!"

I turned my bike around, rode up to where she was hiding behind a lunch table, evidently expecting a tongue-lashing, and simply stated, "Yes, I'm gay." I then wished her a good afternoon and went on my way.

I wish I could say that we all lived happily ever after, but unfortunately that was not the case. Three times during the last three years I have found the word FAG written on or in my classroom—two of those times were just this past year. The most recent occasion was on the second-to-last day of school, written on the outside of my bungalow door.

I have taught the students that the word *faggot* originally referred to a bundle of sticks used for kindling, and that during the middle ages when women accused of witchcraft were burned at the stake, sometimes men accused of homosexuality were covered in oil and used to start the fire, thereby serving as the kindling or "faggot." "So when you call someone a fag you are saying that they deserve to be burned alive," I tell them in the hope that this will impress upon them the horrific evil of the word.

Yet this last incident has opened my eyes to the reality that my casual "Yeah, I'm gay. So what?" attitude, an occasional discussion or article related to the subject once or twice a year, a yearly visit to the health class by members of a gay speakers bureau, and a general air of tolerance for all groups that are discriminated upon in our society is not enough to completely defeat the ingrained homophobia that still persists among some of the best-educated children in this most enlightened of cities.

So during the summer I contacted Kevin Gogin and Olivia Higgins at the Support Services for Sexual Minority Youth and the School Health Programs Department, the dedicated people who provide the LGBT education services in our district. With their help, I became the Sexual Minority Youth Liaison for my school, which means that signs are posted in every classroom letting kids know that I am there if they need to talk about issues of sexual orientation. My new responsibility also requires me to start a "diversity club," which I have begun with the help of the after-school program coordinator, and to organize Violence Prevention Month and gay pride. I am also a resource for my fellow teachers, providing them with age-appropriate materials to help them teach students to understand and respect LGBT people.

And so the school year began. Now once again I was faced with a new version of the age-old question: How and when would I come out to this new batch of students? And how could I do it in a way that would help them not only to understand and respect LGBT people, but also to make valuable connections to their own lives so that the message would sink in? I had an idea about how to approach it, but I needed a catalyst, something that would set the proper tone and help pave the way.

Fortunately, Olivia had recommended a novel called *The Misfits* by James Howe, the main characters of which are all different in some way from their seventh-grade peers. One of them, Joe, is an out and proud gay boy, who improbably but wonderfully finds that the boy he has a crush on likes him too. Together, the group of outcasts start a campaign to stop name-calling at their school.

Each of my seventh graders read this book, and we discussed the issues it raised. When one of my classes started an impromptu discussion about whether people are born gay or lesbian, I knew that the time had come to make my big speech.

"Today I have something to tell you about myself," I began. "I'm a misfit too. I'm a misfit in the same way as Joe. I'm gay.

"Now, my experience was different from Joe's. When I was a teenager during the '70s I didn't accept myself the way he does. When I was growing up the only gay people I knew about were the men marching in the gay pride parade wearing dresses that I would see for a few moments on the news. I thought that that was what it meant to be gay, and since I had no interest in wearing dresses I thought that I was some kind of freak that didn't belong anywhere.

"Everything around me told me that it was wrong to like boys, and that I was supposed to like girls. So from around the time when I was about 11 to around 21 I would go to bed every night wishing that in the morning I would wake up attracted to girls instead of boys.

"But eventually I came to realize that I was not alone, that gay men and lesbian women were all different kinds of people, most of whom were like me: just like everyone else in every way except that we are emotionally attracted to people of the same sex. I came to accept and celebrate who I was instead of fearing and hating my feelings because society had taught me that what I was was 'wrong.'

"Then I met a man that I now share my life with. We held a commitment ceremony that all of our friends and family members attended. We've been together for 16 years now.

"Now, I'm not telling you this because I have some need to unburden myself to you. I am telling you this because I want you to have what I didn't have: a gay role model, a successful, respected member of the community whom you know personally and whom you can't stereotype or easily dismiss as some kind of oddball but whom you are getting to know as a fully rounded individual.

"I am also telling you this to make it very clear that I will not allow anyone to use the word *fag* or *gay* as an insult in this class, just as I will not allow anyone to use words which insult people of different races, cultural backgrounds, genders, religions, or abilities.

"I am also telling you this because I want the children in this classroom who have family members or friends who are lesbian or gay to know that their families will be respected in this room.

"Also, statistically speaking, about one in 10 people all over the world are lesbian, gay, bisexual, or transgender, and so, statistically, there are students in this school who are, or someday will be, dealing with this issue. I want those students to know that they are safe here.

"I am saying to all of you that no matter what kind of misfit you are, whether you think you are overweight, or too short, or not good-looking enough, or anything that makes you feel different, be proud of who you are. Don't let anyone tell you that you aren't a good person, or that you have to be something that you aren't. Be proud to be yourself. That's my message to you today."

This particular class applauded heartily when I finished, and I spent the rest of the period answering some very insightful questions about my experiences and opinions. The responses of the other classes, when I gave them the same speech, ranged from enthusiasm to indifference, but I felt that I had done all I could to come out in a way that would connect with their lives and help them to understand and respect LGBT people.

As you might expect, I got a little flack from parents for this. I heard from some supportive parents that there had been "discussions" among the parents about me, and one parent wrote a very detailed anonymous letter to the principal demanding that I be reprimanded. My principal was very supportive and gave a great deal of her valuable time helping make certain that nothing came of this.

Out of all of this has also come what for me is a rather astonishing thing. Throughout my teaching career I have always had difficulty feeling truly relaxed and comfortable around my students. There has always been a distance between us, which I believed to be because of the needs of classroom discipline and my demanding academic requirements.

Yet suddenly, I have become aware that the wall separating my students from me has disappeared, even though the need for discipline and my high academic expectations remain. Now, for the first time ever, I am able to laugh and joke with my students without feeling awkward. I am my naturally silly self with them, and they have responded by showing affection in return.

Why has this finally happened during my eighth year of teaching? There may be many reasons, yet I cannot help but think that finally opening up to them fully, baring my heart to them without fear or restraint, might have something to do with it. I feel confident and secure with my students in a way I've never felt before. I no longer have to be afraid that something I say will trigger a raised eyebrow and a question that I don't feel ready to answer.

Ironically, it may be the act of opening up, perhaps more than the message itself, which will hopefully keep someone from writing FAG on my wall again. But if someone does, I will know that it isn't in any way because I have failed to do everything I can to prevent it.

✳

The preceding was written during 2003. It is now late February 2004 and Ted and I are legally married! On February 12 we went to the annual Valentine's Day protest at San Francisco City Hall: A group of us ask for marriage licenses; they say no; we demonstrate and make speeches. Except, as everyone now knows, this year they said yes, and we were among the first 20 same-sex couples in the country to be officially wed. We were stunned and overjoyed.

Afterward, I told my students about it, but it turned out many of them had already seen me on the news. Parents have been coming up to me every day since to offer their congratulations. I have told the students that we are living in truly historic times, and that is how it feels, like we are being carried along in an unstoppable flood of freedom and equality.

And so the marriage question can finally be answered, with no ambiguity or asterisks attached. The struggle for true equality is just beginning, of course, both inside and outside of the classroom. Hopefully, someday in the near future, when a student asks if I am married, and I answer "Yes, to a man," every middle schooler in the room will have the same thought: "Whatever. Big deal."

LIVING SIMPLY AND OPENLY

Kathleen Crawford
Math teacher, drama teacher
Jefferson County public schools
Louisville, Kentucky

I think the biggest reason I became a teacher is because I knew if I did, I would never stop learning. In college I could not decide on one specific content area to major in, and I would routinely take 18–19 hours each semester because I enjoyed the coursework and academic environment. I loved to read and spend time pondering, sharing great thoughts in study groups, and quoting Ralph Waldo Emerson: "What lies behind us, and what lies before us, are tiny matters compared to what lies within us."

I was so young, yet I thought I was so wise. Ha! As I have grown older—I've taught for 19 years now—I've realized that academic work is a tiny matter compared to the life experiences on my journey. So, if I may borrow from the *Gilligan's Island* theme song, "Now, sit right back and you'll hear a tale…"

During the summer of 2001, I realized, accepted, and embraced the fact that I am a lesbian.

When I look back on my life, I know that I felt those first inklings in junior high, but I was a tomboy and athletic and it was the mid '70s, so I just didn't pay too much attention to those feelings. I viewed the boys in the neighborhood and at school mostly as competitors. I was determined to always show them up in one way or another. I don't remember having true feelings for them—though I "played" that I did. I enjoyed my friendships with girls and remember having crushes; but in that time of innocence, I thought of those feelings as admiration. I did have a fascination with Wonder Woman's background as an Amazon princess. I remember fantasizing about a world, a community of strong and beautiful women. But I never consciously thought of myself as homosexual. Whenever the topic of homosexuality came up, it was typically something joked about or talked about in hushed tones.

Back then, I didn't spend much time concerned about what I was feeling. I just sort of went along with what was considered "acceptable" and "normal." So I finished my undergraduate degree and married a nice guy. I was drawn to his gentle manner, plus he was not macho and condescending like so many guys I had met and known. I wanted children and a good life.

But there was an emptiness deep within me.

To fill this void, I developed a pattern of throwing myself into things, learning as much as I could, and getting very involved in my children, work, church, and personal development. This culminated after attending an educational conference in 1998, when I seized a new venture that came my way—writing, editing, consulting, and new professional opportunities with a Catholic publishing house. I cut back to part-time teaching at the Catholic high school where I'd been employed for the past 11 years.

The world had opened up! I was learning and growing so much in my new work and meeting some amazing people. Over the course of three years, I grew very close to one amazing person in particular, the design director at the publishing company. We clicked intellectually from the very beginning. I often traveled on business to Minnesota, where she lived. Over the course of time, we began carving out time for just the two of us, and so our emotional and spiritual connection grew. The friendship was pure joy.

However, it was still a big surprise when I realized that I was falling in love with this amazing woman, Cindi.

Neither one of us were consciously aware of what was happening when we dove deeply into an intimate, whole, and connected relationship. However, when the physical dimension developed, everything made sense to me. I had never known what it was like to feel so whole, so complete, so *me*. I realized that I was a lesbian.

By this time, Cindi and I had fallen in love. We wanted to spend the rest of our lives loving each other. It sounds simple; it seems like a fairy tale and the beginning of a beautiful love story. But to get to what our vision of a relationship would be, it was not going to be easy because of what we not-so-jokingly called the "practicalities." We were colleagues at a Catholic publishing company. I had been teaching at a local Catholic high school for 11 years. I loved my classes and my students. We were both women with heterosexual pasts. I was in a 15-year marriage and had three kids. We knew that if we were to really be together, both of us would need to find new jobs. This would mean Cindi leaving Minnesota and moving 600 miles to Kentucky. Not your typical love story.

One October afternoon as we walked, I was keenly aware that we were choosing what was choosing us. She said, "We'll live it simply and openly."

I looked into my beloved's blue eyes and repeated what she had said. "Yes, we'll live it simply and openly."

Two weeks later, after we made the commitment to live *it*—our lesbian relationship—simply and openly, the major life changes began. We knew that it would mean some painful situations and endings in our lives, but the seven months between that late October and May were more difficult than I had imagined. I came out to a husband, three children (then ages 13, 11, 8), friends, and family. And it was not an accepting and positive experience. I heard the most hateful things.

The following month, while I was on a business trip, my ex-husband scheduled a meeting and outed me to an administrator at the Catholic school where I taught. When I got back to town I had a conversation with the assistant principal that was very painful. I was told that I was touched by "an evil spirit." I was told that I would live the story of Hamlet and "leave nothing but dead bodies in my wake." She questioned my spirituality, my teaching ability, and whether or not I could actually teach in a Catholic school.

I was filled with hurt, disbelief, and anger. How could I go from celebrated teacher at the school one day to the next day having my life judged? I had already come to the conclusion that I would leave the school at the end of the academic year because I knew if I didn't it would be impossible to live openly in my relationship with Cindi. But after hearing such hateful things and knowing that it would create a "scandal," I resigned in the middle of the year. I was not asked to leave, but I would have been if I'd stayed there and claimed my homosexuality. I handled a hard situation the best I could, but looking back on it it still feels raw and painful.

In the late spring, Cindi left her position as design director and moved to Kentucky. It was wonderful to finally be together. We began the process of becoming a family. Shortly after Cindi's arrival I resigned from my editing position and applied for a job in the public school system. I got the job almost immediately.

I started teaching drama at Westport Middle School and Fine Arts Academy and was filled with enthusiasm. I started to network, wanting to meet other teachers in the system who were gay and out of the closet. I talked to Natalie, a friend who was the director of the Louisville Youth Group, a support group for LGBTQ teens, and she gave me the names of two teachers at my school that she had heard good things about. I looked these teachers up immediately and found they were out to colleagues, but not students; both were in long-term relationships and were wonderful, healthy individuals. We became a good support system for one another.

But I wanted to network beyond my school, so I went to a couple of meetings of a Gay-Lesbian Teacher Caucus that was sponsored by the teacher's union. I found teachers who were out to colleagues but not students to be the norm. Throughout the year I had conversations with only two teachers who were out to their students—one of whom told me that the more out you were, the more protected you would be.

That was not what I heard at my school. I heard various "warnings" from my principal about not sharing my sexual orientation with colleagues, and certainly not students. She said her concern was that I would not be accepted and that I could get hurt. The principal also made comments about parents and the community not accepting gays and lesbians. I remember telling her that after all I had lived through over the past year or so, I could handle some remarks at the copy machine. Later that year we had a conversation in which she told me not to deny or affirm or validate when asked about my sexual orientation. She also told me not to promote it.

I felt a profound sense of sadness and frustration at the injustice and craziness of it all. I had left Catholic institutions where the "don't ask, don't tell" policy was securely in place—along with teachings on homosexual activity being sinful. I was not prepared for the same "policy" in a public school system in a city with a fairness ordinance that protects LGBTQ individuals from discrimination.

As the school year went on I became deeply aware of the hatred, prejudice, and stereotypes that pervaded our school. In the halls, at lunch, on the buses, and even in my well-managed and engaging classroom, students would not think twice about calling each other "gay" or "fag." While I would also hear racist and sexist remarks, or even comments on another student's cognitive ability, I heard more homophobic remarks than anything. I began keeping track of how many times I heard these slurs, put-downs, jokes, and comments, and it was averaging about 10–15 times a day. I even heard students make comments about a few of the male teachers using these words.

I knew that there were many teachers who would not address the comments, but I was not one of them. From the first comment I heard that August, I found myself constantly saying to my students, "That is inappropriate and not respectful to your classmate or to this group of people." "I take personal offense at that comment." "We need to respect all people."

Since I was teaching drama, I gave students the opportunity to plan role-plays and participate in improvisational scenarios. During performances, students would often bring stereotypical and prejudiced bias to characters they were developing. They also knew, without a shadow of a doubt, that I would deal with comments, have conversations with them, stop a performance, and penalize their grade if they crossed a line. I felt like I was making some headway, but it was a daily commitment to be consistent and aware. Still, I was not out to students. I had never gone from a reprimand to anything on a more personal level, other than my mantra of "I take personal offense at that comment."

But one early spring day in March 2003, that all changed.

We had been studying character development for more than two weeks. As a springboard for one last character study performance, I wanted students to do some analysis of the movie *Harriet the Spy*. I set the focus, talked about dramatic and production elements, specifically about the stylized Nickelodeon approach to the film, and then began a 25-minute clip from the movie.

During one scene the main character, Harriet, is getting ready for bed and talking to Golly, her nanny, played by Rosie O'Donnell. Once Harriet begins bouncing on the bed, Golly shoos her off the bed, tickling and teasing her on the way to her own bedroom.

The class was quiet, watching and enjoying the movie. Then an eighth-grader (who I'll call Brad) yelled out, "Lesbian!" First laughter, then side conversations started.

I had a student turn on the light and then I asked, "Brad, can you help me understand what would possess you to yell that out? It has nothing to do with the movie."

He then began to explain, "Well, Rosie is a lesbian, right? And so, I was wondering if the people who made the movie knew that. I mean, look at how she is touching that girl."

I said, "Brad, that is inappropriate, and I honestly don't know if your comment is rooted in ignorance, or fear, or what. I do find it personally offensive."

He then said, "But Ms. Crawford, I mean she's touching that girl all like…"

There was growing laughter, conversations, and smirking.

Something inside me just could not let it go with simply reciting my chosen mantra. I was sickened by the connection my young student was making with lesbianism and pedophilia. I was also keenly aware of the moment being a teachable one—and one that would be memorable for my students and for me.

I quietly and calmly said, "I find your comments personally offensive. Do you know why?"

He shook his head no. I took a deep breath and was aware of my heart beating quickly and the catch in my voice. I looked out at my students and gazed into their eyes. Then I focused on Brad.

"I am a lesbian. It hurts my heart, my ears, and my feelings when you say things like that. The role that Rosie is playing is that of a caring nanny. There is nothing about her being a lesbian that would make shooing a child off to bed inappropriate or sexual or anything like that. I don't know what these hateful comments are based upon or why you think they are funny. I really don't."

It was so quiet in the classroom. Eyes were wider than I had seen them all year. Some students did not make eye contact. I saw Brad gulp.

Then I finished, "I want you to be more careful when you choose words. You do not know who you could be offending. I am a good teacher, a good mom, and a lesbian. The slurs, the put-downs, and the misconceptions you have are not who I am or what I am about. I want you to understand where I am coming from. I want you to think about a real, live gay person's face when you say homophobic remarks. They hurt *me*. Do you understand?"

He said, "Yes, Ms. Crawford. I'm sorry."

I then continued on with the movie. The class was quiet, did the analysis questions at the end, and was dismissed.

As I moved to the door to see students out, I noticed Brad hanging back. When everyone had left the room, he looked down at me—he was over 6 feet tall—and said to my face, "I'm sorry. I didn't know. I don't have anything against gay people."

I said, "I hope not."

He continued, "I was just trying to be funny. I am really sorry, Ms. Crawford."

I told him that I accepted his apology and I thanked him for his maturity.

During my planning period, I immediately scripted the events of the class and put them in a memo to my principal, just in case there was an onslaught of parent calls. I said I would discuss what had happened with her, provided that my union representative was with me. Once my principal read the memo, she came up to my room. I could tell she was not pleased with what had happened, but she surprised me and said that she saw it was a teachable moment and she would support me.

The onslaught of parent calls never came. I was later told of an "anonymous" parent complaint, but when I asked to speak to the parent, it was not brought up again.

The next day or two, the class seemed a little different. I told them that Brad had apologized and I thanked them for handling that moment in a mature way. A little comic relief later and the class went back to dramatic presentations. The major difference was that the homophobic remarks became the exception, as opposed to the norm, as they had been before. Students had a good-natured rapport with me about not "crossing the line" and we enjoyed one another so much during those last two months. On my final exam, I asked a question about what they had learned during the trimester about respect and diversity. A number of students commented on my coming out in class and said that as a result they stopped prejudging people or making fun of them. Brad's answer was most poignant: He commented that before, he'd made homophobic remarks 10 times a day, whereas in the past two months he had only said them twice, and afterward regretted it.

As the semester went on, kids being kids, the word got out about Ms. Crawford being gay. There were whispers and looks— but of course, in middle school, you never know what those whispers and looks mean. In April I came out to my sixth-grade class in a similar teachable moment that stemmed from students calling a male teacher on the floor a "faggot." I sent a memo to my principal, and even though my assistant principal told me of another anonymous parent phone call, I was never called into the office for a conversation.

One other defining moment came in May, during the week of statewide testing in Kentucky. I was proctoring a class in another teacher's room and all the students had finished testing except one in the back. The test booklets were collected, and students were getting restless. I moved to the center of the room and as I did so, there was a lot of commotion and noise from the right side. And then a voice yelled out, "Hey, lesbian." I was surprised and tried to locate the student who said it.

I asked who said it and a couple of girls said, "Don't tell her."

Then I heard more comments and words like "nasty," "gross," "lesbo," "filthy" and full sentences such as, "Being gay is gross. I've seen *Jerry Springer*." "It's nasty, wrong, just bad."

The noise level was starting to build and becoming unmanageable. Students on the other side of the room were playing and bugging one another. As I walked to the side of the room with all the comments, a girl named Alexandra started speaking: "Yeah, I heard you were gay. I don't care. Shouldn't matter what people do."

I asked, "So, you've heard all this where?"

She said, "On the bus, in the halls, all over the place. It doesn't matter to me."

I told Alexandra I respected her beliefs and complimented her on a mature understanding of diversity. Then another student asked, "You are gay?"

And I said, "Yes. I don't believe it matters. I'm a good person and a good teacher."

While some students were obnoxious, still muttering words like "gross" and "nasty," other students added some positive comments about respect.

After that experience, whenever comments occurred in any of my classes, I would have conversations with small groups about the use of the word *gay* as an adjective, asking them why they choose that word, and what other words really describe what they are saying. I explained to them how sad it makes me to hear them using that word as an adjective meaning "weird," "gross," "bad," "disgusting."

*

I believe in these young people and I think our society commonly sells them short. I value my relationships with my students and colleagues. I am hopeful that each school will be a place of growth for young minds and attitudes. They are questioning and can be taught, but we must model for them what is appropriate and right. How? By addressing the issue of verbal violence and harassment, by educating students about the connection between attitudes and thoughts and words and behavior, by modeling and witnessing what it sounds like and means to speak in respectful and dignified ways. Gay and straight teachers need to speak out. It really doesn't seem as much of a gay issue as one about basic respect, human dignity, and tolerance—values that are always age-appropriate, values that will make the world a better place.

*

A couple of girls stayed after one of my classes one day and said that they had heard some students talking about me being gay. She and the other girl told me that they said to their peers, "Yes, she is, but it doesn't matter. Leave the judging to God."

I said, "Exactly."

*

My relationship with Cindi is one of profound happiness and joy. We are creating new circles of friends and extended family. My children have adjusted well and are thriving in a loving home. I am teaching math at a different school in my neighborhood, and I enjoy it a good deal. My parents and siblings keep moving more to a place of acceptance and love. Life is good.

I want to live authentically.

I want to live my life openly and simply.

I will. I am.

WHY I DO WHAT I DO

Roberto Wheaton
Ninth grade earth science teacher
Cathedral City High School
Cathedral City, California

It seems like dealing with my sexual orientation began in (of all places) a small university in northern Idaho in 1984. My final education class assignment was to identify a controversial issue in education and to present an argument for or against, with a personal opinion supporting my argument. Growing up as a Latino/Native American mix in an inner-city barrio and on a reservation, the one thing I knew was how to fight, so being one of two males in a class of 75 women (and gay at that), I decided to write my paper on the issue of gays in education.

After three hours of typical education talk, my presentation really woke up the class and the professor. Every word I uttered seemed to flow with conviction. When I was finished, the class gave me a standing ovation. The professor called me into his office to tell me that he would be giving me an A for the class and thanked me for addressing a unique issue we would all have to face someday.

In many ways this was the my first "coming out," but I knew it wasn't going to be the last time I would stand among strangers and admit I was a gay teacher. Why this is necessary, I don't know. Perhaps I have always felt like I didn't quite fit into either the Latino or Native cultures completely, but my sexual orientation always seemed to be a complete fit.

In 1984 I left the reservation with a bag of clothes in the trunk of my old Ford Fairmont and headed for Seattle, where I accepted a teaching position at a Native American high school in south Seattle. During my first two years of teaching, I didn't address my sexual orientation—one, because it never came up and, two, because I was too busy surviving from day to day as a beginning teacher. Then one day in class I overheard two 16-year-old boys talking about meeting in front of a bar on Capitol Hill to find a "runner" and score. I knew from my days on the reservation that finding runners was a way for teens to have adults buy alcohol, in return for money or sex. These boys were talking of giving up their bodies for alcohol and drugs, and they knew exactly where to loiter. I knew this because coincidentally, I was moonlighting at this particular bar at night, and I knew what was taking place outside its front doors.

I casually asked the boys to remain after class, but they left as soon as the bell rang. After class I stopped by to speak with the counselor and nurses about my concern. The nurse told me she would speak to the boys, but the school had few resources to deal with these kinds of problems.

That same week, I received a note in my box from the visiting physician at our school about a meeting I might be interested in attending. A group of physicians, therapists, and administrators were forming a group to work on LGBT issues for adolescents. I was invited to join but was told not to tell anyone about the group.

I attended the meeting; indeed, there was a support group starting at the local university and a possible youth group for teens. I was impressed with the group, but admission to it was a very private affair as they wanted to keep out any possible pedophiles. I was accepted because I was a gay teacher (although not an out one at time).

My journey toward coming out was just beginning.

In 1989 I left the school for another small community public school where I knew there were a number of out gay students. The teachers seemed supportive and tolerant as all the rooms had signs of some type advocating peace or "Diversity Welcomed Here." I met a couple of gay teachers, but they were in the closet and seemed to have no intentions of ever coming out—even though in their dress and behavior they embodied every gay stereotype. The students and staff "knew"; the teachers themselves seemed to be the only ones who didn't think that they were "out." While it was healthy for the school to have out gay and lesbian students, I was told that for teachers, the answer was a clear "no." I took their advice and decided to feel out the community before making any decision about coming out.

During this time my work with the LGBT group seemed to increase, as we did community trainings, established an information line, and sponsored dances and a support group. I began to identify library resources and reached out to my own school librarian. She greeted the LGBT books I brought with open arms and invited me to bring even more resources. Eventually she even set up an LGBT presentation to the school librarians and developed a LGBT resource list for the school district.

Then one winter day in my ninth-grade environmental class, a young girl with an ACT UP shirt ask me if I was gay. Shocked, I responded with a loud "No," then watched her face shift from anticipation to disappointment.

That day was one of my lowest points. I had compromised my advocacy and the beliefs that drove it to hold on to my job. I had not been truthful to the very students for whom I was advocating in my community work. I had let fear guide my decision, rather than my principles. And I don't think I fooled anyone: Gay students know which teachers are gay from the first day of the school year. I vowed never to lie to students again about my sexual orientation.

The moment of truth came the following October.

I can remember that fall day like it was yesterday. I arrived early to school, parked my car, and was gathering my book bag when a teacher parked beside me yelled, "Great job, Bob!" I replied "Thanks," even though I didn't know what had motivated his comment. Then, as I proceeded through the parking lot, another teacher commented how proud she was of my work. I was still puzzled at these comments. It wasn't until I entered the school and was greeted by another colleague with a hug and "Nice interview! We're so proud of you," that I remembered the interview I'd done with a local public radio station back in the spring about LGBT youth issues. Apparently, it had finally aired the day before.

I guess I had outed myself on National Public Radio—without even knowing it.

Walking down the hallway toward the office, I felt a sense of relief about coming out to my colleagues. I knew too that I had to deal with my fears about losing my job, what my administrator would say, and what to expect inside the office—it could be the warmest of places or sheer hell, especially when you had a SEE ME! posted on your box. I wasn't in the mood for a SEE ME! day, so I tried to sneak by unnoticed. But my friend, the attendance secretary, saw me and yelled "Bobby, I just knew you were! I am so proud of you." My heart started racing as I tried to quiet her down and not draw attention from the principal. I knew it was only a matter of time before a SEE ME! would appear on my box; I just wanted it to come another day. I was feeling so good, thanks to the support from my peers, and I wasn't ready for the heavy-handed reprimand I was so sure I would receive.

Making my way up the stairs to my classroom, I realized that some students had probably heard the interview, and I pondered how I would respond. My first three periods were 7th–8th grade, and I was hoping that they didn't hear it or simply forgot, since that's what they commonly do at that age. As expected, no one said a word for three periods.

Then my fourth period—a 10th-grade class—came stumbling in. I could hear them talking about the interview and knew the question was coming. Most of these students had been in my 9th-grade class the year before, when had I denied the question; now they were unusually silent. Ten minutes into the class, a young man raised his hand to ask, "Hey, Bob, were you on the radio today?" I responded with a "As a matter of fact, I was," and I complimented him for listening to NPR. Then the class went dead again and a young woman (who was holding her girlfriend's hand) asked, "Are you gay?" I responded that "I would love to answer that question, but not during class time." I invited them to stay after class during part of their lunch, when I would give them the answer they wanted to hear.

The hour seemed to fly by. My nervousness was building, but knew that I had to be truthful with the students, even if it might mean I'd lose my job, my career, my reputation in education. When the lunch bell rang, I expected the class to bolt, but every last student sat quietly in their seats, with their eyes fixed on me. Trying not to sweat or show any emotion in my voice, I waited for the young girl to ask the question again. This time I took a few seconds to breathe and answered, "Yes, I am." It was the most empowering moment of my teaching career.

I broke down and apologized for the previous year's denial. I explained my fears about job security, but mostly I spoke about my feelings of my own betrayal of my beliefs—and of my students, who are the reason I was teaching in the first place.

The next 15 minutes were filled with stories about dads, moms, friends, and family, and the pain and fear they all had to live with on a daily basis. A male student yelled, "It shouldn't matter what a teacher is, but how they do their job." One girl, who identified herself as a lesbian, spoke of her fears at our school and how she had no place or person to go to for help. Another student described how her sister, an A student in an outlying high school, had come out and been beaten up and hassled until she dropped out of school. When the second lunch bell rang, I fell to my chair in disbelief that the students had been so supportive. They'd had so much more compassion than I expected. That is when I realized that the youth of today are pretty genuine about acceptance: It's the family and organizational leaders (school administrators) that create the intolerance for LGBT students.

For the next couple of weeks, students stopped by at lunch or during passing time to ask if "it" was true. I always answered that it was, and asked if this was a problem. I received no negative responses. I thought that my coming out was a nonevent—until Halloween weekend.

When I returned on the Monday after Halloween and entered my classroom, I was shocked to find my desk turned upside-down and the room scrawled with antigay graffiti. I knew that there might be consequences for coming out, but I hadn't anticipated anything like this. I called security to report the incident. They did the usual district write-up and went their way.

I went downstairs to the office and asked to meet with the principal. I informed her what had happened. She looked at me and said, "Now you know what women teachers go through when they find BITCH scrawled on their blackboards, or are called it to their faces." I tried to explain this incident was different than that, but the principal replied, "I can barely deal with teenage pregnancy, let alone this issue." And the meeting was over. I left feeling completely on my own and knowing that I would have to find some other way to report this incident if I didn't want it to happen again.

It's interesting how fate works when you least expect it. The next month, a student placed a poster for a city-sponsored LGBT dance on the bulletin board at another school and was harassed by the principal. I was called to help advocate for the student. After calling ACT UP, the Gay News, and other activists, I called the district office and demanded a meeting with the superintendent, telling them that we were going to blow this story to the press and unleash ACT UP if we didn't get an immediate response. Within hours we had a meeting with the superintendent and two school lawyers. We came up with a plan that included a letter of reprimand for the administrator's file and mandatory training for all administrators on LGBT issues. The district agreed. Guess which out gay teacher was asked to serve on the panel for these trainings? You got it. And my story was used in the training sessions.

Interestingly, none of the administrators from my building made it to any of those sessions.

In the following years I experienced few antigay incidents, other than having my windows egged a couple times and finding BOB'S A FAGGOT written in the boys bathroom. I found myself working under a constant pressure from my unsupportive principal. Nevertheless I hung in there, feeling that my presence was important both for my students and so that our school might become a safe place for LGBT youth, families, and teachers.

During my 12 years in Seattle I was fortunate to have colleagues who were supportive, compassionate, caring, and loving individuals who spoke up for LGBT rights without hesitation. I now think of my coming-out as being like the experience of a student on the first day of a new school year. You enter with many fears and hesitations but if the building is affirming, supportive, and respectful, you have opportunities to grow.

For me there is nothing more beautiful than to see at graduation that LGBT youth who arrived at our school door battered, defeated, and neglected has grown and blossomed thanks to a nurturing, caring, and loving staff. I smile as these confident, proud adults leave the stage with a diploma and college admissions and a will to make a better world. They are why I do what I do.

ONE OF THE BOYS FROM THE BAND

Michael Fridgen
Music teacher
Pinecrest Elementary School
Hastings, Minnesota

"Mr. Fridgen, I want to ask you a question," said Zach after class. "Some of the other kids say you're gay. On the playground I heard this one kid say that you're a fag. Is that true?"

"What?" I replied, pretending I did not hear him. Actually, I'm a music teacher with above-average hearing, but I needed to buy some time to consider my answer. Zach repeated his question as my mind raced to discover a reply.

Man, this kid's got guts, I thought to myself as I looked at his extremely serious face. I was openly gay to most everyone who knew me, but this was the first time a student had broached the subject. I had lived under the assumption that as an elementary teacher my students were too young to be concerned with the intimate details of my personal life; I'd thought that was for high school teachers to deal with. However, Zach's question immediately informed me that fifth graders are definitely not too young to be wondering why their handsome music teacher is unmarried.

*

Times have changed since I was in fifth grade 18 years ago.

When I was Zach's age I sang with the St. John's Boys Choir in Collegeville, Minnesota. Twice each week my parents drove me to St. John's Abbey to rehearse with 35 other boys; I loved every minute of it. It's true that I liked to sing; it's true that I liked the serenity of St. John's; and it's true that I liked learning from the Benedictine monks. But none of these reasons explained why I loved the boys choir with all my heart.

I grew up wanting to play with dolls rather than dump trucks and being extremely careful not to get my dress clothes dirty. Until I joined the boys choir, I was not the typical "snakes and snails" kind of guy. But now, for the first time, I was one of the boys. That is why I loved it so much. Nobody thought I was strange for wanting to go to rehearsal; nobody thought it odd that I dressed in a tuxedo and smiled for the audience. In the boys choir, we all looked and acted the same.

Damn that puberty! I was at my peak enjoyment of being one of the guys when adolescence hit and took it all away. First, my voice changed; goodbye boys choir. Then, as I entered high school, it became obvious that I was no longer one of the guys. I needed to seek out a new place to hide. I found it on the street.

I loved marching band: the pageantry, the music, the chance to wear a huge feather on my head. It was absolutely my favorite thing to do. By the time I was a junior I became drum major. People respected me as I marched down the street in front of thousands of spectators. Wearing my white uniform, I was one of the guys again. In the marching band we all looked and acted the same.

Damn that graduation! Leaving high school meant leaving marching band. Once again I was in search of a safe place to exist. I found it one Sunday at church. It seemed so obvious to me; I would love to be part of the clergy. Priests get to sing all the time; they are respected; they're invited to dinner parties; and they get to wear gaudy outfits in front of thousands of people. It would be perfect.

I began going on retreats and meeting with vocation directors; I started hanging out with seminarians. I was one of the boys again and was anxious to put on the Roman collar; all the clergy looked and acted the same.

During this time of discernment I was compelled to finish my degree in music education, a degree that has turned out to be my greatest blessing. God works in mysterious ways, and He knows what is best for our future. While waiting for the appropriate time to enter the seminary, I began teaching elementary music. After a few years of watching the children interact with one another I made the greatest discovery of my life: If you are feeling like you're not one of the boys, perhaps you should change your concept of how boys look and act.

I had spent my life attempting to look and act like everyone else, when what I really needed was to simply look and act like me.

✻

"Mr. Fridgen," said Zach. "I'm not going to get in trouble for asking you this, am I?"

"Of course not, Zach," I replied. "In fact, I'm proud of you for having the courage to talk *with* me instead of going to the playground to talk *about* me."

After considering my life, I knew how to answer him. More importantly, I learned that gender identification issues cannot wait until high school; I needed Zach to know that you do not have to be what society says you are. I stood before him not as a choirboy, drum major, or priest, but simply as me.

"Zach, yes, I am gay. I have been for all my life, and I do not wish to be any different; this is how God made me. I am not the only gay teacher in this school, and you may someday learn that many of your classmates are gay. In fact, you are going to meet gay people everywhere you go throughout your whole life.

"I know that you are a great kid, Zach, and I hope you will remember that there are many different kinds of people on this planet: black, white, blond, brunette, the list goes on and on. There are men, like your dad, who want to make their lives with women.

There are women, like your mom, who want to be with men. But, Zach, don't forget that there are also women who want to make their lives with other women, and men who want to be with men. There is enough love in God's heart for all the different kinds of people; I hope you will have enough love in your heart as well."

I could tell from his face that Zach had been expecting a simple yes or no answer; he got much more. As a teacher of primary students, the impact I make on academic skills can be observed daily. But the difference I make in personal development is never immediately evident. It may be years—if ever—before I find out whether Zach learned my real lesson: Don't worry so much about being one of the boys. Just be.

MY DOG DYKE

Julia Haines
Music teacher
Stratford Friends School
Havertown, Pennsylvania

As an out teacher working with elementary-age children with learning differences, I always look for that teachable moment. My students, never ones to disappoint, gave me a teachable moment that I will always cherish.

One morning in the spring of 2003 one of my most challenging students, A., came into my room muttering "dyke...dyke" over and over again. He was really taken with this word and kept remarking on it, sometimes under his breath, sometimes in a stage whisper.

I asked him if he knew what it meant. In fact, I asked the whole class of 10- and 11-year-olds if anyone knew what it meant. One student, Z., raised his hand. " I think it means demented," he said.

"No," I told them. "There are two meanings of the word *dyke*. One meaning is a wall to prevent flooding."

I then asked if anyone had ever heard of the story from Holland about the boy who prevented a disaster by putting his finger in a leaking dike. None of my students had heard this story. I found this to be very interesting as this was an archetypal story that had been repeatedly told to many of my contemporaries in the baby-boom generation when we were kids. I had grown up with this story, a parable about a young person who suffers discomfort in order to help safeguard his community. (I later found out that this was a fictional story by the American writer Mary Mapes Dodge but that it had so much impact that the Dutch actually built a statue to commemorate the story.)

The students started looking askance; they had no relationship to this story. Meanwhile, A. kept muttering "Dyke…dyke…I like this word, I think I'll name my dog Dyke."

Then, one of the other students asked: "Teacher Julia, what is the other meaning?"

I looked around and said: "It is a slang word for *lesbian.*"

The silence was delicious as you could see the students digesting this new information. Then A. started muttering "Dyke, Dyke, I'm going to call my dog Dyke. Hey, Dykey, come here…that will sound good in the park." His fascination with the word seemed to be fueled with this new information.

At this point, I told him directly that no, he couldn't do that, as it was offensive and inappropriate. He looked shocked and asked "Why, Teacher Julia?"

So I said: "I am a lesbian, and I don't want to hear you using the word in that manner."

Now the silence rang deeper. All the students, including one who had lesbian moms, were looking at me incredulously. I waited.

And then, dear Z. raised his hand and said quite sincerely: " But Teacher Julia, how come you didn't tell us this at the beginning of the year?" This question got some of the other students nodding and talking in agreement. It was all I could do to contain my delight.

Now I had the floor. I just looked at my students and said, "Oh, right, I'm going to stand up in front of the class in September and say, 'Hi, I'm Teacher Julia, your lesbian music teacher.'"

Everybody started laughing except for A., who looked flustered. He sat back for a minute and then raised his hand. "Why do they let you teach here?" he asked.

"Because I am a good teacher," I replied.

He then asked, "But, um, don't you, um, bother, um, you know, the other girl teachers, don't they get, um, upset…um, ah, because you, um, bother…" to which I asked him, "Do you mean harass?" This young boy knew this word quite well, as he had been to the assistant principal's office more than once for harassing girls at the beginning of the year, and he nodded his head vigorously. I looked at him again and said, "No, I am a good teacher, and good teachers don't harass other people."

Then he wanted to know if he should tell his mother. I told them all that this was a good topic they could go home and talk to their families about. Later, I heard from one of the parents that her daughter had come home and said, "I've known Teacher Julia all my life, and I can't believe that she never told me this before. How come I didn't know?"

But A. still wanted to know how I could teach at the school. I let the whole class know that not only was I a lesbian, but we also had gay and lesbian parents, and it was important for our school community to be welcoming to all families.

Then E., who is usually very quiet, raised her hand and said, "My moms are lesbians." Almost all the class knew that, as her moms had visited their classes to talk about their family and many students had been over to her house. To empower E. to speak her truth was the most rewarding part of this experience.

When I am open to my students, it makes it safer for them to be open in our school community. I know it is essential for me to continue this journey, not only working with teachable moments, but also making sure that I bring my experience to the students so that they can feel safe and affirmed in our school community.

MY JOURNEY IN EDUCATION

Jannette Manuel
Family and consumer science education department head
Garfield High School
Seattle, Washington

I was 10 years old when I realized something about me was different from all of the other girls in the neighborhood. It wasn't a question, nor something I needed to rationalize, but rather a statement to my own self: "I am gay!" At the same time, though, I knew that I wanted to be a teacher one day, and that brought up so many more questions—it was more of a complicated process than my own coming out. Am I going to be a teacher in my native Philippines? What subject could I possibly teach?

Throughout my life I have always admired my teachers and thought of nothing more profoundly significant than to be a teacher myself. They have in their many ways given me so much hope and support and such a sense of belonging. It's amazing how even their smiles at times allowed me to not feel not so alone.

When my family and I moved to Seattle in 1989 I found a "home" in Eileen Knobbs's classroom at Ballard High School. Though I can't remember much of my high school years, I'll never forget Ms. Knobbs. I was extremely shy and even though I could speak English, the difference in language and culture made school difficult. In her classroom she allowed me to be who I am and to succeed at my own pace.

It wasn't until I was attending North Seattle Community

College, when I worked as a mentor for the Higher Education Project, that I knew for sure that I would become a high school teacher. Working with those high school students was a revelation: It brought me immense satisfaction. Their energy, curiosity, and growth were something I wanted to be a part of. I finally settled on a degree in human development, specifically family and consumer science education (FACSE) at Washington State University. I couldn't wait to get started. I knew that from then on, my life would be full of excitement, growth, and revelations.

I began my teaching career at Garfield High School in Seattle. It is one of the most diverse inner-city schools in the state of Washington, with more than 1,700 students. Though I was not extremely excited to be at Garfield (simply because I had my heart set on teaching at the high school I went to, Ballard), I really didn't have time to mull over the situation. Not only was it my first year of teaching but also the department head and one of the teachers in the Seattle School District who were just starting ProStart, a culinary-hospitality program for high school students. It was a crazy year, but support from my administration, my mentor—Mona Mendoza—and my FACSE colleagues allowed me to survive and also grow from the experience.

Though I knew that I was different from everyone else, it was more apparent than ever when I first went to a conference for vocational educators. I walked into a room full of FACSE educators who were mostly Caucasian middle-age women. I felt self-conscious of the fact that I was a Filipina and that I was probably the only gay woman in the room. Although there were many who were welcoming, there were (and still are) women who give me second looks or question my presence at these conferences. It irks me when this happens, yet I have to stop myself from becoming upset, for I have to realize that some of these women have never seen the likes of me in their daily lives. I have to educate them.

I feel quite fortunate to be working with a group of women in my school that is extremely supportive. Since FACSE is comprised of a specialized group of vocational educators, we find ourselves working together in many different situations. I know that I can approach anyone with anything. How many people can say that their colleagues offer them advice on artificial insemination and give them a turkey baster to use during the insemination process? How many can say that their colleagues are offering them their husband's or boyfriend's sperm? In fact, even Ms. Knobbs, my former high school teacher and now my colleague, offered to ask her son for a "donation." I never really had to come out to these women; it was simply a fact that needed to be known. It was as simple as the day I told myself that I am gay.

It is hard to see some of my colleagues who are extremely scared of others finding out who they are. Their fears consume their energy and constrain their ability to function properly in their careers and in their lives. It makes me feel free and scared at the same time. I am glad that I long ago acknowledged and accepted who I am, and it is that comfort that makes me free to be who I am as a person and as a teacher. Consequently I find it easy to encourage my students to be who they are and to become what they want to be and to be happy. I find it easy to be honest—sometimes brutally—to those around me. I find it easy to be able to point out to my students that sometimes their behaviors are not that appropriate.

Though it is not common knowledge, it is also not a big secret in school that Ms. Manuel is gay. Some students figure it out the first day in class. For some, their friends tell them. Yet, there are those that do not have a clue and still to this day ask me if I have a boyfriend. I have never pretended to be anything less than who I am. I am not the most feminine woman, which I suppose makes it easier for them to guess.

I have come out to a number of students, male or female—sometimes out of need and necessity. During my second year of teaching, I had a student who I suspected was gay. She showed signs of a person who was going through the coming-out process and I noticed that she was spending a lot of time in my room. She needed and wanted someone to talk to. One afternoon she stopped by my room with another female student. She looked extremely sad and before she left, she informed me that she would not be here the following day. I told her that things would get better and that she would survive whatever it was that was bothering her. I didn't think much of what she said until the next day when I didn't see her in class. I started panicking and soon found out that indeed, she had tried to hurt herself. She was in the hospital for about three weeks, and during that time I made sure that I was there for her. I was one of the few people she allowed to visit her, and at times we even talked about what happened. Even though she survived, to this day I feel guilty about ignoring what she said to me that day in class. I promised myself that after that incident, never again would I ignore such comments. From then on I've created an environment that is more welcoming and a "home" to my students.

Since then I have had the opportunity to have real conversations with students about feelings, relationships, and family. Yet there are still times when fear outweighs everything else. Sometimes nothing is guaranteed. My confidence as a person and as a teacher was tested a couple of months ago. It was one of those things that teachers would consider as their worst nightmare—certainly as a gay teacher I considered it my worst nightmare. A student started a rumor that a female student had a crush on me. When I found out, I was more scared that I'd ever been in my life. Though it wasn't as bad as if I was the one rumored to have a crush on a female student, I still felt completely paralyzed. And even though the student assured me that whoever started the rumor was just an immature and selfish person, and that this was just a moment where we were being "tested," it was still hard to function properly with something like that looming over my head. For months I kept waiting for something to happen—difficult conversations with the administration, perhaps an investigation, perhaps even losing my job.

Though none of these things happened, I felt vulnerable that something like this can happen again. I could be shattered so easily. Even with the support system I have, there are still many things unclear and undefined as I continue my journey as an educator.

Though I have never considered myself an activist, I have found myself becoming more and more vocal about diversity, acceptance, and tolerance. Whether it is talking to a student about why he or she called someone a "fag" or advocating the need for the inclusion of LGBT issues in the family and consumer science education curriculum, I have started to make these things my responsibility and will continue to do so. I do it not only for the sake of my students but also for my colleagues. As I am about to end my fourth year of teaching, I am excited. Even with all the uncertainties of this world, I know that I can count on the excitement, growth, and revelations that this teaching brings. I look forward to the day when I can say that I have journeyed a million miles, a journey that has been full of rich experiences and lessons, all of which started because I wanted to become a teacher.

I'LL SEE YOU THERE

Malana Summers
Eighth grade core teacher
Rivera Middle School
Merced, California

L'audace, encore de l'audace, toujours l'audace! I can't believe that I'm actually doing this. By now, of course, I'd heard this refrain from the little voice inside me too many times to count. The Rubicon had long since been crossed. The only thing left was to follow through.

It had been months since I'd somewhat reluctantly told Sallie, my therapist, that I needed to transition fully. Already having been sobered by a painful divorce as well as the estrangement of my children, countless hours of electrolysis, and more than two years of hormone replacement therapy, I'd had plenty of opportunities to reflect. Somehow, this had to work.

Outing myself was not something I really wanted to do, but it had to be done. There was no other way now. I had seen others try and fail, had learned from witnessing those mistakes, and I had a plan. I would go straight to the most senior officials, promise to avoid publicity whenever possible, and be a team player. And so on May 11, 2000, I met with my superintendent and his personnel associate. Holding my hand was a union representative who also happened to be a colleague and friend. Pushing copies of a letter outlining my clinical history and professional assessments across the table in reply to a "Why are we here?" was like the opening ante of some surreal poker game. (I would come to realize just how apt the analogy was as spring warmed into summer.)

By August my assignment had morphed from eighth-grade teacher at the school I'd been working at for 20 years to being squirreled away as a teacher on special assignment in the district's profession development center. The concept wasn't so terrible. Both the district and I had sought a "win-win" situation—that is, of course, after both they and I had sought legal advice. The reality turned out to be less appealing. My duties were not very well thought-out. One long year was spent in a series of largely menial functions. One particularly frustrating example was spending several days removing staples from collated paper packets so that the paper could be recycled. Was I being nudged into giving up? I thought so.

Meanwhile, word of my transition didn't take long to spread through the local educational community. During the months of my mutually agreed exile, I endured looks of questioning, astonishment, and disgust. Lord only knows what was going on behind my back. I tried not to imagine. During this phase, the worst thing was being condescended to. No longer a respected veteran educator, I was now a neophyte bimbo. I thought I was mentally prepared for what would happen. I was not.

I should interject at this point that I am no transsexual poster girl. In my 40s, over 6 feet tall, and by any objective assessment quite the plane Jane, I was attempting what even kind supporters in the trans community would suggest was nearly impossible.

My "passing" was called into question. Well-meaning friends privately suggested that I needed more time to present convincingly. Ironically, stealth—a prized attribute among many transsexuals—is nonexistent in any on-the-job transition. I would probably never completely pass in an environment where coworkers at my school were so grounded in my "him" past. Regardless of any cosmetic image, how could I ever pass in those people's eyes?

Further, I would not be in an insulated private setting. The prospect of public scrutiny, ridicule, and condemnation was quite real. More than one sister predicted that right-wing protests would make themselves felt in one way or another. Ultimately, so conventional wisdom ran, even if I could personally endure the stress, the school system would bow to pressure from parents and other outside forces with political and moral agendas.

Finally, I had a long history in the educational community here. Never mind that it was a positive one. How would the whispers of siblings, ex-students, colleagues, parents, and staff allow me to successfully function teaching adolescents? Problematic or not, I had to try.

By the spring of 2001 I was ready to return to the classroom. Senior school officials still seemed unsure as to how to proceed. On the one hand, I was told to apply for any and all transfer vacancies. On the other, middle-level administration privately suggested to me that I should consider the more low-profile field of grant writing. (For my own sake.) This was the central San Joaquin Valley, after all, the reasoning went, "And you know how people are." At one point I was even called into the assistant superintendent's office for an exploratory conversation as to whether I might be interested in a two-year severance package. Thank you, no.

I'm a Capricorn, and stubborn as any goat. I teach middle school. It's what I know; it's what I do. I'd like to think I'm pretty good at it—every evaluation I've received in my career has said so. Therefore, it's not surprising that I should be determined to return to the classroom. Curiously, this made sense to virtually no one that I talked to.

In any case, after prioritizing the available vacancies, and though I preferred a new school, I was informed that I would be returning to my original school and assignment. Oh, joy! To face people, some of who'd known "Butch" (couldn't you just die?) for two decades, now as Malana—fresh from breast augmentation and on the verge of the big snip-snip—was daunting. Where were Toto and that wizard when I really needed them?

During the first few days, if I hadn't had a sense of humor, all would have been lost. Reactions from staff ran the entire gamut. I'm still awaiting the appropriate offer of a doctorate in humanities. Seriously. One of my favorite reactions was from a sincerely concerned colleague and friend who took me aside and in a quiet moment asked, "Haven't you thought about moving to San Francisco?" Another was, "Now you know how it feels to be black." That one took a while to grasp as I'm one pale-complexioned, fair-haired honky girl.

I was going back to the classroom, though. Or was I? At the 11th hour, the school district got cold feet. I was called in and begged to accept an on-campus position as a nonteaching programs facilitator. I would learn later that downtown was getting phone calls from "concerned citizens." Another Chernobyl? Sensing the pervasive mood—that the sky was indeed falling—I reluctantly agreed. This time—with the demand that I be given a signed memorandum of understanding that should I so desire, I would be able to return to full-time teaching duties for the 2002–2003 school year—I agreed. Patience can be a virtue. It was noted that this would facilitate a less-demanding recovery from my scheduled gender reassignment surgery, set for December 2001. This was in my best interest…at least that's what I was told.

Fast-forward to today.

At the time of this writing, March 2004, I am in the middle of my second year back in the classroom—at my original assignment, eighth-grade language arts and social studies, at my original school. My students seem to have forgotten, if they ever knew, that I was a "him." Occasionally, other students will hear the rumors and catcall my former name and gender from a distance in an attempt to get a reaction. And yes, it hurts.

Even though California's education and legal codes protect me from harassment and employment discrimination, I can't pretend that it doesn't exist. School officials are wary of taking forceful response for fear of opening a can of worms—and I understand their plight, to a degree. One needs a thick skin to transition on the job!

Nobody would choose my life. At one point a school official spoke of my journey as a lifestyle choice, and I nearly became unglued. Anyone who would suggest that is, to put it tactfully, ill-informed. To spend the first half of my life in the anguish of the wrong gender was ghastly. To try and fashion a "normal" life in denial of a powerful internal reality was destructive, not only to me but ultimately to those I cared most deeply for. And then to risk all that I had managed to acquire—love, family, friendship, career, economic security, and respect—in a leap of faith that seemed akin to leaping from a Cessna without a parachute. There was no choice involved, only an imperative.

Today I am consoled by the fact that I have persevered. I never went on *Oprah,* and I haven't even been mentioned in what passes for a newspaper in my locale. People who were radically opposed to my return to the classroom have receded into the forgiving veil of time. I have lost friends and made new ones on my journey. Those who I thought would rally behind me didn't. But supporters from unexpected quarters have shown great compassion. In each case, they know who they are.

If, in some small measure, my experience can make it easier, or provide some inspiration for the next trans person, then maybe I've helped. I'm still looking for "Happily Ever After," and I hope to see you there.

FEELING ALL RIGHT ON
THE RELIGIOUS LEFT

Patricia Lyons
Religion teacher
St. Stephen's and St. Agnes's School
Alexandria, Virginia

Seniors in high school used to wait for the mailman to hear responses from colleges to which they applied. I hear that now you can find out on the Internet, which is an amazing change. Back in 1990 I thought I was a high-tech senior because, rather than stalk letter carriers near the official notification date, I picked up the phone and called the only college to which I had applied.

"Harvard University, Office of Undergraduate Admissions. Can I help you?" What an understated request. I gave my social security number while I listened to my parents whispering in the next room, waiting to hear the news. I had called from the privacy of my bedroom on my Garfield the Cat telephone. I remember spending the time on hold by looking at the bulging white eyes of that faux feline and thinking, *Why I am making such an important call on this ridiculous phone?* Then, out of the silence, the words: "You were admitted. Do you have any other questions?" I gently hung up Garfield, looked at myself in that old full-length mirror, and whispered the words, "They can't touch me now."

What a sad first reaction to such wonderful news—especially since I've always been known as a lighthearted and hopeful person. To this day I know my parents would be shocked to think that when I entered that room to share my college news, the smile on my face did not represent the first emotion I had felt. I applied to Harvard for many reasons, most of which my parents and my friends knew about and understood. But no one but Garfield had any idea that on the top of that list of reasons was: armor in my adult life.

How naive I was to think that an Ivy League education would somehow take away the threat and dread I felt as a teenager when I thought about how the world would see me and treat me for being a homosexual. I did not have the word *homosexual* back then for my feelings, but I knew even as a child that I was different than most of my female peers, and I felt that difference getting stronger and not weaker with every new day of my life. Who was I afraid of? Everybody, I guess. But most of all, as a person of strong faith since childhood, I was afraid of those who would reject me in the name of God. Growing up as a Catholic and looking at crucifixes all the time, I was a very young child when I first thought about what religious people do to people whom they reject. I never questioned God's love for me, but every glance at Jesus on the cross was a kind of signpost to me of where my future might lead.

Today, I am a much-loved teacher in my school. I enjoy what older teachers call "the young-teacher honeymoon." This is the phenomenon of students seeing young teachers as infinitely cooler and more hip than any gray-haired teacher could ever be, no matter how interesting their classroom actually is. Every time I find a lonely gray hair in my head, I pluck it out quickly and am forced to admit that these honeymoon days may soon come to an end.

I also think the subject I teach also makes for easy friends among students. All religion classes in my Episcopal school are electives, which the students must take a number of in order to graduate. The idea of mandatory religion classes is a chore for many, but it can also be a break from the major academic subjects that they have been taking for years. I have always seen the unpopularity of religion as a challenge to take on. I bring in doughnuts and engage in near stand-up comedy acts to introduce the topics and ideas of my classes. I run my religion classes like philosophy seminars, with lots of debating, laughing, and talking about contemporary films and television shows. We talk about music videos, Internet surfing, politicians, and professional sports figures. We talk about Thomas Aquinas, Martin Luther, Nietzsche, Foucault, and *The Simpsons.* I will use any medium to generate interest in spiritual ideas.

I am committed to making the classroom a space of safety and enjoyment—where the talk is not of the dogmatic force of religion but rather of the dynamic creativity of spiritual ideas. I go out to dinner with students of other faiths to hear about their upbringings; I read the religious texts that communicate their faith traditions; I go to synagogue with Jewish students to affirm their faith; I attend the confirmations of Christian students; and I have seized every opportunity to speak at youth conferences in the area on interfaith dialogue with Muslim, Sikh, and Hindu teenagers. I do all this to show every student that the Christianity I practice does not fear the faiths of others but, on the contrary, rejoices in common ground.

Most of my students are Christians, and many are politically center-right Catholics or Protestant evangelicals of many flavors. Most have had a fairly conservative upbringing on social issues. Prior to this past year, I had never considered coming out to this community because I'd convinced myself that I could do more to broaden their understanding of Christianity by becoming their (heterosexual) hero. I have always known the importance of teachers coming out to their students and to their schools, but my deep fear of being attacked for being different led to many years of hiding and rationalizations. I convinced myself that my circumstances—and not my actual fears of being rejected—were the reason that I could not speak. After all, I am a teacher of religion in a church-affiliated Christian high school. Nevertheless, teachers who dared to come out have always inspired me. But whenever educator friends of mine would question me about why I had not taken that step, I would launch into an explanation of The Strategy.

The Strategy was to get kids excited about a version of Christianity that is inclusive of people of all sexual orientations. I worried that "waving my banner" could start rumors and ruin The Strategy. I rationalized that I could do more "on the inside" of conservative Christian circles, rather than coming out and being banished from that subculture for good. I believed that if I came out, many of my students and their parents would shut out my voice and put up walls around their spirituality to avoid my influence on their fairly rigid religious assumption that homosexuality is, at best, displeasing to God.

Hiding my sexual identity by trying to be a spiritual superhero was exhausting. I preached at our weekly school chapel sermons, full of jokes and stories and accessible spiritual messages. I prayed at football season opening dinners, led a community service trip to Honduras, trekked across Europe with history students, chaperoned dances, visited students who were sick or depressed in their homes, baked brownies for student birthdays, and went to the funerals of parents and grandparents. I walked the sidelines of sporting events and approached parents about their moral concerns for their kids, or even for themselves. I took all the esteem that came from this superhero reputation as a sign that The Strategy was working.

It has pained me, though, to be in the middle of conversations with parents and students and to listen to them spew rants against "pro-gay books in the library," "sex-promoting gays," "the homosexual agenda," and "the abomination of homosexuality." I have had dozens of students and parents say point-blank that "a person cannot be a true Christian and a practicing homosexual." I would try not to blink while offering tacit thoughts on inclusion and then changing the subject. I never lied about my sexual orientation, but I never spoke of it either.

But this last year the students have pulled me to a new place. In my Christian ethics class, I ask kids every year what mentors or role models they did not have but needed along the way. More than one student wrote anonymously, "I wish I had a gay teacher." The handwriting alone made me skip a breath. Another student wrote on an anonymous form, "I wish the gay teachers here would say it, because when they don't it sends the message that they are ashamed."

I don't think these students were baiting me to come out. I felt like I had betrayed them. The Strategy required silence so as not to lose any popularity or influence with the students and parents who already enjoy the privileged status of heterosexual and Christian in America. My conscience began to whisper, *Whose side are you on?*

What began last year was a maddening conversation in my head. For the first time since I began teaching Christian theology to young people, I was seriously questioning The Strategy, which said that telling people I was gay would do more damage than good by possibly limiting my audience. I thought back to the people who had made the most difference in my own spiritual understanding of myself and God and how they had handled the issue of coming out. One name and one moment walked to center stage in my memory.

I had been a freshman at Harvard for one month when my father died of a long illness. The morning after his funeral I left my home in New York and flew back to college to try and restart my college experience and the rest of my life. I did not have any real peers as friends yet, but I had made a connection at the University Church, where a dynamic seminarian had gotten me involved in teaching Sunday school. I had also heard three weeks of incredible preaching from Harvard's famous chaplain, the Reverend Professor Peter J. Gomes. I loved his vision of life and God from the start. Working in his church was the most exciting decision I made that first month. I was too scared to shake his hand at any public event, though, and felt it would be a year or two before I got up the courage to introduce myself.

When I came back to college after my dad's funeral, I was stunned to be approached by Reverend Gomes at the coffee hour after church the following Sunday. He had heard about my dad, and he expressed his deepest condolences. I was speechless. And then he really shocked me by inviting me over to his house for tea the following day. Of course I accepted. His house even had a name: Sparks House. I had never been personally invited to a house with its own name. I was definitely one of the most famous freshmen in my dorm.

I paced the floor for hours before the meeting, then walked to his residence so elated and so nervous that my palms were sweating. What could I possibly say to one of Harvard's most renowned professors? I practiced conversation ideas all the way over.

Tea, as I remember it, was not long, but it was definitely an oasis of attention and warmth. It was a very rainy day, and Reverend Gomes met me at his front door with a loud but warm greeting, whisked me in, and took my coat before I could say a word. He poured out words about New England weather, and by the way, did I like sugar in my tea and would I please, please, please take a seat anywhere I felt comfortable. His house was a totally overwhelming and poorly lit museum of artifacts, 19th-century furniture, and photographs on every surface. Every available space bore some honorary plaque or signed paper or framed image. There was more than one picture of Reverend Gomes with every president since I was born, members of royal families, military figures, social activists, the Archbishop of Canterbury, and dozens of mysterious people who looked important and whose identities I hoped a Harvard education would someday reveal to me.

Although I had worried about what we could talk about, I should have remembered that this preacher was, according to *Time* magazine, one of the best talkers in the world, and so the time passed quickly and gracefully. Soon, I was at the door saying good-bye and walking on air back to my dorm.

Perhaps because I was still dealing with my father's death or maybe because I was focused on adjusting to college life, I do not remember too many of the details of the following tumultuous week at Harvard. However, the whole country would soon be embroiled in the events that would occur.

There was a student-run conservative political publication called *Peninsula* that few people read, though it had a loyal following among conservatives of all ages at the university. The November issue came out on more or less the same day as my tea with Reverend Gomes. The entire issue was devoted to homosexuality—essay after essay attacking the gay community with rhetoric from every academic discipline. It was cold, calculating, and disturbing, with lots of talk of "tough love" and "eternal truth." I found the whole issue scary because of its systematic warnings and shady statistics that presented homosexuality as our society's most pressing social evil.

Needless to say, the university was up in arms. I was walking back to my dorm one day that week when I came upon a support rally for gay, lesbian, and transgender members of the university community. The crowd had gathered on the steps of Memorial Church. I only stopped to listen because I saw my new friend Peter Gomes standing on the stage near the microphone. When he took the microphone, I expected to hear kind words of support from a minister who had long been known to be politely supportive of minority groups.

His first words were of sadness about hatred in all forms. He spoke of a more loving and inclusive Christianity. Then I heard his historic words fly through the air of Harvard Yard: "I stand here a Christian and a gay man...that which is irreconcilable for some, is reconcilable for me." There are no words to describe the reaction of the crowd. People were just plain stunned. The Plummer Professor of Christian Morals, the Preacher to Harvard University for over 20 years, a man who had prayed at the inaugurals for both Reagan and George H.W. Bush, had just announced that he was a homosexual. I remember thinking that I had just witnessed a man change his life forever.

Looking back, I am sure Peter Gomes had something of The Strategy for himself during those two decades of stunning popularity in all theological circles across the globe. But one day he dropped The Strategy—and in so doing, radically changed my life and countless others. He was a teacher of the Christian faith who did more than send coded messages of support for all: He also spoke the words to name his life and its vocation as a gay man.

The sad cries for gay role models from my students and the memory of Peter Gomes's coming-out slowly brought me to a point where I realized that my Strategy had to go. I did not know how I could ever find the courage or even the opportunity to come out, but I could feel in the depth of my being that it was the right thing to do.

Then I was asked to speak on a panel with three students at a schoolwide assembly on diversity. The invitation was to speak for three to five minutes about a personal experience of prejudice and/or why it is important for people to be allies in social justice. From the second the offer was made, that voice of conscience started screaming at my fears: *Why not?*

It was a Thursday afternoon, and I'd been asked to speak the following Monday morning. I didn't sleep that night. I thought of every senior class that had graduated in past years and how guilty I had felt at every graduation to say goodbye to students who I knew felt ashamed of their sexual identity and to whom and for whom I had said nothing. By sunrise Friday morning, I knew I had to come out. I met with the Head of School, who spoke kind words of respect for me as a teacher and wise words of confidence in me as a professional to speak appropriately about my sexual orientation.

Looking back on that weekend, I think I was in a state of mourning for the coming death of the safety that had always come from The Strategy. I went to every athletic event that Friday afternoon and hung around with every parent and child I could until I was the last person to leave the fields. I went to more school events on Saturday; in fact, I just hung around the school building and exchanged small talk with anyone I could because I believed that such mindless and pleasant chatter would never be possible after the assembly. It was a busy weekend of what felt like packing for a trip or moving away. I felt more determined as each hour passed and each to-do item was crossed off the long list, but also I felt sad at every step. The long honeymoon, in my imagination, was going to come to an abrupt end.

Monday morning came and I was nervous beyond description. I sat on the stage during that assembly and listened to the three students speak before me about their experiences of economic and racial discrimination. Their words were beautiful and I tried hard to listen to them with full attention and forget my own impending words, which were boiling in my head and causing my sweat to drip from my neck down my back and chest. What kept me sane was looking at all of my students. I hoped they would hear what I'd heard that day from Peter Gomes: that honesty is a greater gift than strategy.

After sharing my story, in which I spoke the words, "I am a homosexual," I ended by saying,

> Those of you who are minorities of color are my heroes. It drives me crazy with anger that people hate me for the way God has made me, but I can hide the truth if I want to. It makes me so sad that some people don't believe me when I say that God and I have studied, prayed, and talked together a great deal about the person I am and that we are both proud of it. But people of color cannot hide their oppressed status like I can. That's what this word *privilege* is all about. I have the privilege of hiding what people might discriminate against if I want to, and that means I have more power to protect myself than those of you who cannot hide. But today I have decided to lay down that privilege and walk away from it so that we can work together in honesty about the fact that we all need allies, and that we all need allies desperately.
>
> You asked me what I think "being an ally" means. I think it means giving up the power of any arbitrary privilege or any unearned opportunity to hide from the ugliness of prejudice. When those of us who can hide, do hide, we do it to save ourselves, although it means sitting by and watching others who cannot hide their differences drown in discrimination. Days like today help to break that cycle here and now. Today I jump into the waters of discrimination with you, which means I am going to need as much support as I plan to offer. But that equality feels better than safety. I dare all of you to jump in. Thank you.

The applause came strong and long. Microphones were open for questions, and the first came from one of my Hindu students, who looked right at me as he grabbed the microphone. He spoke loudly, "I do not have a question, I just wanted to say, Miss Lyons, I'll be your ally." I choked as I tried to smile and keep down the sob that lunged up to my throat with my first breath. The applause came again, but now just for him and for me. One thought came to me as I watched him sit down: If *that* is the only student who is left loving me after all this, if that is the only kind of parent or colleague left, if that is how the few who are left talking to me after this day think and love, then just a handful is more than I need to live an incredible life.

The end of the assembly brought a crowd of students to the podium. I thought that they would all have things to say, but instead they wanted to give hugs and kisses and tears, from boys and girls and colleagues alike. I will never forget their embraces. The very first class I had after the assembly had written on the board, MISS LYONS, YOU ROCK. I had no idea that throwing away so much could feel so good.

Who knows what the future will bring for me at this school. The assembly came just before exams, so everyone quickly went back to the business of schooling within a few hours of the event that was life-changing for me. In earlier years there would perhaps have been an outcry, and yet this day seemed to pass as a great success but also as a sort of nonevent as far as scandal goes. The notes and letters kept coming, but the school also just moved on.

Two weeks later I delivered that sermon to seniors at their last chapel, and it was such a wonderful moment. I did not mention anything about sexual orientation, but for the first time I didn't have to. The issue no longer needed to be the silent but forced subtext in every word. Rather, the real truth is now the text of everything I say in this community. In that sermon I shared my hopes and prayers that those seniors see themselves as children of God and people of dignity, and I did it as the person who knows what I know because of, and not in spite of, who I really am. And for the first time, I know many kids and adults had to face the reality that any spiritual wisdom they get (or ever got) from my words or deeds grows out of my loving and serving God as a gay person.

For many, I know that this fact will cause confusion about their religious assumptions, faith commitments, and Biblical convictions. Teachers usually aim to bring people out of confusion. In this case, however, I think some confusion might be a good thing for social or religious conservatives and their ignorance and fears about homosexuality. Who knows, maybe some of them—like the slave owners, antisuffragists, or pro-segregationists before them—might have to face the possibility that much of what they define as "pleasing to God" might instead be a complex collection of cultural wishes pleasing to the Western tradition.

On the last day of school I sat in the same crowded auditorium for an end-of-the-year awards assembly. I listened to the reading of the dedication of the yearbook by its student editors. They don't say the teacher's name until the end, but by the end of the first sentence of the dedication, I knew, and I bowed my head in my hands and whispered, "Oh, my God." As I walked to the stage on which I had shed my armor for love of those kids two weeks before, the standing ovation was enough to make my steps wobbly. I hugged those seniors and knew I was living in a moment that few people will ever experience. That moment, made possible by the love of so many students and colleagues, is why I teach.

Part Two
Lessons Taught…
and Learned

I STARTED OUT BY NOT TALKING TO ANYONE...

Mike Fishback
Language arts and social studies teacher
The Park School of Baltimore
Brooklandville, Maryland

"When I came here in fifth grade, I had a really bad stuttering problem," began Davon.

For all of his 13 years, "Davon" was a wise kid. Our social studies class, which focused on the theme of identity, provided an outlet for Davon to discuss his own unique situation—as a new student, as an African-American in a mostly white school, as a Muslim in the wake of September 11. And now he saw it as his duty to respond when his classmate "Amy" asked, "Why does Mr. Fishback feel it's so important to tell people he's gay? Why can't gay people just keep it to themselves?"

"I started out by not talking to anyone," Davon continued, his voice quivering a bit. "I was too scared to let anyone know I stuttered, so basically I hid. And then I came home one day and my mom told me that I needed to just talk, and once people got to know me they'd be OK with the stuttering and realize that I was a really cool person even though I stuttered, and that's exactly what happened. And now I'm more confident and I don't even stutter as much anymore. And that's sort of why Mr. Fishback needed to come out."

✳

Looking back on my own middle and high school years, I see a closeted gay boy who never seemed to get bullied yet nonetheless felt like a victim. I spent those years passing as straight and worrying about my future. I tried to figure out how I'd keep my dirty secret the rest of my life. Fortunately, my younger brother—whose natural affect made passing as straight more of a challenge—came out during our teenage years, and slowly, with his help and the guidance of a few other friends and family members in whom I confided, I was completely out by my senior year of college.

Yet not one year later, the closet door beckoned once more. I was hired to be an intern teacher at the Park School, an independent school in the Baltimore area. Although I was just getting used to being openly gay, I decided that in my new school environment, I had to proceed cautiously. That winter, scandal broke out within the Catholic Church, and the terms "gay male" and "child abuser" were thrown about interchangeably in the media. And even though our school was "progressive," few teachers were out to their fellow faculty, and none were out to their students.

My youth and Ivy League credentials quickly earned me—or, more accurately, won me—respect among my colleagues. As I gradually came out to my fellow interns, and then to my faculty mentor, I sensed a desire in our community for a more open dialogue about homosexuality. When I was hired that spring to continue as a full-time middle school teacher, to craft a combined language arts and social studies curriculum, the principal suggested that I include a history of the civil rights movement.

"I'd love to," I responded, "and I want to focus not only on issues of race, but also on women's rights, and gay rights…"

The sentence continued in some random, unmemorable direction, but the words "gay rights" lingered in the air, waiting patiently to be seized and dealt with in whatever way fate intended. When

I finally concluded whatever I was rambling on about, she smiled and said, "That sounds exciting. We've never had a social studies class about gay rights before."

✳

Having gained the support of my administration, I entered my first year of solo teaching while planning the first gay rights unit.

Throughout the fall and winter, I kept asking myself the obvious question: Should I come out to my students? I had been developing a very positive rapport with my seventh graders; was it worth risking it all to provide them with a good role model? Or would it be enough to simply teach about gay issues?

I was made aware of the possible pitfalls of becoming an openly gay teacher. My parents, who have always been completely supportive of me, were worried that I could become a target of false allegations of sexual abuse, like other teachers about whom they had read. Some colleagues were cautious about my becoming the sole representative for all things gay. And in a recent school-wide survey, most students had expressed a belief that if someone were to be openly gay or lesbian at Park School, he or she would have a very difficult time being accepted.

But I also received words of encouragement, not only from my parents and colleagues, but also indirectly from students. In March, as part of an eighth-grade unit on persuasive writing, one student presented a speech to her classmates and teachers about homophobia. She argued that the only way to rid Park School of homophobia was for a faculty member to come out. The audience applauded, and I understood that she was right.

✳

By the first week of May, my seventh graders were well versed in identity, differences, and social justice. We had created individual "identity charts" to explore how we fit into society. We had read *To*

Kill a Mockingbird and "The Lottery" to examine the impact of tradition on human behavior. We had studied the meaning of race and the history of Jim Crow. One Friday I gave them a typical homework assignment: They were to read an article about the Florida adoption controversy and summarize the arguments for and against allowing gay couples to adopt children.

That same Friday, after consulting with the Head of School, I notified my colleagues that Monday would be the day when I would come out to my students. I requested that they encourage dialogue rather than stifle it, and I also pointed them to a section of the GLSEN Web site with suggestions for discussing such issues with students.

I started class a few minutes late Monday morning. My emotions floated somewhere in that realm between excited and nervous, recognizable in that it drains all the saliva from one's mouth. I eyed the full bottle of water that I had placed next to me. I would need it. The kids quieted down, and I began to speak.

"Before we begin discussing the homework, I'd like to say a few words about why we are studying the gay rights movement, because many schools in our country are afraid to teach about this topic. I think one reason is that many people see gay rights as being about sex—because the word *sex* is conveniently placed in the center of the word *homosexuality*—and many schools are afraid to talk about sex. But this is not about sex at all; it's about identity, and respecting differences in our society, which is exactly what we've been studying all year. So one reason we're looking at gay rights is that it's very relevant to our class's curriculum.

"A second reason is that the topic is extremely current. The article you read over the weekend was published less than two years ago. The Supreme Court is currently considering a major gay rights case, and just last week a high-ranking senator was criticized for making antigay remarks. We see these issues covered in the media all the time. In the grand scope of the civil rights movement, gay issues are the current battleground."

I took a sip of water.

"And a third reason, which is perhaps the most important one to me personally, is that I myself am gay."

I paused for a long moment to look around the classroom and allow this news to sink in. Some students returned a blank stare, others smiled, and still others began to get teary-eyed, even before I uttered my next words:

"I decided to teach this course on identity and respecting differences because I deal with these issues every day of my life. I'd also like to say that I am open about my sexuality with everyone in my life, including the Park faculty. Over the course of this year, I've realized that I admire and respect my students deeply, and that I can share this part of me with you and feel comfortable doing so. It's really a testament to how great you guys are."

I then opened the floor for questions and comments. I encouraged my students to ask me about anything, no matter how personal, with the exception of questions about sex itself.

The very first question was, "Are you going to adopt a baby from America or from overseas?"

Here are some of the other questions and comments I remember:

"Is being gay scientific or is it something you choose?"

"Isn't it hard to find someone to be with if everyone who's also gay is hiding who they are?"

"Do you hate people who are homophobic?"

"That guy who visited our class…is he…?" ("Yes, he's my boyfriend.")

"Do gay men like a different kind of guy than straight women do?"

"Did you get girlfriends when you were in school to cover up that you were gay?"

"I heard there are kids in the lower school who have same-sex parents."

"What do your parents think of you being gay?"

"What do you do about being Jewish, if the Bible says homosexuality is a sin?"

"How did you and your boyfriend meet?"

"At my old school there was a lesbian teacher who got fired when a student said she tried to hit on her."

"Are you going to get married?"

"What do you mean you're not allowed to get married?"

"When did you know you were gay?"

"Is it true that all bisexual women are really straight?"

"Did you ever like girls?"

"Were you nervous telling us?"

"You should add GAY to your identity chart now that you're out."

My seventh graders explored this issue with incredible maturity, thoughtfulness, and—most important—open minds. In retrospect, I should not have expected anything less. The week we spent studying the gay adoption battle, examining the life of Harvey Milk, and illustrating essays by adolescents about coming out was by far my most exhilarating and inspiring experience as a teacher.

That Thursday happened to be Grandparents Visiting Day. Members of the "Greatest Generation" observed a dynamic classroom conversation about gays in the military, for which my students and I earned many compliments. In fact, I received only positive feedback about the week, from parents, colleagues, and students. I am still dreading the first negative note, but it has yet to arrive.

But Amy, who was one of the deepest and most articulate thinkers in the class, and who never shied away from taking opposing viewpoints, was a bit uneasy about our study of homosexuality: "Why does Mr. Fishback feel it's so important to tell people he's gay? Why can't gay people just keep it to themselves?"

Yet rather than hiding her confusion or erupting in angry outcries over our lessons, Amy returned to class each day to ask her question again, each time in a sincere attempt to "get it." And each day I attempted to help her get it. I rehashed the hardships of my life. I referred back to the stories we'd read and the films we'd seen, trying to draw parallels. But it finally took 13-year-old

Davon, sitting her down at the end of class to tell her about his stuttering, to give it to her.

What I realized in that moment was that, as much of an advocate as I thought I had become, I was really only a teacher—a teacher with a powerful message and trusting students. The real advocates in that classroom were the students themselves. One who got it helped give it to his classmate. And the next Monday, that classmate, Amy, excitedly reported on the weekend's conversations, in which she had enlightened her family about homosexuality. She had gotten it and given it to others.

WHAT DO LECTURERS WEAR?

Josephine Allison Wilson
Guest lecturer
The London School of Economics
London, England

"What do lecturers wear?" is the question that I half-screamed at my flatmates the night before the first lecture I would ever give. I had been going to university lectures for six years at that point, I had been a full-time student all that time, and I had very rarely missed a scheduled lecture. However, on that particular night, I simply could not dredge up from all that experience what it was that these lecturers actually adorned themselves with before stepping up before any number of students to impart upon them the information that they had garnered from their years of experience—I had no idea what to put on.

Let me clarify.

I am a Ph.D. student at the Gender Institute located in the London School of Economics. My thesis concerns the construction of a theoretical framework, which can adequately account for the variety in trans subjectivities. This probably requires a much longer (and possibly quite dull to some, possibly even many, maybe even most) explanation, but suffice to say I am writing what I know about—namely trans people and their variety, being as I am quite a varied trans person.

One of the things that I have always wanted to do is teach. Luckily, being a Ph.D. student, I'd been encouraged to teach, which suited me fine—at least right up until the point someone actually asked me to do it. It was a lucky accident, really. An e-mail came through the ether to all the Ph.D. students in the Gender Institute asking if there was anyone interested in lecturing on qualitative methodology part-time at the South Bank University. Well, I quite like a bit of qualitative methodology—I have studied it, utilized it in a lot of work to date, and had even published a working paper the previous year on the difficulties in research methodology (specifically qualitative) as it relates to studying trans people. So I thought, well, I'll send her a quick e-mail. "Great," came the response, "We would like you to give a lecture/seminar on Visual Analysis in a few months time. Oh, and we like our lecturers, if they are researching, to utilize their own research as an example or case study."

I wrote back and agreed and then promptly forgot about it (primarily, I think, so I would forget to worry about it) and continued with my day-to-day Ph.D. work. When it came to be about a month away, I started to think about writing the lecture. A lot of things started to cross my mind, in fact. This wasn't a "gender" seminar, this was a lecture/seminar which was part of a qualitative methodology course at the prestigious (and therefore likely "serious" in a sensible-haircut, tie-wearing, briefcase-carrying kind of way) South Bank University. That's not to say that the London School of Economics doesn't have a similar reputation. But I live in the Gender Institute—something of a safe space for varied trans types like myself, and while there are some here with sensible haircuts, ties, and briefcases, they are very friendly and don't intimidate unless required to do so.

My worries began something like this: The person running the course at South Bank knew that I was going to talk about images of trans people, but nonetheless this is a classroom full of people who likely have never met a trans person, let alone considered studying them. I mean, maybe they aren't even sympathetic to the idea.

Let me clarify (further).

I consider myself to be lucky in many ways. I am aware that I have managed to avoid, so far, many of the pitfalls and discriminations in opportunity that trans people often face in all walks of life, let alone in academic or educative spheres. I certainly know of cases—from trans friends, from the media, through the "grapevine" and so forth—that prove I could have it a hell of a lot worse than I do. Don't get me wrong: I have had a trouble or two that I have had to overcome. But that's another story, which I will leave for another time. I have been accepted and allowed to work on my Ph.D., I have a job that pays for my rent and food, occasionally I have an opportunity to have a social life, and now I have been asked to lecture and teach—which, as I have already noted, is something I have always wanted to do.

I started to worry not only about this one lecture/seminar but also about my whole career. Through my own studies and through my own life (as it were), I am aware of the discrimination faced by trans people in any form of employment. Am I asking for too much? I mean, I think of myself as a pretty open trans person. But does this make me completely unemployable? Will this first lecture be my very last?

There have certainly been people in my life who have told me that I will not be employable anywhere, that if I don't "change back" I am going to end up in the gutter ("they" can be very melodramatic, can't they). I try not to listen. But maybe in this instance I am asking for too much. To be openly trans, to talk about social science to sensible, suited people, to talk about bringing the study of trans people and its implications into their sensible sciences…am I going to be taken seriously? Are they even going to listen to me? Who am I kidding?

What am I going to wear?

Now, I am not much of a psychologist these days (I studied it for my first degree, quite some time ago), but I think there may have been some psycho-ma-logical stuff transpiring when I poured all of my insecurities and doubts into the question of what I was going to wear that night before my first lecture, the lecture that I was now not sure I had the courage to go through with. I was starting to question myself in lots of ways, but the only way in which I seemed to be able to communicate this at that moment was through my inability to dress.

Was there something I could wear, I frantically tried to think, that would make these people see beyond what I was sure were their preconceived notions of who—or even what—they thought I was? Was there a special outfit for such an occasion? I didn't know, and I am a little embarrassed to say that I was literally running around, far too late the night before the lecture, shouting at my flatmates. It was one of them, Verena, who came to my rescue. She stopped me in my tracks, sat me down, and started to pull garments out of my closet after I quickly and incoherently tried to explain my dilemma. She pulled out a calf-length black pencil-skirt, my only black "suit" jacket, a cream blouse, and a red scarf. She told me to wear my knee-length boots to add a touch of "funk." This would let them take me seriously, she thought, and allow me to feel "professional" and "confident."

I had never worn these things together. I didn't even know I owned a "suit," and so I'd never considered myself to be someone who could or would wear one. So it was thus, suited and booted, if you will, that I went to my first lecture—essentially appearing as a serious, tie-wearing (or, in my case, scarf-wearing) professional.

I was terrified going into the building. I had straightened my scarf several times before even entering the lobby of the reception that I had been directed to. The lovely person at the desk had called the person that I was to be meeting and I waited, quaking in my boots, as the person descended the stairs to meet me. She seemed OK. Said very pleasant things about being interested in my topic and asked me whether I needed anything. But I had yet to meet the students. That was going to be a whole other thing.

They were lovely.

They were attentive, interested, and vocal. I started the lecture and felt that I had their complete attention as I ran through the theories of Visual Analysis, feminist uses thereof, and finally its application to trans people. They didn't seem to drop off at all when I started to talk about the varieties in trans people's experiences and identifications. I talked about the ways in which trans people often do battle with doctors, psychologists, social scientists, and sometimes even some feminists and lesbian/gay/queer theorists. I talked about the stereotypes of trans people, how they are perceived in academia, the media, politics, and law. And finally I talked about myself, as an educator. The students had responded so well and seemed so invested that I felt comfortable letting them in on my little secret: I wasn't really a suit-wearer by nature. I had constructed this image in order to overcome the prejudices that I imagined they might have. To create an acceptable image in their minds so that they would at least give me a chance. To combat their images of what trans people are like.

The lecture ran late because we had so much to talk about, and I am elated to say that it was a success. It made me feel that I could talk about these issues, to try and educate in these environments, and also to work in academia in general. I was very happy when a few months later I was invited to give the lecture again because the faculty who ran the course had received such good feedback.

It hasn't eliminated all my concerns, but this experience has gone a long way toward making me feel confident about teaching. Of course, I still know that there will be challenges ahead. I still work in a field where trans people are not fully accepted, but I have been lucky to find my niche here, supported as I am, and I feel like I have a real opportunity to change people's minds. I feel lucky in that respect and grateful to those who have helped me get here. I hope that that I can help other people who, like me, love to work in these and other areas of education. I know that is a bit of a grand mission, but if I can achieve that, I think I would be a very happy woman indeed.

PROUD TO BE A FAGET

Dan Woog
Varsity soccer coach
Staples High School
Westport, Connecticut

As an openly gay soccer coach and writer on gay issues, I often talk with students about my experiences, and about gay issues in general. The discussions that follow are intriguing, but the questions are often predictable. So are the notes I receive afterward: "Thanks for coming. I learned a lot. I'll try not to say 'That's so gay' anymore."

Not long ago, however, I spent the day at a Connecticut middle school, talking with eighth-grade classes. Their responses were a bit less scripted. In fact, they were so honest and raw that I saved them. Here are my favorites, along with my reactions to them.

> Dear Dan Woog,
>   Thank you for coming to our class the other day. Although some people in the class didn't agree with you (Matt), who cares because he is stupid. I think its all right so keep going! To me there is nothing wrong with it. Thank you! —Bridget

Ah, eighth graders! They are nothing like the audiences of adults (mental health professionals, fellow teachers, church members) and high school students I am used to. Eighth graders inhabit their own planet—if not an entirely separate universe.

Dear Mr. Woog,

Thank you for informing me about homosexuality. Some of the things you told me informed me. Thank you very much. You have a lot of courage to be gay. Some people would kick your butt if you told them. It should be left that way. Just to let you know, I think that some people in our class are gay. Sincerely, ?

I agree with his or her last comment. I am thinking of the boy in that class who sat directly in front of me. Throughout the entire 40 minutes he never made eye contact—but the tilt of his head told me he was absorbing every word. Come to think of it, perhaps "?" is that boy.

Dear Dan,

Hi! Thanx for coming. I really injoyed you talk about gay people yesterday. I really learned that there can be different people in life, and sorry for laughen at you because It was the first time I ever talk to a gay guy like you so I hope you forgive me. Sincerly, Chamone

All is forgiven. I also forgive the two boys who walked into class holding hands and smirking. I hope they didn't mind when I casually mentioned that many times the ones who make fun of gay people are those who are least sure of their own sexuality.

Dear Dan,

Thanks for coming in and telling us how it is in the gay life. And from now on I won't make fun of people like you. Well try to come back. See ya, Casey

P.S. I am not gay.

Interesting, isn't it, that Casey felt compelled to add that postscript. I hope the next time he hears a homophobic joke—or encounters a homosexual classmate—he remembers my talk, and his pledge.

Dear Dan Woog,

Thank you for coming into our class and talking about gay and lesbian people. I am homophobic, but if you want to be gay you can be gay. Sincerely, Mr. Sullivan's 8th grade class student

Well, eighth graders are nothing if not honest—and uncertain. They also do not censor themselves. When they wrote anonymous questions on note cards during my talk, one youngster wanted to know, "Do you masturbate frequently?" However, that question does not even come close to the one at the end of this note:

Dear Daniel Woog,
   Thank you for coming into our class and informing us about homosexuality. I know that it must have been hard to admit your homosexuality to our eighth grade class. Not many people would have had the courage to do this. Sincerely, A Student
   P.S. Do you think that size matters?

But my favorite thank-you note of all was written by this girl:

Dear Mr. Woog,
   Thank you very much for comming to visit us. Your talk was very interesting. I'm glad that your proud to be a faget. There aren't many people who are. I feel bad for the people who tease gay people. They're regular people. No different. Except for who they like. But I really respect gays as well as others. —Kimberly

Kimberly does not quite get it yet—she must have zoned out during the part in my talk when I mentioned the power of words like "fag" and "homo," especially when spat out by middle-school boys and girls—but she clearly is on her way.

It's notes like hers—and those by Bridget, Casey, and "?"—that keep me going back to talk to eighth graders, year after year. I know I shouldn't stereotype, but it continues to be true: They're funny. They're energetic. They're eager to learn. And—most important— they give me great hope for the future.

CHASING MY OWN TALE

Judee King
Director of after-school programs
Redwood Day School
Oakland, California

1989

Around and around I go, in my career in education, staying just this side of straight and, narrowly, missing. Coworkers, questioning. "We should all go out for a drink after work. Want to?" "Do you have to check with your man?" "*Are* you married?" The eyebrows rise curiously in sync with the virtual theatrical curtain of *The Judee Show* as I mentally and physically rev up to begin the chase.

The tale gains momentum when I find myself needing to quicken the pace as I lose sight of what the actual end of my tale truly is. The sound of laughter soothes my uneasy discomfort of yet again passing for straight. I slyly sigh and slowly grin as questions are soon forgotten.

School events and coworker's parties required being surrounded by a pit crew of my gay male friends. Hair, wardrobe, made up and over from lesbian to thespian. Priming my selected male companion with the script of the screenplay of "our life." Depending on the depth of the current relationship, my girlfriend would be sulking on the couch or pacing and cursing about what a lie I live in order to be in the low-paying field of education. Oh, the exhaustion of make-believe.

Ten years later...1999

The exhaustion of chasing my own tale caught up with me in 1999. I was stopped in my tracks with the news I had breast cancer. I contracted three separate cases of breast cancer within a four-year period! Initially, I went spinning out of control, questioning all rhyme and reason. The direction of my chase took a 180-degree turn. It was time to reevaluate the "who's," "what's," and "where's." The "who": me, a woman educated both formally and by social experience into a real understanding of the challenges of being true to yourself and your sexual orientation and what the denial of the latter can cause to the essence of one's soul. With my newfound awareness, the "what" seemed so clearly defined. As a three-time breast cancer survivor I could use my new lease on life to help others begin their journey. As a second-generation San Franciscan, I wanted to stay local and have the "where" be in the Bay Area. So I sought out opportunities.

The new direction of my chase has drawn me to seek opportunities to support LGBT adolescents through a variety of venues. My experience as a chaperone for the Gay Prom, where teens and young adults from all over California came to share the authentic experience of attending a spring high school prom. That warm spring night was filled with the sweet scent of jasmine carried on the same breeze as the venomous voices of the Caucasian, conservative, corrosive contingency that pressed in mass against the legal barriers, shouting, "God hates you queers, you're all going to hell!" Waving their ignorance on signs that read the same. I joined the welcoming committee, and in our formal wear we made a human barricade encircling the elegant teens in tuxes and gowns, shouting our greetings and compliments over the protesters with their hateful eyes and surgical masks—to keep from getting AIDS, they yelled. Inside, I paused to smile at the young happy couples, capturing memories, posing for prom pictures.

Frannie's voice still rings in my ears filled with sorry surprise, hurt, and anger. "Judee, you're gay! Hey, how come you never said anything? Especially when I came out to the therapist and then they wouldn't let me be alone or near any girls after that." The accusations stung; I remembered how I'd shrunk away when the administration was up in arms and so disgusted and obviously homophobic. Before I could respond, Frannie exclaimed, "Wow, I wonder who else at our school was." I felt so feeble when I explained how much I regretted being forced by our unspoken school policy, "If you are gay or lesbian, you'd better stay in the closet and never disclose your sexual identity to the children or you will be terminated immediately." We hugged and Frannie smiled, forgave me, and danced off into the night to the beat from the turntables of famous San Francisco disc jockey Page Hodel. As the classy-clad crowd moved to the rhythm, I felt the pull of the chase quicken: *It's time…*

I put pen to paper and devised a plan, complete from career to courtship of the woman I'll share my life-dream beside. Shortly after my blueprint was drawn, a beautiful woman walked into my life, bringing love, laughter, and inspiration. All these qualities helped me keep an eye on the prize during agonizing hours of operations and recoveries. Just last December, grinning and kissing, we exchanged rings on the warm sands of Waikiki Beach. Hibiscus and plumeria softly scented the tropical breeze as the moonlight followed the gentle rhythm of the waves as they slid upon the sand. One day we will live together on the island in the sun.

In a fast-paced series of events, I discovered my "where." After chasing my tale through a variety of challenging career choices, I was ready for Redwood Day School in Oakland, California. Their mission statement is in line with my motivation to make a difference in our children's life experience: "Engage, Prepare, Inspire." During my second interview, I stood and watched beautiful children of diverse backgrounds playing in and around the shadows of the filtered sunlight of the towering redwood trees. It was then that I knew this was the place. When I received my new hire packet I nearly choked in an astonished excitement akin to that of a dog who finally has achieved the perceived unachievable: "catching my own tale." For there, printed under the section of "Frequently

Asked Questions," was the answer I have been looking for over the past 22 years of my educational career:

> *Do you have any gay and lesbian staff and families in your current school community?*
> We have faculty, staff, and parents from these communities who are active and vital members of our school. We support community understanding of many kinds of families through curriculum, assemblies, and Gallery displays.

2004

As the dust from my chase begins to settle, my purpose for reaching and teaching is so clearly defined. I have joined Redwood Day School at the right time. My coworkers, both gay and straight, are in the initial planning stages of creating a GSA for our growing community of children and adolescents. I welcome the challenge of making a difference. Timing is everything. I've just been notified I have stage IV breast cancer, my fourth case in five years. I am now more determined than ever that my tale ends with LGBT and straight students and educators all living happily ever after...

TWO YEARS IN THE LIFE OF A QUEER TEACHER

Tarah Ausburn
Language arts teacher
Rose Linda Elementary School
Phoenix, Arizona

October 29, 2001

"Instructor Ausburn, I have a question."

"What is it, Carlota?"

"Are you a lesbian?"

My plan was never to fight this battle so directly. My first battle did not start with my "coming out" at school, nor did it start with "concerned" parents; it started with my car. I take pride in decorating my beautiful silver Honda Civic with progressive bumper stickers, dealing with issues such as animal rights, education, feminism, homophobia, military policies, and racism. To date, there are 62, and I have 18 more sitting in my glove compartment, waiting for the opportunity to make their debut on my moving billboard.

Everywhere I go, my car makes an impact; experiences range from people refusing to park next to me, to throwing gum on my windshield, to asking me out, to thanking me for stating my opinion, to expressing dismay at the lowered resale value, to groups crowding around my car in dozens of parking lots, to honks and thumbs-up on an almost-daily basis. At school, the students competed to find out who owned the car, and then when they figured it out, they bombarded me throughout the year to ask for clarification of my purpose, as well as the meaning behind some of the phrases plastered to the doors, hood, trunk, and bumpers. I once gave my language arts students the opportunity to gain 50 points if they could find the simile on my car; surely enough, Suzanne proudly handed me a slip of paper the very next morning: "A woman without a man is like a fish without a bicycle."

The administration's relationship with my car has not been nearly as friendly.

We were sitting in my classroom, our small bodies easily lounging in two students' desks. Ann, our school's coprincipal, was barely five feet tall, a tiny pale creature with flaming red hair, yet she possessed a respectful air of authority about her.

"I've been asked to talk to you about your bumper stickers," she said.

"What about them?" I asked.

"I want you to know that I'm only passing along a message to you, that this doesn't have anything to do with my own beliefs. Dr. Stanley [our superintendent] is furious about your bumper stickers. He wants you to remove them."

"Well, that's not an option." My blazing eyes challenged her to argue with me, not quite realizing whose side she was on.

"I know what you're going through…" My skeptical expression indicated I thought otherwise of this seemingly straitlaced principal in her gray suit and bright-pink, collared shirt. "No, I do. When I first started teaching I used to get in trouble all the time for my clothing. Even though I was a music and theater teacher, and we were always sitting on the floor in a circle, they thought my overalls and jeans were inappropriate. I constantly got into battles with my supervisor. In the end, you just have to figure out whether the battle is worth fighting."

I hardly recognized the underlying synonymy between wearing jeans to work and being ordered to remove bumper stickers from one's car, but I struggled to keep the cold fury out of my eyes.

She continued, "I want you to know that I support you, but I am not going to fight this battle for you."

Something in the way she told me this softened my hard defense. Perhaps I thought that her status as an administrator automatically put her on "their" side. Knowing her support—albeit silent—was there enabled me to open myself up enough to talk to her. I understood the precarious position she was in. She had been given orders from her boss, and it was not in her own best interest to help me fight the battle. So she passed along the message, while subtly giving me another message of her own.

"So, he wants my bumper stickers removed. Did he say which ones?"

"He did single out two," she admitted, "but I am not sure how many he wants you to remove. He did mention VEGETARIANS TASTE BETTER, and he was particularly outraged by SORRY I MISSED CHURCH. I WAS BUSY PRACTICING WITCHCRAFT AND BECOMING A LESBIAN. He said that it was 'offensive.' Anyway, like I said, I am just passing along a message from him. It's your decision what you want to do. He wants to know your decision tomorrow."

I did not give a decision the next day, simply because I had not had enough time to discuss the situation with any private attorneys or the ACLU. Luckily, a First Amendment rights specialist did return my e-mail, and he provided me with support and ammunition as to why the school district could not force me to remove my bumper stickers. When Ann approached me again to ask what my decision was, based on suggestions from the specialist, I told her that I would not remove any bumper stickers, that all requests or mandates needed to be put into writing, and that they needed to come from the person making the orders.

But Dr. Stanley would not contact me directly, despite my request. He told Ann to tell me to park off campus, on a side street. I refused to do that as well and again reiterated that I needed all mandates in writing.

His next step was ordering Ann to write me a formal directive—in her name, not his—requiring me to write out a list of all my bumper stickers and the interpretation of their meanings. This list was to be turned in by the next school day, less than 24 hours later. At this point I knew I was being harassed and again sought legal counsel. I ended up writing the school district a three-page letter detailing why I thought this was inappropriate and unethical. I did submit a then-current list of my bumper stickers and an interpretation of their meanings. The meaning was the same for each bumper sticker: "Guaranteeing freedom of speech for all humans and animals." At the end of the letter, I announced firm intentions to legally fight this battle, if the school district was that adamant about forcing me to remove my bumper stickers.

I waited for a reply, which never came. Weeks went by, and not another word was said about my bumper stickers. After six weeks, I knew that there would be a new form of harassment in the future and waited for it to arise. I was not disappointed. Throughout the rest of the year, I was shunned by my coworkers and mistreated by the administration. At one point, when I questioned a shady decision made by the assistant superintendent regarding one of my ED (emotionally disturbed) students, I was written up for "questioning authority."

My reaction was to put a bumper sticker on my car that stated in bold, red letters: QUESTION AUTHORITY.

❋

"Shut the fuck up, stupid faggot!" Dishawne yelled at Doug, seemingly for no reason other than the fact that Doug kept walking around the room talking to himself in that naturally psychotic way of his. My blood went cold, and my underarms immediately started to sweat. This was the first time I would address queer-related hate speech with my students, and I wanted to make an impression that lasted. Amazingly, my voice remained calm and unwavering.

"Dishawne, how would you feel if I called you a nigger?"

He stopped dead in his tracks. My assistant stared at me with wide eyes. Was some white girl teacher from Pennsylvania really going to open her mouth and say "the *n* word" in front of black people? Other students who had not yet left to go to their buses whipped their heads around toward Dishawne to see what he would do.

"But you wouldn't, Instructor, because you're not like that." Still, his face showed disbelief and outrage.

"Dishawne, you calling Doug a faggot is no different than me calling you a nigger."

"That's not the same at all," he said. But I had his eye contact, and he was engaging in conversation. I pressed on, hoping to get through to him. He knew I was angry—he could hear it in my icy voice—but he did not understand why.

"*Faggot* is a word that was used in the Middle Ages. Gay men were rounded, tied together, and set on fire. They called homosexuals 'faggots' because the word *faggot* means 'a bundle of sticks,' and they tied them up just like they were a bunch of sticks."

"It's still not the same as *nigger*. It's just not right for you to call black people niggers."

I had used so much passion in my explanation that I felt defeated when he didn't immediately make the connection. I turned my back to him and said, "Go home, Dishawne," in a frustrated voice. He knew I was mad and did not know what to do. "Sorry, Instructor," he whimpered and ran out of the room, relieved to be away from my disappointment and my historical references.

The next morning, Dishawne tentatively approached me in class before school started.

"Can I talk to you, Instructor?"

The previous day's events had already washed away in my dreams, stored away as memories to potentially be retrieved later. I knew better than to take the whole matter personally; I was fighting a battle that was far older and stronger than I was. "Of course you can talk to me. What's up, Dishawne?"

"I told my mom last night about what happened yesterday."

A range of thoughts sped through my head. She misunderstood my reference with "the *n* word." She didn't like that I was teaching homosexual history at school. She was angry and was going to take it to the principal or the school board. These are the paranoid thoughts that float daily through the mind of any teacher who fights for LGBT rights on school grounds.

"It turns out my uncle is…that way."

"That way, Dishawne?"

"He's…you know…gay. He has one of those key chains with all the colors on it, like yours. He has a bunch of rainbow stuff, but I didn't know that meant he was gay. My mom and I sat down and talked about it. She told me it was OK. She still loves him, and I should too, and there isn't anything wrong with him being gay."

"Do you love your uncle?"

"Yeah."

"Even if he's gay?"

"I don't care!"

"I think that's great, Dishawne. Not everyone would be so mature about it. I'm proud of you."

Dishawne can't handle compliments, and he grew quite flustered. "I'm sorry about yesterday, Instructor."

"Thank you, Dishawne. It's not easy to apologize. And thanks for telling me about your uncle. I won't tell anyone, though—don't worry. That's your business."

He left to go hang out with his friends before the morning bell rang, and I spent the rest of my morning prep time floating on clouds. I'd finally gotten through to *someone*.

*

Throughout the year, I had intentionally treated my sexual preference as a mundane characteristic, hoping to normalize such a taboo concept. I never had a formal coming-out speech, but I answered my students' questions honestly. When they asked why I didn't have a boyfriend, I told them. When they wanted to know about my girlfriend, I gave them any requested information that did not relate to sex. The assistant superintendent did not agree that sexual orientation or preference and sexuality are completely different matters. She also did not see the connection between having positive LGBT role models and a subsequent campus decrease in hate speech, homophobic attitudes, and middle school children getting beaten to a pulp simply because they are or are perceived to be queer. I was reprimanded for letting my students know about my sexual preference and given the formal directive not to discuss sexuality with any student on campus.

✳

"Dishawne, what's wrong?"

"My mom went to go see my uncle. He's in the hospital, and he has AIDS."

"Is this the uncle you were telling me about before, the one with the rainbow key chain?"

"No, this is another one. But he's that way too."

"Are you upset that he has AIDS?"

"I don't know him…but my mom goes to visit him in the hospital, and she hugs him. I don't want her to catch what he's got."

"Dishawne, you can't catch AIDS from hugging someone who has it."

"Yeah, but she kisses him too."

"You can't catch it that way either."

"How can you catch it, then?" he challenged, fighting back the tears forming in his eyes.

There it was, that paralyzing fear of saying the "wrong" thing and being written up or sued for it later. Why does the truth carry such fear and risk of consequence? Why can't I just answer a question to a scared teenage boy who thinks his mom is going to die just because she visits her sick brother in the hospital?

✳

At the end of the year, the assistant superintendent informed me that my contract would not be renewed because she did not think that I could "deal well with children."

Never mind that, according to our state's Department of Education guidelines, this was illegal, for the simple reason that they told me they would not renew my contract after the state-mandated deadline. Never mind that their statement did not even make any sense, as my most significant gain that year had *not* been standardized test scores, grades, attendance, or objective assessments but rather a connection with a group of special-needs students who had so few positive experiences in a public-school setting. Never mind that their statement is also ridiculous and irrational because it is ambiguous and lacking in any concrete support; she could not give me one example to support her slander. Never mind that this administration was lying about the real reason they wanted to get rid of me, but they needed an excuse that was somehow related to the children. Never mind that this administration is scared to tell me the real reason because they are already sitting on two potential lawsuits—due to the fact that two of our students had committed suicide in the previous three weeks—and they wanted to avoid a third potential legal battle. Never mind that they could have gotten away with telling me, "We are firing you because you are a lesbian." Never mind that the statement is preposterous for the additional reason that my cumulative end-of-year evaluation by my school principal states: "Instructor Ausburn clearly has an exceptional ability for handling troubled youth."

Never mind that what the assistant superintendent really meant to tell me was, "It is not that you cannot deal well with children. It is that we cannot deal well with you."

✳

If I had not been only 22 years old—and devoid of union representation, financial support, or higher connections—I might have fought back. Instead, I left quietly and applied at another school district. I felt kicked down and humiliated, but I rationalized that there would come a time when I would have to fight again; next time I would be stronger. In some ways the next year was better. I accepted a teaching position at another school in South Phoenix, with a population that had similar demographics.

My reading class was made up of mainstream junior high students. They were a delight to interact with; unlike my previous students, they weren't imprisoned in a self-contained ED classroom. I became that positive role model I hoped to be, and I had some impact on their language choices. Most of my students would not have even considered calling someone else "gay," "faggot," "dyke," or "homo," at least not in my presence. I also became the confidante to about half a dozen questioning eighth-graders. I even received community support when I discussed a controversial curriculum with two dozen parents and guardians. When I wanted to implement a yearlong diversity curriculum into my junior high reading class, complete with a month on gay and lesbian history, I began to circulate amongst students' guardians, trying to gauge their reaction. In some cases, I met with guardians in their homes; others came to meet me in my classroom. I discussed my intentions with 23 guardians altogether; only one mother refused to support my curriculum. The other 22 mothers, fathers, and guardians signed a written statement, asserting their support.

✳

It had been a particularly difficult day. A parent came in to yell at me about his daughter's math grade on her progress report. I didn't drink water all day because the vending machine kept spitting out Minute Maid Fruit Punch in a can when I pushed the button for purified water. I was coming down with a cold *again,* drained by stress, moldy classrooms, polluted air, and germy kids. It was only 11:55, and I still had hours of teaching and grading ahead of me. Kids were in my classroom—writing on my white board, gossiping about friends and new dating partners, eating and making a mess, and manipulating the surroundings in order to get my attention. Even though it was lunchtime, and the students should have been eating in the cafeteria, there was always a select group of students who would eat lunch in my room and spend their "recess" sitting inside the classroom rather than soaking up the sun's vitamins out on the playground or basketball courts.

I always tried to appear busy when I was in a foul mood, hoping the students would not talk to me as much when I needed the solitary downtime that simply was not available. Walking toward my desk, I stopped at a white table that held our classroom suggestion box. Shaking it, I heard the scratching sound of paper hitting cardboard, so I flipped the latch and opened the lid. Two papers, white, each folded and refolded half a dozen times, lay in stark contrast compared to the fluorescent orange bottom, and I opened each paper, always curious to read what the students thought they wanted, needed, or deserved in order to make this a better class.

"We need some tissues, Instructor. Real tissues not hard toilet paper."

Fair enough. If I don't blow my nose using bulk supply toilet paper, I should not expect my students to. I made a mental note to stop at the grocery store on the way home.

"Do you date students? My friend likes you. Hint-hint, it's a girl."

I looked around, paranoid that this was a joke and I was not going to handle it properly. Everyone was immersed in her or his own business, and no one but me felt the pounding in my chest. I folded that paper back up and stuck it in my purse. There was no point in trying to deal with the comment until my head was clear.

Two days later, Mireya mentioned it over a delicious cafeteria-provided lunch of taco boats, one of the few vegetarian dishes provided at RL Elementary. Mireya always tried to keep secrets, but the truth was she had no will power. She also wanted to be the important person who spread the grade's gossip, so I learned many a story and junior-high truth from her.

"How often do you read your notes in the suggestion box, Instructor?"

"I check it twice a week, on Tuesdays and Fridays."

Carlota and Mireya exchanged a look, and Mireya continued to pry. "Did you check it this Tuesday?"

"Yes. Why?"

No answer. No answer. Still, no answer. I repeated my question, more persistently this time. "Why, Mireya?"

"I know who wrote it."

"Who wrote what?"

"The note."

"What note?" I could see her frustration, and it was the highlight of my entire day.

"You know."

"Mireya, I get notes almost every day [this was a lie]. What note are you talking about? Did *you* write me a note?"

"No!"

"Oh, OK then. What note are you talking about?"

Mireya had had enough. "It was Darlene. She wrote it. She wrote it for Melosa, because Melosa likes you. She's like that, you know."

"Oh."

She obviously expected a bigger reaction than that. I knew I was torturing her. It's not often an eighth-grade teacher has the upper hand over her students, so it's important to take advantage of every available opportunity.

"Are you going to answer her?"

"I don't date students, Mireya. That's against the law, and it's not right for a teacher to date her student anyway. Then, that teacher might give the student special treatment...or fail the student when they break up."

It wasn't the answer that Mireya wanted. "Would you date her if she wasn't your student?"

"Not if she was 14."

"If she *wasn't* 14?" Mireya planned to push this conversation until she extracted the information she wanted; that much was clear.

"That depends on how much we had in common."

"Instructor, you're like that?"

"Like what?"

"You know."

"If you want to have a conversation, Mireya, you need to be able to say what's on your mind."

"Melosa's a girl."

"That's true. Rose Linda Elementary is giving you a wonderful education."

"Aw, Instructor! Do you date girls?"

"I date people, Mireya. Would you date someone who was black?"

"Yes."

"Native American?"

"Yes."

"Poor?"

"Who cares if they're poor?"

"That's the way I feel about dating girls. Who cares? They're people, all the same."

"I don't care either," Carlota piped up. "What difference does it make?" It was the first and only thing she said during the entire conversation.

❋

Of course, the students are not really the problem; it is the society and the system that engulf and train them to repeat history's mistakes. I cannot say that my administration was any better this year. They would not permit me to teach Gay and Lesbian History Month as part of my yearlong diversity curriculum; when I put up a fight and started gaining community support, they switched me mid-year from being the junior high reading teacher to teaching eighth-graders math. Throughout the year, my homeroom students read stories from a book published by Teaching Tolerance; the stories focused on struggles and achievements made by various minority groups. We read the stories together, discussed their implications, and followed up with relevant projects. When my principal heard that we read a true story about a Utah lesbian teacher fighting against a gag order her school district issued her, I was reprimanded for not getting prior approval of the book first, despite the fact that the assistant principal had approved the book for the social studies teacher the prior year. The discrimination was not as blatant the second time around, but that did not make it any better; it actually made it more difficult to deal with. I would have preferred the in-your-face, "I don't like you because you're a queer" approach, rather than the more subtle tactics used by this second administration to silence me and all LGBTAQ students on school grounds.

*

This morning one of my students approached me before school. The night before, she had gotten a phone call from her aunt. Apparently, two teachers approached Ebony's aunt Tanisha, who also works at our school, to discuss some accusations concerning Ebony and me. There were two comments mentioned: (1) Ebony sits between my legs at the school basketball games; and (2) Ebony hangs out with me, alone, in my classroom.

Tanisha called another one of Ebony's aunts, who proceeded to call Ebony. According to Ebony, this conversation consisted of her aunt passing along the information and warning her to stop doing anything, if she was.

Ebony was embarrassed to admit this, and she usually confided all of her 14-year-old secrets to me. I tried to appear lackadaisical, hoping it would rub off. Casually I questioned, "Did you tell her there is nothing going on between us?"

"Of course!" she exclaimed. "All she said was, 'Well, you'd better stop, if there is.'"

I knew exactly who had started this, as there were only two teachers who consistently attended the basketball games: the cheerleading coaches. I had been informed on more than one occasion that they had a problem with me teaching at the school; they thought it was "inappropriate." By this time I was used to the fact that teachers used my sexual orientation as an argument to declare me "unfit" for teaching. Up until now I never bothered to approach any of the teachers, as I knew all would vehemently deny having made such bigoted remarks. This time I immediately approached Tanisha to discuss these allegations. She agreed with me, so we went and talked it over with the administrators. It turned out that the administrators had already been approached, and my principal informed me that he had looked into the situation.

Incredulously, I asked, "You heard this too? Why doesn't anyone inform *me* of these accusations?"

A strange look passed across the principal's face—guilt, mixed with…disappointment?—before he lamely replied, "Well, I looked into it and didn't find anything. If there had been a problem, then you would have known about it." I couldn't help but wonder if he was disappointed that he found nothing to persecute me for. I left the office continuing to feel suspicious but proud that I handled the rumor directly and efficiently to the best of my ability. Nothing ever came of the rumor, but I did start to notice the way certain teachers watched me whenever I talked to Ebony outside of the classroom.

✳

The relatively supportive response from my principal made it quite an interesting turn of events when I discovered that my principal did not plan to renew my contract. It was déjà vu: For the second year in a row, my contributions to my students were thwarted by politics and irrational fears—and the administration had again failed to follow legal procedures required for not renewing my contract. According to the law, I should have been informed by April 15, via writing, if they did not plan for my return to their school.

It was more than simple legal procedures that frustrated me, however; it was, of course, principle. My standardized test scores on the SAT-9s rivaled that of the two other eighth-grade teachers, who had decades of experience compared to my two years. My math test scores alone were a vast improvement from the 0% of students who had achieved grade level in the past three years; my classes' test scores indicated that 17% of the eight-graders at RL Elementary were now on grade level, mathematically speaking. In my homeroom, I tripled the number of honor roll students. I was popular with the students; they both trusted and respected me, a difficult feat to achieve simultaneously amongst kids of their age. I averaged 11-hour days and 60-hour weeks, working overtime to find ways to get my students interested in learning.

None of that mattered, though, when the administration was dealing with a polysexual-but-lesbian-to-them teacher who had the audacity to drive a car saturated with "offensive" bumper stickers, teach gay and lesbian history, and not feel ashamed of her sexual preferences.

Remember, though—the past year's experiences had made me stronger, and I took advantage of that strength to fight back this time. After discovering that my contract would not be renewed, I involved my union and made plans to sue the district, battling loudly enough that my principal rescinded his decision; he filed a "Recommendation to Hire" form at the district. I signed my contract. I did not even want to return there, but there was no way I was going to allow them to make that decision for me, not when I'd dedicated a year of my life to helping those kids achieve beyond their perceived capabilities.

If there is one thing all of this has taught me, it is the importance of developing patience. I want to make change overnight in my classroom and on school grounds, and of course I cannot. If I do not learn patience, my frustration will erode both my idealism and any chance I have of improving conditions. I also understand now that I am seriously not going to have any impact if I am in this alone. I would like to think I am important and extraordinary enough that I could be that *one teacher* who changed my students' lives. The truth is, unless there are other teachers, leaders, adults, and peers confirming my lessons on diversity and tolerance, my progress will be minimal. It is often disheartening to look around at my staff meetings and see the walls of intolerance that have been built around the public education system. It is frightening to see other queer colleagues look away in silence instead of speaking up. I see that I am literally the only one at our school fighting against gender conformity, sexism, and heterosexism.

I do feel alone. I am lucky because I don't need to have a lot of support in order to have my beliefs validated. Not everyone feels that way. Validation aside, though, I know I cannot make the necessary progress if I fight alone. We need other teachers also paving the rainbow way for true diversity and tolerance when it comes to sexual orientation or preference. We need people in power, working on the system from the inside. We need resources, volunteers, secure organizations, and community support in order to make any of this work. Change is not going to naturally occur *for* us. If we are not actively working toward solving the problem, then we remain a part of the problem.

*

Dario and Chale approach me, the smirks on their faces an obvious sign that they are up to something. Chale, always the more outspoken one of the pair, speaks up first. "Have you ever heard of Flexx, Instructor Ausburn?"

"No. What is it?"

"It's a gay club practically right across the street from me."

"How do you know it's a gay club?"

Dario jumps into the conversation, eager to contribute. "'Cause there are all these guys walking around funny and holding hands with other guys."

"What do you mean, 'walking around funny'?"

This time, it's Chale's turn. "You know how gay guys walk…all funny, and then they talk with that weird lisp, and they do that hand thing…" Chale proceeds to make one of his wrists go limp, and Dario bursts out laughing: "Chale, you look so...flexx...when you do that."

It was blatantly clear by now that they were baiting me, so I decided to retaliate in my own way. "Well, Chale looks flexx no matter what he does."

There are definite benefits to working with adolescents who are old enough to appreciate sarcasm. Before Chale could recover with a witty remark of his own, I reminded both of them, "There are some gay people who 'look' gay, but there are also lots of people you'd never know were gay. Don't go thinking all gay people look and act the same."

"That's messed up, Instructor," whined Chale. "I don't look flexx."

"Hey, you never know, Chale," I replied. "You never know who's flexx and who's not. That's the point I'm trying to make." I walked away, leaving two students who love to antagonize me standing there, mouths agape and at a loss for any retaliation. The battles I win are slow in coming and seemingly miniscule—but I'm making progress.

ARE THOSE REAL?

Anafaith Lubliner
Theater teacher
César Chávez Elementary
San Francisco, California

I can still remember the moment before I came out as a lesbian to my students. I was sitting on the dirty floor of the cafeteria/auditorium. There was that familiar strange aroma of garbage and kids. It was dark, with dingy faux theater lighting. I looked around at their distracted faces, poking one another, thinking today would be just another day in acting class. I was anxious. But there was a little glimmer of hope. Hope that I was about to do something…good. Life-changing. They had no idea what was about to hit them.

How did I come to this decision? I came out because of a realization. I am an after-school theater teacher in the Mission District at César Chávez Elementary in one of the most gay-friendly cities in the country, possibly the world.

Now, let me tell you, scratch the surface of any school in San Francisco and you will find a large queer population—from the teachers to any part of the administration. So many people have migrated to this gay mecca in order to be free and open about their sexual orientation. Yet here is the conundrum. While most of the people on the staff are out to one another, they are still closeted with the students and the parents. In general we know who is a cross-dresser, who is a lesbian, and who is raising a son that has two daddies. But we're hush-hush when it comes to the students we see day in and out.

This may not seem so strange in Utah, but in San Francisco? Why would we be afraid here? This is the town where we see men in dresses and dyke lesbian leather daddies with their "boi" and we do not bat an eye. Yet the teachers and staff are still afraid to tell their students.

Why are we hiding from children? I believe the answer is internal. It is the inner child that still lives in the schoolyard—the child that has been bullied and pummeled into corners and hard pavement for being different. Too swishy, too butch, too, too, too anything…just too. We do not want to be teased, to be the weak one, to be taunted and humiliated again and again, or worse, to be the one totally left out. We are afraid if we are exposed, the parents, the teachers, and the kids will hate us. We won't be allowed to play with our friends anymore.

I came out because I finally decided that I did not want to let these old fears win. It was time for me to face the bully in the schoolyard. The day I made this decision, a student of mine made a gay slur toward another boy. Instead of responding immediately, I became numb and did not say anything at all. I froze.

Afterward, I was very disappointed in myself and tried to look at why I had been so unable to respond. Had the slur been toward any racial group, I would have acted immediately. Yet a gay slur hit my core: He was talking about me. This was when I realized the depth of my hiding. I had to take action. If I believe in freedom and equality for all, what better place to start than in my own classroom?

My first plan of action was to speak with the staff at Jamestown. I told my supervisor, Katie Brackenridge. I sat her down in the school therapy section, surrounded by little toys, African-American and Latina dolls, and various stuffed animals. Katie was a phenomenal supervisor: sharp, strong, and an excellent educator. She still floored me with her response. Katie looked at me and immediately told me she would completely support me. She even offered to sit in with the kids when I came out. I was thrilled.

I also spoke with my teaching assistant, who was only 15 and had been raised Catholic. She was intelligent and scrappy and the kids loved her, but her Catholic upbringing made me cautious. She quietly told me that she had been raised to accept everyone, that her uncle is gay, and that it was no big deal to her. She also offered to support me. This had been one of my anxieties around coming out in my school. So many children in the Mission District are raised in a Catholic or Christian environment, which I assumed was generally homophobic. Once again I was happily surprised. Together we picked a specific date.

When that day finally came, only half the kids showed up, so we decided to wait until my next teaching day. That was when the anxiety and tension began to build. I had to wait two more days!

Finally the day came. I sat in a circle with the kids, Katie, and my TA. My first line was "I need to talk to you all about something that upset me." They were immediately on alert, sure they were in trouble. I assured them they were not in trouble. Then I said, "There was something that one of you said that hurt my feelings. When I heard one student say to another student they were gay in a mean way, that hurt my feelings. Because you were talking about me; I am a lesbian."

Shocked looks, silence, gasps, and wide-open eyes.

"Who did it?" they asked, looking around.

"I am not going to say who did it, but does anyone have a question?" That is when the flood of questions began. Their curiosity was amazing.

Question: Who is the girl and who is the boy? Answer: We are both girls, no one plays the boy.

Question: Are you really a man? Answer: No.

Question: Do you kiss her? Answer: I don't talk about private things...

Question: At what age did you know that you liked girls? Answer: About 18.

Then, my favorite question: While pointing at my breasts, one girl asked: Are those real? Answer: Yes, my breasts are real, and I am a woman!

One student said, "That's OK, Ana, you are still the nice person you always were…"

Then they asked why Katie was there. Katie said, "Because I want everyone to know I support Ana. She is gay, and it doesn't matter—she is still my friend."

Another student said, "My uncle is gay." A few others chimed in with stories about gay relatives, or how their parents relate to gay people. We were done.

Then the most extraordinary thing happened. Afterward, I was still anxious, my heart was tight, my breathing shallow. I was afraid that I would be rejected, thrown out of the house, so to speak. We went outside for our break, to let the kids play in the yard, and two of the girls kept on hugging me over and over, giving me "love bombs." It was as if they felt closer to me because I had opened up to them.

Then came the biggest surprise of all: The kids decided to improvise a play in a talk show format. Here was the setup:

Title: *Bullies on the Playground*
Characters: An upper-class English girl, a Southern girl, a bully, best friend to the English girl, two talk-show hosts, a *gay character,* and the studio audience.
Story: Gay character and all the others had been mercilessly mistreated by the school bully. Characters come up to be interviewed by the hosts. One by one they tell the story of how they have been bullied. The bully comes onstage. The studio audience all began to boo. Then when the gay student is telling his story onstage, they all began to cheer. Then they all began to chant "Gay is good, gay is good." Then the bully apologizes to the gay kid and all of his other victims. The end.

It was unbelievable. I could not have planned it better myself. That was how the day ended.

The following week the resistance began. One of the children, Pablo (all of the children's names have been changed to protect their privacy), was absent the day I had come out. When he returned he came back to *Bullies in the Playground* being played out again. He began to turn the chant around into "Gay is bad," and some of the students joined in. We had to stop class to talk about it.

The honeymoon was over. It seemed like a metaphor for society. Often when there is an opening, there is also a closing down in fear.

It was not all easy after that. That same student, Pablo, was mysteriously and suddenly pulled out of my class. My own identity issues came up: I am married to a woman, and yet I consider myself bisexual. Should I have come out as bisexual? Or would that have been too much for me? For the kids? I do not know. Maybe I was still hiding.

Still, the ice had been broken. They all expressed an interest in meeting my partner, Katrine. They were as intrigued with her being a juggler as with her being my partner. A week later I brought in Katrine to meet them, and as promised she taught them how to juggle. They all seemed both intrigued and shy. They were thrilled with the juggling.

My being out eventually faded into the background of plays and sets and regular day-to-day activities. I have since come out three other times, with varying degrees of drama.

Years later, the third time I came out, there was an interesting development. I told this new class that they could meet Katrine as well. But Katrine was not able to make it that semester. Yet one student, Angelica, bothered me over and over. She was beyond fascinated: She was borderline obsessed. She bothered me every time she saw me. "When am I going to meet Katrine?" "When am I going to meet Katrine?" Finally Katrine came to a performance to meet her. When she met Katrine, Angelica was shy beyond belief.

Will Angelica be a lesbian? I do not know, but her level of interest made me believe that by coming out I had stirred some possible inner recognition in her. She also told me she wants to be a teacher. If she is a lesbian, she will have a role model of an out gay teacher who was not ashamed of the fact that she loves a woman.

I believe without a shadow of a doubt this is the best lesson I have ever given.

TRUE COLORS

Chip James
School social worker
Clarkstown Schools
New City, New York

Having cleaned up their places at the table, my fifth-grade boys, in a five-member group for children of divorced parents, bounded out the door to recess. I faced my desk to phone my friend Jane—also a school social worker—and tell her I'd be a bit late for our lunch date. When I turned to leave the office, however, I discovered that Jason remained seated at the table. I'd known Jason since he was 9, early in fourth grade; he was referred by his teacher due to his "poor self-image" and ongoing conflicts with peers. At times the conflicts were initiated by other boys' taunting, and at other times they were initiated by Jason's vigilant defensiveness. Underneath the conflicts, however, was the pain and confusion of his perception of himself as "different." A slight, olive-skinned boy under a pile of dirty-blond hair (complete with a hastily made cow-lick in front, a feeble attempt to fit in), he sat waiting for words to come. Below his faded blue T-shirt and his jeans were the new sneakers he'd negotiated with his mother as an early birthday present. Already he'd learned from a classmate that the stripes were "all wrong."

He said nothing and didn't look up at me. I pretended to arrange some things on my desk to give him some time to get his nerve up. Finally, given my time constraints, I offered, "So, Jason, usually when someone stays at my table, they either have something they need to say, or something they need to hear."

"First," replied Jason. The sound of spittle punctuated his speech, which had been increasingly pensive and measured and was especially so today.

"OK," I continued, "is it about school or home?"

"Home," he said, nodding his head, lips pursed in anticipation and concern.

"Is it about something that happened or something you wish would happen?"

"Something I wish." His direct eye contact told me that I had his full attention. We might actually get somewhere. With each answer known and expressed, he was closer to something that's difficult to get at. He turned a corner to find a corridor, and not a dead end.

"Does it involve Mom's house or Dad's?" I continued.

"Mom's."

"So, Jason, what is it that you wish would happen with you and your Mom?" The right question is always more than half the battle.

"I want her to watch a movie with me."

"Is this about the movie or about spending some time with her?"

"Well, kind of both, but more about the movie," he clarified.

"So, what's the movie, and what's important about it?" I asked.

"Have you seen *Bring It On,* Mr. James? It's about professional cheerleaders and what they go through to compete. It's really, really hard to do."

"I haven't seen it, Jason, but I'd like to. What is it that you'd like your Mom to get from watching this movie with you?"

" I want her to see how hard that stuff is. I want her to know that's what I want to do."

"Wow, so you want your Mom to respect what you want to do."

"*Exactly,*" exclaimed Jason, awed by my insight.

"Have you tried to tell her before?" I asked.

"Well, yes, but she didn't have time to listen to me." While this may be the perception of many kids, I knew it to be true in Jason's situation.

"Then that's what we have to work on first, right?" I asked, with Jason's immediate agreement. "We have to come up with time when you're alone with your mom. How about homework time?"

"No, that's crazy time in my house."

"OK, how about some time in the car?"

"Yes, that's it—before we pick up the others!" Ah, my crystal ball is in tune now. "But I don't know what to say."

"All right, it's best to be clear when making a request. I'll try it on you and you see if it fits. You drive, and I'll be you. If the radio's on, you may want to turn it down so your mom hears and listens. It's a good signal that you're going to say something serious. 'Mom, I really want you to watch a movie with me, because I want you to learn something about me.'"

"That's perfect, Mr. James!"

"Now I'll drive, and you're you…go," I directed.

"Mom, I really *need* you to watch a movie with me, because I want you to know something about me and what I want to do." This time he personalized and empowered the request with his substitution of "need."

"Great. Jason, is there any reason why you've hesitated about doing this?"

"Well, most people think that cheerleading is only for girls, but there are boys who do it," he answered.

"Of course there are boys who do it. Is that why you want your mom to know that it's hard to do?" I asked.

"Yes."

"Brilliant," I replied, "and very creative."

"Mr. James, why do people think that cheerleading is only for girls?"

"I think it's because cheerleaders cheer for players, and originally all the players could only be men. So, the women took over cheering. After a long time of seeing it this way, people just think that's the way it is…even though it's not that way anymore. It's pretty dumb, and, unfortunately, some people believe a lot of dumb things, just because it's what they've learned. A dumb thing about how somebody's supposed to be is called a stereotype. Stereotypes confuse people because they always have a little piece of truth, so it seems like it could be true. But, a stereotype also has lies. I'm always proud of people who follow their own heart and don't let a stereotype boss them around. I'm proud of girls who join the little league team, and I'm proud of boys who follow their interest onto the cheerleading squad. I'm proud of you."

"Thank you, Mr. James."

"I'm also proud of being chosen for this discussion, and I'm glad that you want your family to know you better…and to respect you for it. Will you let me know how it goes?"

"Yes."

"Good luck, and let me know if you need more from me?"

"I will." He thanked me and went off to join his class.

When I arrived at the diner, Jane was already seated. "I just had an amazing conversation with one of my fifth-grade boys," I began, and proceeded to tell the story. As I continued, step by step, Jane's eyes widened, as did her pearly smile.

"I can't believe this!" she exclaimed. "I just can't believe this." She was laughing. "My son, the fifth grader, had me sit down with him this past week to watch *Bring It On*." More bursts of laughter, and tearing eyes. "He wanted me to know that he wants to be a cheerleader, and that it's hard work."

"You've got to be kidding me." I took her hand, and we both squeezed through heartfelt laughter.

Jane continued. "He asked me where there's a high school that has a coed cheerleading squad, and whether he could go there one day. I told him we'd explore it, and that if it didn't happen in high school, he could take gymnastics and we'd look for a college where he could do it." I could only hope that Jason would receive half as supportive a reception from his mother.

When I saw Jason the next week for his regular group meeting,

I asked him to stay behind after the other boys left. He wanted to get to recess and could only spare me a few minutes, his coolness belying some potential discomfort.

"You're wondering if I spoke to my mom…well, I did. And no, we haven't watched the video yet, because my mother can't find the time," he said, rolling his eyes dramatically.

"Jason, I'm proud of you for following through, and sad that she's disappointing you. She doesn't even get it that she's missing out. Do I call her for an appointment, or do you want to step it up and try a note this time? You see, if you give up, you join her. You both deserve for her to listen to you."

"I'll write a note. If it still doesn't work, you can call," he decided. I admired his desire to handle it himself and told him so.

"But that's not the only reason I asked you to stay," I broke in as he darted a glance at the door, recess still beckoning. "I wanted to tell you about an interesting conversation I had recently with a friend of mine." This potential window into my personal life stole his attention away from recess and he settled himself on the chair. "You see, after our last talk, I had lunch with a friend of mine who is also a school social worker like me. I was still thinking about what you and I discussed and thought that it was an important talk. So, without using any names, I told her the story. She became stunned and couldn't believe what she was hearing. It turns out that she has a son in the fifth grade, and this past week he asked her to watch *Bring It On* with him."

This time Jason's eyes enlarged as his mouth hung open in absolute disbelief. "Really? Did she do it?" he asked with hope and anticipation.

I momentarily considered whether I could do harm by answering this question, concerned that his mother's reception may not be as fulfilling. Understanding that he still needed to know that *some* mom would be supportive, I answered him, "Yes, she did, and now she knows that her son wants to be a cheerleader, and she wants to help find ways to make it happen."

Jason grew quiet, as I watched his shoulders drop with his silent pondering. "You know, Mr. James, maybe he and I could get along." (An important consideration for someone who felt largely alien with regard to his peers.)

"I bet it's a good possibility," I said. Then I dismissed him, and he floated to recess in a stream of new consciousness. It struck me that he was a new boy—a boy who knows there's another boy in the world like him, with a mother who supports him.

After a faculty meeting, I walked Jane to her car. We both started speaking simultaneously. I let her go first.

"When I got home on the day of our lunch date, I told my son about our conversation and the story you told me. He was so excited to hear that there's another fifth-grade boy who wants to be a cheerleader. His very first response was 'Maybe we could get along.'"

Now it was my turn for the wide eyes and the slack jaw. Jane's son said what Jason had said verbatim. Now there are two boys in the world who will never be alone again, regardless of whether they meet.

✳

Rigid social expectations regarding gender roles have been so unfair to human beings for a long time, and kids pay the price. At the potential costs of taunting, rejection, and isolation, kids are often fumbling their way through the "mind" field of gender roles that don't reflect them either as individuals or, more basically, as people. While taking on the complexities and contradictions of Western gender politics and sexism as a whole would overwhelm these young pilgrims, trimming off the crust and cutting it up into chewable pieces can change the world...one bite at a time.

"Hey! Mr. James, how can you do that?" asked a boy in the third grade, first to arrive of six boys and girls in a weekly counseling group. I had no idea what he was referring to. "Your cup, you're drinking out of a pink cup!" With his permission, I brought the question to the group when they arrived with lunch bags and styrofoam trays of mass-produced food. "Yeah," they chided, "how *can* you drink out of a pink cup?" Their incredulity was unanimous.

"Well," I told them, "it's got a bottom, a handle, and it's filled with coffee exactly the way I like it, so I don't have any problem drinking out of it. What could be the problem with me drinking out of it?"

"It's a girl color," they agreed.

"Oh," I said, "you mean there are things only for girls and only for boys?"

"*Yes*! Duh!" I clearly needed some training on the matter.

"OK, so let's do this so I can get really clear." I drew a line down the center of the black board, labeling one side BOYS and the other GIRLS. Then I said, "Let's list as many girl things and boy things as we can." They instantly began calling out items for the lists—seemingly without dispute. Of course, the lists began with colors. Girl colors were pink, red, yellow, and purple, while boy colors were blue, green, brown, and black. Boys are faster, stronger, better at and more interested in sports, and they like tools and cars. Girls, on the other hand, like to play with dolls, dance, clean, cook, and sew, and they care more about their looks.

Though there were no overt challenges to individual items, as the lists lengthened the group became increasingly polarized, and the tension was palpable. They began corralling their lunch materials into small, identifiable "territories," circling the wagons. Accidental foot touching under the table became kicking, and a defensive atmosphere enveloped the room.

"OK, stop," I said. "Let's forget about the list for a minute. What's happening in this room at this table?"

Silence. They looked at me and at one another.

"We're getting angry at each other," offered Anna firmly.

"Why?" I asked.

"Because there are things wrong on those lists," she said. I breathed a private sigh of relief. Perhaps we had moved somewhat beyond those antiquated and limiting stereotypes after all.

"So," I proposed, "how about we go back to the lists, and if you can tell me what's wrong with an item, we'll agree to take it off the list." We began to dismantle the lists. The girls were quick and clear about owning things on the boys' list. Girls can also be strong, fast, and can like and be good at sports. After all, that very morning Claire had beaten Thomas at a race in the schoolyard…three times! With examples agreeable to all, these items were removed from the list. The boys sat silently as their list grew shorter. None of the three boys attempted to dispute any items on the girls' list. I wondered if they were feeling emasculated. They needed help.

Knowing them all rather well, I encouraged the boys to own something on the girls' list—something they needed but were terrified to do. "Now, listen here, you guys," I cajoled, "I happen to know how long it takes to make those perfect little spikes on top of your heads with gel, tie laces like that, and make sure that pants hang right up top and at the bottom. I also happen to know that you wouldn't even *think* of leaving your house unless they were all perfect. So don't even try to tell me otherwise. Am I right?"

The boys looked at one another, blushing, with chirps of suppressed giggles. The girls were thrilled with the suggestion, and they joined the boys' chirping, till they were all laughing together at the truth of the situation. They seemed thrilled and supportive of the boys' acceptance of my use of humor to weather the vulnerability of potential humiliation in owning girls' list items. "Girls care more about their looks" was removed from the girls' list without opposition.

I pushed again. "And you, Tony, brought me spaghetti that you made so I would know what a good cook you are, right?" Again, laughter, and still lighter spirits. "Cooking" was removed from the girls' list.

There were only a few items left on the lists, and time was running out. "I have another idea," I said. "Tell me what you think about this." I erased the line dividing the board into two lists.

"That's it," Anna cried out, "we'll have only one list!" She got it immediately. They all excitedly agreed. All seemed relieved to find a solution that saved them from the limitations and pain of the rigid and unrealistic lists.

I continued. "If it's going to be one list, it has to have one title," I stated. "What will we title the list?"

Again, silence. Then, Anna (on a roll...and I swear I didn't pay her...though I was moved to!) stated with certainty, "Let's call it 'Humankind.'"

"Yes, yes. Humankind," the rest chimed in. I wrote HUMANKIND over the remnants of the torturous lists, turning the remaining items into one list.

They literally bounced, giggling, out of my room, like they had just won a team sport. They looked as though pounds of extra weight had been taken off of them. There was such relief in surviving and even flourishing through the process of constructing, then consciously *de*constructing a system that is experienced as oppressive. As it turns out, there are all kinds of boys and all kinds of girls, all kinds of things for them to like and do, *and* it feels good to remember that.

Two weeks later I played a board game with this same group of kids. Anna stopped the play for a moment, saying, "Hey, look what we did!" She pointed to the plastic pawns on the board. "We all chose opposite colors." We all looked at the pieces to see that, indeed each child had chosen a color from the "other" side of the original two lists. We all laughed, and we reminisced about how fun that meeting had been in the end. Privately, I feared that once attention was called to their "gender-atypical" choices, something tantamount to a crime, they would rectify this by trading colors. They laughed and maintained their "new" color choices. They seemed gratified, as I certainly was.

Early in my career as a school social worker, I couldn't imagine being out. Now it's hard to imagine not being out. This doesn't mean that I make a general and regular announcement, but rather that self-censorship is not an automatic process. My being out is much more about comfort in my own skin while being out on the issues as an advocate, mental health consultant, educator, and colleague.

Well, time for a cup of coffee...in my pink cup. Join me?

AN UNCERTAIN AND BRILLIANT WORLD

Elizabeth Katz
Teacher
Phillips Exeter Academy
Exeter, New Hampshire

For my teachers, and my students

When I was in high school it felt like almost nothing outside my books was true. I looked out the windows of my school library into the abandoned parks of Boston, and the world seemed distant and unreal. My own life too did not seem real; it was a combination of hiding myself and hiding other people. I had just figured out that I was gay and that I could tell no one. In the library, I sat underneath desks and read Walt Whitman and Adrienne Rich. I had to believe in books; if it was my furtive life that was true, I would have to listen to the radio through headphones for the rest of my life, lie about the people I talked to on the phone, hide the magazines I bought. Every morning, I put on my jeans and my black T-shirt. It was easy, invisible. I could save my thinking for the brave lives I wanted to learn about in books.

The only people who seemed to live beyond the stories that surrounded me were my teachers, and especially the women who taught me English. It was my teachers who convinced me that my own life was full of possibilities, who showed me lives full of integrity and courage outside the books they taught.

Seven years after my own graduation, I came back to high school, this time as a teacher myself, with memories of what my own teachers had been to me. I started my second year of teaching, September 2002, in limbo. I had taken this position in the English department at Cranbrook Kingswood Upper School to be near my partner, who was still in graduate school at the University of Michigan. Eight months after she moved in with me, she left. I was alone, almost a thousand miles away from my family and friends, in a school and a profession where I wasn't sure I belonged. My summer had been spent trying to put my life back together, filling the holes in the apartment where her books and picture frames had been. I knew this year would be my last in this school.

As the school year began, the English teachers settled into our first department meeting. We ran through book orders, department policies, and class sizes, and then one of my colleagues announced a visiting author, an alumnus, a man who had made his reputation by writing novels about being gay. My colleague ran through the publications, the prizes the writer had won, and then paused. Because this writer was "a proponent of the gay lifestyle," he said, we could mention the writer's lecture in class but could distribute none of his writing.

I did not know what to do. I wanted to cry and, realizing I couldn't stop myself, I left the meeting. The only place to go was the bathroom, just like all those times in high school when my friends and I fled to the girls' room for an inadequate privacy. I was ashamed to be part of a school that did not want students to read about people like me. The school had invited this man back because of the recognition he had received as a writer, and yet they wouldn't allow students to read his writing.

I thought about my own visibility; I had never lied to my students, and when they asked about the ring I had worn on my left hand, or the woman who answered the phone at my apartment, I had told them about my partner. I had been visible when necessary. Now, it felt like what was necessary was changing. Angry and sad, I went to my friend Tim, one of the faculty advisers to our school's gay-straight alliance. As we talked, I could feel him becoming outraged.

A few days later, Tim confronted an administrator in the faculty room. "Why can't we pass out excerpts from the books? We know what's appropriate," he said.

The administrator shuffled his feet. "We're just not ready for this yet," he said. Tim looked him straight in the eye. He did not raise his voice. "Then when? I mean that. I want a date for when we'll be ready."

I had come out in high school for a lot of reasons, but mostly because I believed the personal was political. I believed in the power of visibility and the obligation to raise one's voice against injustice. The day after I came out, my younger sister found an anonymous note in her mailbox that read, "Tell your fucking faggy sister to go to hell. That's where she belongs." At that moment, everything stopped being theoretical; the personal was all *too* personal. My sister and I ran to the English teacher who was the adviser to the school GSA. She interrupted a meeting of school administrators to hand over the note and demand to know what they were going to do about it. A school assembly was held, the note was read out loud, and the head of the school said, looking out at all the students, "We do not tolerate this. This is not what our community is about." Suddenly, being gay was more important, and even more difficult, than it had been. There were things that could be done, that had to be done.

I went to my first meeting of the year as coadviser to the gay-straight alliance feeling again like the girl who had needed community and comfort and acceptance. There were more than a dozen students at the meeting. Some were my students, others were strangers. The room was full of a tense excitement; you could feel the students' relief in the safety of the meeting, in meeting other people like themselves, in seeing the possibilities of what and who they could be. They needed mirrors. I thought about that writing we weren't allowed to pass out and went back to my reading list for the year, adding *The Hours* by Michael Cunningham, a novel in which one of the central relationships is between two women who have been partners for 18 years.

The autumn moved on to Homecoming Week, capped off by the junior-senior girls' football game and the fall parents' visiting day on Friday. As an adviser to the junior class, I felt the tension rising between the two classes until, on Thursday afternoon, more than 30 cars in the parking lot were vandalized with shaving cream and motor oil. An all-school assembly was called for Friday before the game.

On Friday, parents' visiting day, I walked into my classroom, arranging my books and waiting for parents to arrive. On my right, I could hear a soccer player and a football player arguing.

"All soccer players are foot fairies," said the football player. I could see his mother cringing as she looked at her hands.

I froze, then said, "You know that kind of language is unacceptable in my classroom."

"Yes," said his mother, weakly. The football player stuttered an apology; I swallowed, then started to teach. The day passed in introductions and awkward pauses, and by the time we got to the assembly, I was exhausted.

I stood with the other teachers on the far side of the gym and listened to a dean talking about the vandalism. "It is not acceptable to destroy people's property. It is not acceptable to write obscenities in the parking lot. It is completely inappropriate to write FAG on a person's car." I heard the distinction: not "unacceptable," "inappropriate." For the second time that day, I felt my stomach churn. I walked out of the gym.

That night, after the homecoming dance, I sat talking to Suzanne, one of my former students. A week ago she had come to find me in the faculty room, asking, "Ms. Katz, when did you know you were…different?"

"I knew when I was 14, but I've had friends who didn't know until they were out of college, and others who felt they knew when they were really young." I looked at her. "Have you been thinking about that stuff?"

Half in tears, she did not meet my eyes as she said, "Yes." Suzanne had spent that night at the dance tentatively dancing with another girl, but had been unable to ignore the stares, the people laughing and pointing. "I thought I could do that here," she said, "but after what happened in the parking lot, I just don't feel safe anymore."

Saturday morning I called Tim, and I told him about what had happened in my classroom, about what Suzanne had said. "I've been thinking about what happened on Friday, and I think I need to come out at school, to the kids. Being silent is hurting me, and if it's hurting me, it must be hurting the kids. They need to know that their words are hurting real people."

Tim paused; I could hear him breathing on the other end of the line. "I won't let you do this alone. I'm going to come out too. We're in this together." That weekend, I couldn't stop thinking about the anonymous words that had shaped my experience of being gay in high school. After striding to the head's office, the gay-straight alliance's adviser had sat me down in an empty classroom. Looking directly in my eyes, she said, "You know you're not going to hell, don't you?" With her words, I felt the shame of being a target lift away.

Monday morning, class meetings were called. I did not know what I wanted to say about the graffiti until I looked at the 11th graders. "When someone uses anonymous and hateful language, because there is no name attached, the entire community is responsible for it. I know that you are better than these words. But what you need to know is that these words hurt. They hurt me as a member of this community, they hurt me as your teacher, and they hurt me as a gay woman. I know you are better than this, and I want better things for you than this language. I don't want to be part of a community where these words are used, and we have to work together now to reject this kind of language. You are going to be leaders, and this is the time to become leaders, to act with honesty and integrity and say that we do not allow this in our community. We do not destroy property, and we do not destroy people.

We are better than this. You are better than this." Next to me, the class president, Emily, began to clap, and the entire class joined in.

That week, at the gay-straight alliance meeting, I said to the kids, "What do you guys think about what happened in the parking lot?" They were silent; I pressed. "Were you surprised? Or was it not a big deal?"

One of the girls looked at me, stonily. "I hear those words so much I don't hear them anymore," she said.

"Do me a favor," I passed out some scrap paper, "and write down the things you hear other people saying about being gay." For a few minutes, the room was silent, and then slowly they began to pass me the pieces of paper.

Faggot.

Dyke.

I'll pay you two girls to have sex if I can watch.

She's gay? I never listened to her anyway.

Across the room, my student Peter was still bent over his paper. I kept going through the pages.

Homo.

Fruit.

You don't belong here, dyke.

That's so gay.

Peter handed me his paper, folded up.

Cocksucker Pole blower Gay freak Fruit Homo Queen Fudge packer Dick licker…

The list kept going. There wasn't room on his page to fit another word.

A week later, the gay alumnus writer visited the school. After many, many discussions—and some student activism—suitable passages had been agreed upon to pass out to the students. In his classroom, Tim had passed out the writing, saying, "When I read this, I know exactly how the character feels. Growing up gay in a time when no one—I mean *no one*—talked about it, I understand his secrecy and his desire for companionship. So it's important to me that we read this, because it's a story you very easily might never hear." His students had listened, respectfully, and then, one by one, in the days afterward, approached him to say how they appreciated his honesty.

In the gay-straight alliance, the writer sat down with the kids. "What are your lives like?" he asked, and their faces were filled with pleasure. So few people wanting an honest answer asked what their lives were really like.

Peter spoke up. "Last year, I was walking down the hallway and these senior guys, for no reason, just looked at me and said, 'Faggot.'" He looked at his hands.

"So what did you do?" asked the writer.

"I just figure that they must be gay too, if they know what to look for." Peter looked up and tentatively smiled. The group began to laugh, slowly, and then, both incredulous and excited, Peter grinned.

Every week, I watched the kids in the gay-straight alliance walk into the meeting and relax. They let go of the masks and guards that even the ones who were out wore; they were giddy and earnest. They began to share their stories with one another—their first visits to gay bookstores, their fears about coming out to their parents, their first dates. They began to share their stories with me. Sometimes Tim and I didn't leave school until 8:30 or 9 at night because the kids didn't want to leave the room, or one another, or sometimes us. I began to recognize the lag and pause of a student who wanted to talk privately, like Victoria, who said, "I need to tell you this story, and I've only told one other person."

Slowly, the story unfolded, of being forced to watch as her boyfriend walked up to another boy, and saying, "I hate you, you faggot," began to beat him. Victoria had been held back as she watched the fists, the scalp splitting open, and the blood running down. Suddenly, the other boys were gone and Victoria and the beaten boy were alone, his split head in her lap, covered in blood. "You have to go to the hospital," she said to him. "I can't go to the hospital. What would I tell them? I can't tell them." She sat holding him all night, and the blood dried, stiff, all through her jeans.

She looked at me. "I never talked about this before without crying," she said, and I held out my arms to her. She grabbed on, and I held her; it was all I could do. I could not forget what she had said, earlier in the meeting: "Words hurt us. Our skin isn't this thick."

In class, we began *The Hours*. "Is everyone in this book gay?" my students protested. "Are these people gay or bisexual? Can't they make up their minds?" The students needed to label the characters, to fit them into boxes. I sighed and tried to talk about contradictions, about fluidity, about identity. Sitting across from me, I watched Gwen and Evan lean toward each other and then toward their books. They were the two who never stopped talking in class, pulling ideas out of each other and the books, swift and sure. Some days I would come into class and see Evan asleep on Gwen's desk; other days, they faced each other, Gwen twisting her hair around her hand until her fingers turned white. In class, a month ago, Evan had looked up from *Mrs. Dalloway* and said, "They are all outsiders. Septimus, and Clarissa, and Sally—they are all outside." How sad he seemed to be saying it.

Now with *The Hours*, Evan and Gwen's eager participation had become ardent. There was hardly a moment when their hands weren't up to say something. One day after class they came up to my desk.

"I have a problem," said Gwen. "Here. See, Clarissa says that she and Sally are married. But people won't let them get married. I don't get it. How can she use that word, when no one will let them do it?"

"OK," I said, "tell me about Clarissa's world. Who are her friends?"

"Richard, and Louis, and Walter, and Mary Krull—"

"And what do they have in common?"

"Well, *they're* all gay too."

"So what's normal? I mean, for Clarissa and Sally, in their world." Gwen's smile became keen. I went on. "So for them, they are married. Everyone sees them that way, and they see themselves that way."

Evan interrupted. "Like when we date people," he said to Gwen. "We don't care whoever we date. But bigger, whole neighborhoods of people like us." He turned to me. "This book, it's everything; it's about everything."

I borrowed a line from *The Hours* that we'd discussed the week before. "It's the book of your life," I said, and I hoped he understood that when I said "your," I meant "my" too.

Spring semester's parents' visiting day crept up. I looked at my syllabus and realized that day's reading would focus on Clarissa and Sally. I thought of the fall, of my student's comments, of Homecoming, of the administrators who had told me that two students were doing poorly in my class because of their discomfort with my coming out. The discussion, with my students' parents watching, would be difficult.

We started class and began to talk about Clarissa and Sally's relationship, about why it worked, about why Clarissa was dissatisfied. Even in front of their parents, my students talked about these relationships without being self-conscious or awkward. The characters were simply people, and being lesbians was just part of who they were. The lives in the book had become real to them, and they could not imagine being dishonest or secretive about those lives.

I watched my students' parents leave the classroom. The only one to come up to my desk was Peter's mother. "I'm going to have to read that book now," she said, and I smiled at her, and then at Peter's quietly pleased face behind her.

When we finished *The Hours*, Evan asked whether he could write a personal response rather than a critical paper as his final project. It was going to be really personal, he warned me. It might not be like a real paper. It wasn't like anything else he'd ever done before; he might fail completely. "Evan," I said, "it'll be OK, I promise."

When Evan handed in the paper, placing it on my desk skittishly, he apologized again. That night, I read the essay: his moment by a pond, with the only girl he had ever loved, telling her that he likes boys, and knowing nothing would be the same after he had spoken. I wanted to tell him that the book made me remember what it was like to be in love for the first time, that it made me remember moments by water with women I had loved. I wanted to tell him that this book made me believe in love again, that it made me believe that Evan and Gwen, and all my students, would find a way to love another person.

"Did you read it?" Evan asked tensely before class the next day.

"It was beautiful," I told him, and watched him release his breath. Evan had always been not evasive, but elusive, always guarded. That was gone. His smile, for the first time in days, was easy instead of anxious. I handed back the first of the papers I'd graded, including Evan's. I'd paper-clipped an envelope to the back, and, from the corner of my eye, I saw him take the envelope with my note and slip it into his backpack. His paper needed more than the comments in the margins about run-on sentences and word choice. Instead, in the envelope, I wrote to him: *You are going into an uncertain and brilliant world. Find books and cities you love. Find a person to love who will make you happy, who you will love with integrity and bravery. I want these things for you, and I know, in time, you will have them.*

A few days later, I went with my classes to see the movie of *The Hours*, and I watched Evan and Gwen watch me. One of the characters had the name of the partner who had left me almost a year ago. I felt myself cringe as I heard her name, over and over again, but was determined not to let myself show that ache. There were a lot of things I was willing to give to Evan and Gwen, but my sadness wasn't one of them.

I began to go on job interviews, and every time one of my students began a sentence with "Next year…" I felt guilty. On my interviews, I talked about my students, about the gay-straight alliance, about the need to listen to their stories. When the school I'd been dreaming of for months called to offer me a job, I was elated and sad. I thought back over the year, about the students who hung in doorways to ask, "Do you have a minute?" when they needed half an hour, to the three-page letter one of my students wrote, telling me how she had begun to realize she was gay. I thought of the boy whom I had never met before he came up to me at a dance and said, "I think someone's going to tell my dad I'm gay. What do I do?" And I thought of myself at the beginning of the year, quiet, frightened, crying in the bathroom. I thought of the emptiness I had felt when my partner had left, and the loneliness of doing things by myself that I had done for years with someone else. I had needed to fill that emptiness, and I had filled it with my students. They, in return, had reached out to me. Helping them was a way to say thank you to my own teachers in high school, people who I knew believed in me beyond all reasonable understanding. I had known that, if I needed them, they would be there.

The memory of those teachers was never closer than the May night my friend Kate, who worked in admissions, picked me up for dinner, and telling me that she needed to check out some equipment, drove me to the student center. We walked in, and from a corner of the room, 40 of my students shouted in unison, "Surprise!" I looked at the kids gathered against the walls. I saw Tim and the kids from the gay-straight alliance and students from my classes. I saw the kids from the diversity program I advised. Some I knew well, others only from editing their papers or passing in the hallways. I saw Peter and Victoria, Gwen. ("Evan couldn't come," she told me, "but he sent the cake.") One by one, they came up to me and hugged me fiercely. I didn't know what to say except, "Thank you."

"Who put this together?" I asked Kate.

She pointed to Emily, the junior class president, and Brianne, one of my academic advisees.

Emily came over. "Were you surprised?" she asked.

"I don't even know what to say," I told her.

"Everybody's signing a book for you," said Emily, pointing to a cluster of students in a corner. "We wanted you to have something to remember this."

I smiled. "I don't think I could ever forget it."

After the party, Kate and I helped Emily clean up. As we boxed up the leftover cake, I turned to Emily. "I wish I could explain how much this means to me. I feel overwhelmed, but what I keep thinking of is when I was in high school, I had these amazing teachers, and I thought they were the most incredible women in the world. My senior year, one of them—she advised the gay-straight alliance—was leaving my high school, and my best friend and I threw her a surprise party, at the end of the year, with another of our teachers. We wanted to figure out some way to tell her how much we were going to miss her, how important she was to us. I can't explain what it feels like to be on the other side of that."

A week later, a few days before graduation, Emily brought me the scrapbook my students had signed. I could not stop reading it, looking at the pictures of my students laughing, dancing with one another. I loved their happiness. At graduation, I could not stop embracing them all. Minna, a student I had talked through her breakup with her girlfriend, told me, "You're like my mom, here." A student who told me the first day of school that she was stupid in English—it was not her first language—said, "You have no idea how much I learned in your class. Thank you for everything." Katia, a student from my first year who was gay, out, and unremittingly honest about it, said, "I couldn't have done this without you."

Emily walked me back to my car. I thought of what she had given me, and of all of those I had watched get their diplomas, then of not being able to see next year's class in their caps and gowns, and I felt my throat close. On the path in the woods to the car, we stopped to say goodbye. We both began to cry. "Don't go," she said. We hugged, and she walked out of the woods and into the meadow, a girl in a white dress in the sunlight. It should have been an allegory, but it was real.

At home, I took out the scrapbook once more. *If I ever consider being a teacher, I would want to be like you*, wrote Minna. From Katia: *You gave me confidence in the classroom, which I never had.* Gwen's cramped handwriting read, *I have learned more from you*

*than any other teacher and probably any other person, except my par-
ents.* Peter wrote, *You know, you can't tell my other teachers this, but
you're my favorite teacher.* Evan had taken the book home after the
party; he had written, *There is so much I want to say to you: I want
to write how much I will miss you and how important a person you
are to so many people. If I could, I would barrage you with a billion
adjectives and adverbs in an attempt to explain how significant you
are. Thank you for teaching me (I learned much more than English).*
Finally, tucked in a corner, was a note from Emily: *Ms. Katz, you
told me the story of the teacher you respected so much in high school,
and I would just like you to know that from my perspective, you have
become her. When I found out you were leaving, I wanted to make
sure that you knew how much we cared about you, and how much
you have meant to us.*

I don't know how I became the person my students see, but I
trust in this transformation. I learned how to be a teacher by listening to my students, by hearing what they needed, and I learned
how to be a teacher by every day remembering what my teachers
had given to me. I left my first job knowing I could help make my
students' lives better, and I couldn't think of them without hearing
the stories they had trusted me with. Our truths were as brave and
honest as the books we read.

IN THE SWAMP

Cindy Lutenbacher
Assistant professor of English
Morehouse College
Atlanta, Georgia

In November 2002, Morehouse College, historically a college for black men, received a significant amount of media attention when a student took a baseball bat to another student whose glance in the dormitory shower he perceived as a sexual advance. I do not believe Morehouse is any more homophobic than any other college campus; the amount of media focus seemed to me extraordinary. Was it because of the baseball bat? Or because the college is African-American?

I am a white lesbian who has taught English at Morehouse since 1990. Although it is tempting to try to relate some of the experiences of the past few years at Morehouse (for that may be what some would like to hear), I think I have a slightly different story I'd like to try to tell. This one is a story about racism, homophobia, critical thinking, critical living, "engaged pedagogy" (*Teaching to Transgress: Education as the Practice of Freedom* by bell hooks), and how all of those things collide and collude and, I hope, have meaning inside a first-year English composition course, and inside the heart of its teacher.

The story is not a linear one, and the morals within it don't all come at the end. For me, one of the most important morals is that we cannot separate into discrete boxes the many oppressions that

144

inhabit the lives of our students and ourselves. As former Spelman College president Johnnetta Cole used to say, "We are all messed up in each other." For me, this means that I cannot separate the necessity to be my students' ally against the constant tsunami of racism from the necessity for homophobia to end.

As a lesbian, I have a vested interest in seeing homophobia end. Although it may seem perplexing to some, I also believe that as a white person, I have a vested interest in seeing racism end. As the mother of two girls of color, I have a vested interest in seeing racism, sexism, and homophobia end. However, as a teacher, I know I cannot impose my beliefs upon my students. What I can do is to set the stage for critical thinking, for deeper personal and political investigation, for a kind of soul-quest that can open hearts and intelligence to question the roots of our beliefs. For me, the critical piece of setting that stage is that I be at least as willing to live and learn and unearth my own limits as I want my students to be.

When I've presented at conferences about my first-year composition class, I've named the talk "Teacher in the Swamp." What I mean to imply is that I do not believe I can ask my students to be deeply engaged in examining not only the dominant culture but also their own received, unconscious beliefs and values unless I am just as deeply immersed in examining my own received, unconscious beliefs and values. I cannot hope that my students will critically examine homophobia's impact on their lives if I'm not willing to "get down and dirty" with myself and racism, beginning with the mirror and moving through the public sphere of our daily lives. I cannot ask those who are hostile to homosexuality to think about how they may participate in perpetuation of homophobia—and a resultant split in the black community—if I'm not willing to take action against the white privilege that awaits me at every turn.

"We are all messed up in each other." These kinds of profound and critical excavations, reflections, and capacities for change and growth are what I mean by "the swamp," and I know I must be nose-deep in the middle of it—not just because my teacher-self wants students to be thinking critically, but because I cannot fathom any other path to a future.

Backdrop

About three years ago, in the summer of 2000, I decided to revise my second-semester freshman composition course, English 102. It's not that I was desperate for change; nothing traumatic had happened to make me know it was time for radical revision. I had been teaching English college composition for a decade, and I had been having a glorious time of it, feeling useful, successful, and happy.

But I kept hearing a voice that told me I had not gone far enough, I had not risked enough, and that time was running out the front door. I needed to invite my students into deeper territory, deeper terrains of the soul if I wanted them to write more powerfully—and also live more daringly.

I decided to do away with the usual texts of formal writing, research skills, and argumentation, and to begin with content, with some of the most central and ubiquitous matters that impact our lives personally: racism and sexism. *Begin with content that matters,* I kept hearing, *and the form will follow.* Every step of this process has been, and continues to be, just this way; I hear an idea, follow it, and sit with it, and if it continues to speak, then I try it.

Racism

I knew and believed several things in relation to what it would mean to focus upon racism in a writing course. I believed and still believe that racism affects every person in this country, but that it impacts people of color with much greater concrete, dangerous, and deleterious effects than it does people of whiteness. In my 14 years of teaching at Morehouse, I have not encountered one student for whom racism was not a critical piece of his or her life. Thus, I consider my students to be the experts on understanding how racism works upon their lives.

Reckoning with that reality brought me to another pedagogical precept that I hold dear: "Begin with what the students know, begin with their own lives, start with their own expertise and experience, and honor that knowing." From these ideas came the first assignment of the class, what I've called the "class offering." Each student brings in a piece of writing (quote, article, poem, song, essay, letter, story, speech, etc.) that has mattered to him in his dealing with racism. The students share these offerings with one another in small groups, and then we share some of them with the whole class. This assignment usually takes two or three class periods because the discussions are so rich; we invariably articulate a host of the current incarnations of racism and white supremacy, as well as the historical reflections of slavery, lynching, and other forms of white violence, including the ubiquitous experience of racial profiling.

In an additional attempt to accentuate the experiential, I also show the film *Sankofa* every semester. The film is excruciating and powerful, no matter how many times I see it, and I always watch it with them. We journal-write in response to the film, using guiding questions, such as "What do you believe are the messages in the film?" and "What does the film have to do with your life?" And to provide a safe space for students to take me to task for showing the film, I even offer the optional, leading question, "Is there anything you want to say to me?" To my surprise, most students who choose this question use the opportunity to thank me for showing the film, to explain how they've never had a chance to really learn anything honest about slavery, to express the sense of both horror in the history and pride in their ancestors, or to ask me about my own journey to the beliefs about racism that I hold:

I'm glad that I was able to experience *Sankofa*. Being an African-American male has caused me to step back and really review my life. Am I doing all that I can to make my ancestors proud of me? Am I keeping their dreams alive? Will I be able to endure this life and achieve all that is set before me? I think that the answers are yes. With so much pride from my ancestors behind me, why would I fail? I know that they did not suffer in vain, and I'm going to prove that to them.

Sankofa helped me to understand my past and how I should always hold it in a sacred place in my heart because if I forget the struggles of my people, I'm doomed…

When I see injustice happening, am I one to do everything in my power to stop it, or am I someone who would simply ignore it?

The souls of those who were taken from their homeland and brought here to be slaves still speak volumes. I guess their souls will never rest until we, the children of slavery, remember who we are.

Watching a movie like *Sankofa* is very emotional, being an African-American. I wonder how most white people in general react to *Sankofa*? I realize that all people are different and do not share the same opinions. But the white people that I know would state that it was not that bad and it is over. I feel like—no, it is not over. My ancestors were tortured for hundreds of years and to put it in the past and forget about it would be an abomination.

A movie like *Sankofa* is a scream in a room full of people trying to be silent. These movies are necessary so blacks can understand where they have come from, so they can know where to go. White people need to see it to understand, develop empathy, and realize that yes, it was that horrible. People actually went through this and were treated this way. I encourage every white person to try and reverse the role and truly ask themselves how they would feel toward a group of people who did things like this.

The things that students have said in other discussions when they refer back to *Sankofa*, the realities I've come to claim as I learn more and more of history, the vital eloquence I've experienced, from Frederick Douglass to Toni Morrison to my dearest friends—all lead me to a constant encounter with slavery and the past. They lead me to continue showing the film—at Morehouse and in settings with white people.

And they lead me to my own continued encounters with

slavery. To the moment, one hot July night a couple of summers ago, of reading primary accounts of slavery as I held my sleeping youngest child, my child who is African-American, and heard as clear as a wolf's song: "My ancestors did this to your ancestors." Then, later, silently, to the eyes of my students: "My ancestors did this to your ancestors." To the eyes of my friends. My colleagues. My family.

Some white people have tried to avoid any kind of naked encounter with slavery, saying that their ancestors came to this country after the Civil War, so they really don't have anything to face. Or that their ancestors were oppressed too, so they don't really have to claim slavery. But slavery was done in our name and on our behalf, and we continue to gain from it.

If I am to teach young African-American men, I must do so as an ally, and I can only be an ally if I am living—24/7—inside the realities of history and racism and doing everything possible to end it, whether that locus of oppression be in an institution, in the white people around me, or in my own life.

Sankofa opens the door to reclaiming the past, and I try to further that reclamation with what I call "home-town research." Students research the untold histories of racism in their home towns or home states, in order to try to learn something of what their eighth-grade social studies texts omitted. Equally important, I require that they also research the resistance that was mounted, for there's never been an incident of racism to which there was not some form of resistance, even if that resistance was simply to survive. Students have reported that this assignment is both horrifying and deeply satisfying. They say that they learn some things that shock them about the cities that they love, but they are relieved to at least be able to bring them forward and share them with classmates. Furthermore, they see what their forebears have done to resist the madness. In some cases, students have grown to look at their parents and grandparents through new eyes, having learned something of the conditions and times through which they lived.

Sexism

Sankofa offers so many important lessons, but one of the most important and salient is the way that "divide and conquer" worked inside slavery, and it is upon this lesson that I ask the class to move into considering sexism and homophobia. As with racism or any other part of the course, the students represent a range of attitudes, values, and beliefs, from "the man should be the leader and women should be subordinate" to a most sophisticated understanding of the oppression of women. But almost without fail, the students "get it"—that anything that divides African-Americans from one another serves to keep the racist status quo in power. So we begin.

We start with exercises that open up the dialogue, my favorite being "Four Corners," which I've amended to be "Five Corners," in which I post around the room five sheets of paper on which I've written one of the following statements:

- Black women are not really oppressed more than black men are, so I don't really need to be involved.
- Black women need to take charge of their own oppression and not be passive about it.
- Too much fuss is made over the oppression of women, including the oppression of black women.
- The oppression of women will end when men end it, so my responsibility is to do all I can, including challenging my brothers.
- Different genders have different roles in society. I'm comfortable with my role and wish that women would be comfortable with theirs.

The students get up and walk to the posted statement that most closely matches their own feeling, sit down with the others who have chosen that "corner," and discuss why they believe what they do. Each group then reports on the discussion, and the whole class has a chance to respond to one another. From there, we begin to examine the attitudes and beliefs that surface, and I try to be delicate, which is not at all natural to me.

I'm also deeply blessed to have the connection with Men

Stopping Violence (MSV), an organization here in Atlanta focused on ending violence against women, especially domestic violence. Two of their leaders are African-American men who run workshops and six-month groups for men who have committed domestic violence. The two leaders have come to my classes to conduct workshops and allow the students to respond to what they've experienced. They do this without my presence, for MSV believes that it is the responsibility of men to work with men to end sexism and violence against women, just as I believe it is the responsibility of white people to work with white people to end racism and its violence. Then the students write about the workshops, and I'm able to experience it through their eyes:

> The Men Stopping Violence experience is perhaps the most emotionally moving experience that I have ever encountered.... Many males in the world have been poisoned with the belief that a woman must be dominated and abused in order for their manhood to be preserved. It is essential that we as men take a deeper look at our belief system and realize that all that we were taught may not be correct. We should not be afraid to make changes in our mind-set. Instead we should embrace change, for we will all be better people for it.

> Another lesson that I took with me was that change is possible. No matter what happens or what someone does, if they are open and willing to change, then it can happen. I'm very happy to have had this experience.... It makes me think of all the things that I have done and said to offend someone. I am open to change, and I'm ready to start my process in finding myself. Isn't that the point of college?

> I heard one man say, "How could she leave me? She sees that I'm in school trying to better myself, and she still leaves." It amazed me the kind of role that black women are expected to fulfill. Even after being beaten, black women are expected to stand by their man...

Although not all of the responses are so open and favorable, many or most are similar to those of the students above, who see sexism as the logical consequence of a misogynist dominating culture.

I confess: This part of the course is the most difficult for me. Originally, I thought it would have been otherwise, that the discussions in which I had to face my own accountability for racism would be more difficult and painful. But the truth is just the opposite. When I hear students in places of denial or blaming women or jovially bonding with one another at the expense of women and homosexuals, I find myself so very tired. But I take a breath and think of how exhausting it must be for people of African descent and other people of color to hear us white people live in cheerful oblivion (white privilege) and express layer upon layer of denials of their everyday reality.

I remember a Sunday early in this part of the course in which I had read hundreds of pages of their writings, most of which were filled with avoidance of responsibility for sexism. Each page felt like a blow to my gut. Inside every denial and shift of responsibility, every stereotyping, every blaming of women, I felt the millennia of violence, enslavement, and destruction of women.

The following class meeting, I returned their writings with my brief comments, and we turned to dialogue about the connections between racism and sexism, and about what people of color experience when we white folks deny the things that they know in the depth of the body and soul.

The position of African-American men in relation to the oppression of sexism is one full of contradictions: They are perceived as a larger threat to white male dominance, and are thus presented in the media and other public arenas as generally violent and barbaric. As a friend and mother of African-American boys said, "Black women are just ignored. Black men are ignored *and* targeted." Yet, African-American men, like all men in this society, have been allowed to view women as inferior and to collaborate with their own oppression by buttressing the hierarchy of power and allowing "divide and conquer" to persist.

What I ask of them is that they look at the historic oppression of American women and how the stereotypes that continue to plague African-American women are the ones created in order to serve the power of white men and women. I ask them to consider the ways that they may have served the racist, white powers by not being their sisters' true allies. The assignment is to recall and write about an incident in which an African-American sister was disrespected. Did they intervene? If so, what happened? If not, why not? Here are some of their responses:

> By emulating the master, the male slave believes he is gaining a glimpse of power. [Both] the master and slaves viewed African women only as a means of sexual satisfaction and personal aggrandizement…[and are] the foundation of the problem concerning African-American men "bonding at the expense of the humanity of women." African-American males must bond in the healing of our wounds rather than the creating of new ones. African-American males must bond on the concept that the eradication of these two issues are not mutually exclusive but are dependent upon one another…. African-American males must not expect freedom from racism if they are agents of sexism.

> There is a stepladder in this society that currently values black women at the bottom. If black men don't respect their female counterparts, then who will?

> We black males have not even completely overcome our own internal conflicts, yet think it not hypocrisy to complain about the evils of the white man while tolerating the domestic abuse of our sisters, mothers, lovers, and wives on a scale equally as large. We would rather turn our heads and live in our own collective fantasies than let go of our comfort zone and face the reality that surrounds us. Ironically, though, this abandonment of comfort is the exact same mentality that we want whites to have in dealing with racism from our own perspective.

Homophobia

My first semester of this revised course, I found that something exciting was happening, that we were coming together in ways that were even more profound than I'd hoped. Our standing together inside the "swamp" made for a sense of being allies. About mid-semester, as we began struggling with sexism and what it means to be united with one's sisters, homophobia entered the class in ways to which I was accustomed—gibes to one another about being "soft" or "Hey, I don't know about you, but I like girls…"

I always challenged the homophobic remarks; I've done that since I began teaching college, for I want the homosexual students in my classes and on campus to know that they are in a safe space. But the challenges could only go so far, because the need some students have to present themselves as heterosexual is fierce. But something began to gnaw at my bones and would not let go.

I knew I needed to come out to them.

I sat with this knowledge for a while. I talked with a friend, a heterosexual African-American woman whose experience of Morehouse is that it is a very homophobic place. She worried that I might be burying my future there, and was I prepared to deal with possible fallout?

I didn't know what the fallout would be, and I still don't. But one reality kept talking to me from the mirror: Because of the color of their skin, my students cannot hide from the line of fire of racism. How can I be a true ally to them if I am hiding from the line of fire in any area of my life? They have to bear the daily flame; how could I do less?

I couldn't hide, couldn't participate in the lies, and so I told them. I told them of my beliefs about being an ally and how that meant to me that I have to stand in the flame. I told them that the courage I see in the ways they are living their everyday lives, the courage that so many of them have in trying to face their own learned demons of sexism, the courage that some of them have in embracing their own homosexuality, and the simple fact that "you are family to me"—all made it necessary for me to come from the shadows and open myself to whatever might come my way by being a lesbian, openly lesbian.

Silence.

I was sweating and shaking from adrenaline, but we went on to talk from there. I let them ask me questions, the usual things about whether I believed that homosexuals were born or made, what I believed about raising my children, and so on. And then, as I'd guessed would happen, over the next several days a number of students came to my office, wrote in their journals, or sent me e-mails in order to come out to me. Some waited until the end of the course. They told me of their own fears of being open, their choices to remain closeted, and of the many students in the classroom who were "frontin'" about their sexual orientation. These experiences (though I guarded their anonymity) opened the door for further discussions in class, including how difficult it must be to be a gay man on campus. The matter returned us to the very powerful political reality of "divide and conquer," and on that basis, we began to see homophobia's deeper claim upon their lives. Anything that serves to divide African-Americans against one another consumes their energy and keeps them less empowered to struggle in a unified and communal way against the racist oppression that all of them face. As one student said, "We black people have been through so much. How could we put that onto a person because of who he loves?"

I asked them to write about their experiences, the personal narratives of homophobia and their responses to the events; I've kept this assigment in ensuing years. For some, this is their first chance to talk about things that had happened to them as gay men; for others, the result is an examination of their involvement in situations where the psychological violence of homophobia was committed; and for some, the discussions touch off a torrent of rejection of homosexuality:

African-American men have to join together as one whole to fight the bigger issues. This means putting all little social taboos aside. Why should it matter if one guy wears pink while another wears blue? So what, you have more muscles than the next guy. Stop using sports as a fence to hide behind when you talk about what "real men" do. Real men should fight for what is right. Real men should stand against the man who calls him a "nigger" before calling his brother a "punk faggot." Real men stand together in spite of their difference.

My opinion is that the first thing that African-Americans should do is to do away with homosexuality.... African culture does not allow the practice of homosexuality. Homosexuality is something which can never be thought of.... The students should be taught that although they were brought from Africa and are now living in America, they should not do away with their culture.

Similar to racism, homophobia limits the intelligence of humankind. As victims of racism experience discrimination based on their skin color, something they cannot control, individuals who are gay or lesbian are discriminated against due to their genetic makeup. They are viewed by society as being less, when in reality they are just as equal as anyone else. If homosexuals continue to persistently protest, as African-Americans did during the Civil Rights Movement, their voices will be heard, and sooner or later they will be looked upon as human beings...

What is shocking is that the same community who has faced the very same feelings of hatred and bias has now turned a deaf ear to its own people because they have "chosen" to be homosexuals.

Later on, when I found out that my roommate was a homosexual, I was enormously disturbed because of my fear. I recall not talking to him for the first week because I didn't want to come off as "gay." But I am proud to say that I have overcome my fear, my homophobia. I now have a lifetime friend in my roommate. He is the most genuine person that I have ever met. I was able to overcome my fear because I broke down the wall that separated us. I think breaking down that wall is the first step to overcoming homophobia... It seemed hard at first, but looking back, reaching out to my roommate is one of the best choices that I have ever made.

The reason I believe that Morehouse should not really embrace homosexuality is the fact that I think it is morally wrong. I say this because in the Bible it clearly states that men are not supposed to sleep with men and women are not supposed to sleep with women.... On the other hand, as a Christian I believe in loving everybody and caring for one another; the fact that someone is gay does not mean that he or she should be discriminated against.

One of the men (attending the Men Stopping Violence group) admitted that for him attending the class was hard at first because he felt as if men coming together expressing problems and emotions was being weak or a sissy. It is a shame when a man would rather go through the judicial system than open up to another man.... We must stop worrying about what the world is thinking or saying about us, because the world does not care about African-American males. They want us to fight and bicker and kill ourselves.... We must stop viewing gays and homosexuals as weak and start targeting deadbeat dads, criminals, and drug dealers as being weak. We must stop accepting society's views of us and create a new mold. The new African-American man will be strong, responsible, a provider, and a person in tune with his emotions.

The college should not even acknowledge that this issue does exist.

After so many years of suppression and discrimination, we should not have any room to do unto others what was done to us. If no one else can empathize with the homosexual community, we as black Americans should be able. We know what it's like to have to hide, to act a certain way, and to enter through the back door.

Over the years I have been called a lot of things. From sissy, faggot, gay, to gay-ass nigger, I've heard it all. It is hard to hold a straight face, but it is accomplished. I believe it's all about empowerment. Sadly, it comes to the point where you actually get used to it all. Every day I cry inside because of the constant battle I fight, not to be happy, not to be gay, but to be myself.

[*Fall semester*] I know that the Morehouse community will definitely understand that embracing homosexuality will be detrimental to the future success and prosperity of this institution. Morehouse was founded on Christian principles and has traditionally been affiliated with the Baptist Church. It is not time to go against our fundamental beliefs now.

[*Spring semester*] The same United States military that tries to keep black people from reaching high-ranking positions also had a problem with people of homosexual orientation serving their country. The same school system that teaches black people that they can never amount to anything more than blue-collar also teaches the so-called Christian doctrine that homosexuality is wrong, instead of Jesus' top commandment of "Love thy God with all thy heart, and love they neighbor as yourself." The same media that portrays black people as being thuggish and rugged-out also portrays homosexuals as overly assertive and open. And the same "democratic" government that tries to strip away affirmative action and promotes racial profiling also denies homosexual people marriage privileges and custody to children in court cases. When black men can realize that they are in the same struggle, they will be more willing to embrace a fellow homosexual brother.... Black men have traveled through so much together, including everything from shackles as slaves to the current oppressive behavior of incarceration. As a people, we cannot allow sexual preference to stop our fight for justice and equality.

Some students are deeply threatened by this part of the course and seem to shut down their wonderful minds in considering homosexuality. But for most, the frank conversation and the understanding of the ways that homophobia serves the construction of power in this society unlocks doors and windows to critical thinking that was previously inaccessible.

For all the reasons above and for the sake of the homosexual students at Morehouse, I've chosen to come out to every class since that first. The response is nearly always the same. And my gay brothers always find their way to my office.

Since that decision, I've also come out to nearly every group on campus with which I'm associated: faculty, committees, freshman orientation, a meeting with the president. It's never been easy, but it has always felt necessary. Although I think I'm one of the few people on campus who is open about my affectional orientation, I really don't know what the repercussions will be. Tenure? Job security? Will some rabid homophobe with power try to take my children from me? I tell myself that those are paranoid delusions, but "in the community" we know of too many cases of retribution that have come to people who were open, cases that should be completely bizarre, but unfortunately are not.

Family and Community History

The writing for this course comes throughout the semester in a variety of assignments, but the most successful assignment is a portfolio project titled "Family and Community History." The project is intended to be a claiming of both the past and the present as a way of making an offering to the future, "a gift that you are creating in order to honor the ancestors and to give to the next generation so that they can continue to keep the community alive and healthy." It includes letters to the ancestors, letters to our children and future generations, interviews with family members, hometown research of lost histories and resistance, family trees, artifacts, research into world and national events, journal entries, and other writings that can be contained in a notebook. This project is the place where all the lessons at last come together, where we must stand with one another beneath the blessings and the requirements of those who gave everything.

Dear Ancestor,

You are my motivation and my inspiration.... When I think of all the adversity that you went through just so I could be here, it makes me want to do the best that I can in all of my works. When I am in class and I start to doze off, I think of you. When I try to cut a paper short, I think of you. When I receive a B and know that I could have done a lot better, I think of you. When I am able to sit and converse with whites in peace, I think of you... It is key that you stay in my spirit and mind for the rest of my life.

Dear Ancestors,

I will honor you by getting my education. I owe it to you and to myself.... You died for me to have the right to be educated, so I refuse to be one to dishonor you by falling off educationally.... I plan to raise my children right and stay close to my family also. So many of you were sold away during slave trades and...were stripped of mothers, brothers, fathers, sons, or daughters. So many of us today take for granted our family. It makes no sense at all for this to happen when you paid the price back then....

ne teacher in 10

To My Ancestors,

My wish is to become strong and work as a leader in the community like you did in the Choctaw nation. I thank my ancestors who are native to this land for passing down your love.... To my African ancestors who were brought from West Africa, I thank you for staying strong with so much abuse and harassment. I know the fields where you worked were hot and the work was hard, but you kept your faith and passed on a beautiful generation. To my ancestors who stood up in the civil rights movement, help me to show the burning desire you had for equality and justice. I thank all the ancestors who stood up for what is right and fought for it as well. Please help me become a better man so I can raise up a great nation where if any mouth is hungry, let it be fed; if any man or woman is naked, let him or her be clothed; if any unjust problem remains, let there be a solution. This is what I pray.

Dear Children...

From sit-ins to large protests, there are many ways to show resistance to racism. Throughout history, we have seen these demonstrations by African-Americans time and time again. We have seen these demonstrations in both peaceful manners and violent conditions. From students to elderly, politicians to lay leaders, and slaves to free men, forms of resistance to racism have attempted to "level the playing field" among races.... I hope that you all will have this same dedication to your race. Think about your children. Make it a better day for yourselves and them.

The Family History Project is the place where I believe the course comes together most profoundly for the students. And it's the place of the greatest sorrow and most profound hope for me. By far, the part of the work that leaves us all shaking the most is the interview of family members. Constantly, students report that having to ask the questions opens the door to stories that had not been told and a knowledge they fear they would have lost otherwise. In some cases, it has opened lines of family communication that had been closed. Even the students for whom the family history contains things that are difficult to face report that the *telling* of these stories is freeing and gives them strength. This project leaves no one unchanged.

And that includes me. The interviews and the histories shared bring the students and me into an even closer kinship. To witness the stories and histories that they bring is an event of the soul of galactic proportion. It is not possible for me to encounter the story of Great Aunt Sara, who at 10 years of age had to hide submerged in the swamp and walk two days to Gainesville, Florida, in order to avoid the fate of her older sister and mother, who were lynched for attempting to vote, without my becoming a different person. And there are many stories like this one—a seemingly infinite number of stories of murder of the soul, the constant disrespect and disregard of human dignity—that students and their families have experienced, of heart-shattering heroism, the mothers who worked three jobs, the grandmothers who were there to love beyond measure when young boys were dirtied by stereotyping and false accusations, the fathers who faced the mob, the ancestors who refused to be whipped and then made their way to the Underground Railroad.... I cannot imagine any person truly hearing these stories and not being forever transformed, translated into another being.

Nothing in the stories surprises me. Nothing. It's hearing them from men whom I see as younger brothers that makes the difference.

And that is why I know I must do all that I can to be there in that swamp with Great Aunt Sara and with the students in my classes, if I have any interest in education playing a part in making a world that is worth living in. I must be there for my own sake.

If I truly believe that students at Morehouse are family, then I have no other choice, as a teacher or white person or lesbian or human.

That's the story I'm trying to tell. That's the story I'm trying to live.

Part Three
May–September

NO MORE SILENCE

Randall Furash-Stewart
Amherst, Massachusetts

The summit of happiness is when a person is ready to be what he is.
—Erasmus

I had a dream last night. Every teacher from middle school or high school that I had ever suspected to be gay, lesbian, bisexual, or gender variant was in it. We sat around talking about everyday kinds of things: classroom management, the quality of school lunch, the difficulty of balancing being queer outside of school with being a teacher. I saw the pain they felt in living a double life. I understood, and I forgave them.

Growing up in suburban Maryland, just outside of Washington, D.C., in the 1990s, I was lucky enough to be in a fairly safe place to try on various sexualities and gender identities. I proudly walked through school first as an out lesbian in 10th grade and later as an out, gender-questioning queer by the time I graduated from high school. In my searching for myself, I looked for reflections of the possibilities of what I could be in all my teachers. I was looking for a place where I could fit in my high school community.

Not finding one, several other students and I started a gay-straight alliance. We approached several teachers who we were positive would be supportive, but all of them were too scared to support us. Suddenly, my school did not seem like such a safe place. We were assigned a sponsor, a guidance counselor who begrudgingly came to our meetings out of obligation. This, while better than nothing, did not help us find the support we were looking for.

That spring, we organized recognition of the National Day of Silence (a day protesting the silence that many queer and questioning youth are forced to feel in schools). I made stickers for all our supporters to wear. That day the halls were filled with students wearing rainbow stickers, but supportive teachers, especially queer teachers, were scarce. That day I learned a very important lesson: It is all right to be queer, but only if you are not an educator. That summer, I took that lesson with me to my job as a camp counselor. I learned to live a double life.

It did not save me. In fact, I found that it did more harm than good. One day a 6-year-old boy came to camp with a skirt in his bag. He confided in me that he wanted to wear it at camp, but he was scared. I encouraged him to wear it and promised that if any kids teased him, I would defend him. It turned out it was actually my fellow counselors who teased him, at our staff meeting that afternoon. Buried deep in my closet, I could not say anything. I swallowed my objections for fear that I would be accused of being unfit to work with children. The camper never again mentioned the skirt. School had taught me well.

I'd seen the same thing happen in my senior year. During choir practice, one of my fellow students commented on something being "so gay," meaning that it was stupid. I spoke up, objecting to his offensive use of a word I held so dear to my identity. He argued that I was being ridiculous. He made a nearby student, who was also queer, cry. Our choir teacher, whom I suspected was queer, just glared at me, as if I had started the whole disruption, but said not a word to the offending student about his language. I felt betrayed by someone I looked to for guidance.

I carried my bitterness about that event with me to college the next year. I was interviewed by someone writing about queer youth in schools. I argued that teachers needed to speak out more and that I was angry with my high school teachers for teaching the queer youth in our school silence. I was driven to go into teaching to end these silences and educate young people to be fully themselves, responsibly, in the world.

My first year of college, I started a job as a teaching assistant in a small special-needs high school program on campus. I was very closeted at my job. I broke out in a cold sweat any time queer issues came up. I was sure to stop homophobic comments when I heard them, but I always panicked when the need arose. Straight coworkers sometimes brought their boyfriends to visit and spend a day working with the kids. I could not even discuss my primary partner or any of my other lovers with my students or coworkers. I was too scared of having to explain myself.

I had mastered living a double life where the personal and professional were completely separate. My last year there, I was out on campus as transgender. I changed the name I went by and most people referred to me by male pronouns. However, while teaching, I kept going by my old name. I even had coworkers who kept the secret with me, calling me one name at work and another name on campus.

Working in public school that year, doing a prepracticum in a social studies class, the need for my double life was reemphasized. The teacher I was working with was doing a unit on social identities. She included sexual orientation in her lesson, and students were very receptive to talking about that issue, as we live in an area where there are many gay and lesbian parents and youth. She also included gender, but as a strictly unchanging biological fact that we are given at birth. A student brought up that some people have sex changes. Everyone giggled and the teacher responded that we were just not going to go there.

When I approached her after class about the lesson, I made the mistake of coming out to her. I was told that she understood that this was a very special issue for me, but she could only push things so far. I accepted that she was right. The school community just was not ready for that silence to be broken.

When I graduated, I changed my name legally and started looking for work in schools. Every time I went to a job interview, I sweated over what gender I would be perceived as. Sitting comfortably in my double life of silent lies, I let interviewers make their own assumptions about my gender. That is how I got my current job as a female. I work as a teacher in a small special-needs middle school program. In spite of my efforts to appear male, I am a woman there. Still, though, I have been pegged as the queer teacher because of my appearance. I am lucky enough to live in an area where being a lesbian teacher, while not easy, is not unheard of. Under this pretense, I have offered support to students who are going through what I went through in middle school.

"Josie" is a student of mine who immediately started dropping hints as soon as I met her. She talked to me about the Indigo Girls and other gay icons that I am all too familiar with. We spoke in this veiled code at first. I told her she was going to be all right by recommending Ani DiFranco albums, never saying the word "queer" or telling her anything about myself aside from the fact that I have seen the Indigo Girls in concert at least 10 times. I even wrote down the Web site of a local queer youth organization for her, but I could not say anything about it out loud. She confronted me one day, asking why I had responded to a poem she showed me with, "You are not alone." I was flustered. I stuttered out something about how I knew people who had gone through the same tough things she was going through. The next day, she brought in a poem about taking responsibility for guiding kids that are going through the same things you went through. I knew she was right, but old habits die hard. I realized I was teaching Josie the same lessons about silence that my teachers had taught me, and it was not OK to repeat that cycle.

Since then I have started talking more openly about queer issues in my classroom. I also have the Syracuse Cultural Workers Peace Calendar in my classroom, which has a picture of Harry Hay kissing his partner in June. I am both scared and excited about the discussions that will open up in my classes.

However, in spite of all this, I am still living the ultimate double life. I still do not mention my primary partner as easily as some coworkers mention their spouses (he is currently my "roommate"). Nevertheless, there is the much larger issue of pronouns. I am unquestionably a queer guy outside of work. Any time I am working with students, though, I am the queer female teacher. It is better than being perceived as straight, but every time a student calls me "she" or "ma'am," I shiver. Many days I am too distracted to be able to devote my full attention to teaching or planning lessons because something very basic to my self-identity, my gender, is not acknowledged at all. I am playing the same game I played in college. Some of my coworkers acknowledge me as a guy outside of work but participate in my lie by calling me "she" at work.

And what am I getting out of all this hiding and secrecy? Maybe some job security, maybe avoiding alienating some students (or parents). However, I am realizing that it is costing me so much more. I am not able to teach my students to be themselves responsibly in the world when I am avoiding doing just that.

Next month, I am starting my medical transition. I will start taking testosterone, which will masculinize many of my features, like my voice and facial hair. My students will inevitably wonder what is going on. I intend to be honest with them. I do not want to continue the cycle of silence and lies by teaching them shame. Luckily, I have my supervisor's support in this, but I think we are in for quite an adventure. Sometimes I have fantasies of transitioning and then going back to a comfortable double life in my comfortable male body. However, I have made the decision to submit my story to this book because I do not want to live my life that way.

I understand now the pressures my queer middle and high school teachers felt. I forgive them, because their silence was part of something much bigger than they were. In homage to my teachers, I will work to make sure I set a proud example to my students for the rest of my teaching career.

TRANSITIONING IN THE SCHOOL SYSTEM

Gayle Roberts, B.Sc., M.Sc.
Science teacher (1969-2002)
Science department head (1990-2002)
Lord Byng Secondary School
Vancouver, Canada

I began teaching more than 30 years ago, in 1969, at Gladstone Secondary School in Vancouver, Canada. Since that time, the public's attitudes toward homosexuality and transsexuality have changed—for the most part, in a very positive way. Until recently intense pressure was put on everyone in society to be "normal." "Normal" basically meant everyone was expected to pass through our school system, become a productive member of society, marry, have children, and not deviate from societal expectations of heterosexuality and appropriate gender role behavior. Teachers for their part were expected to be society's role models and, as such, could not deviate far from the norm, especially in such crucial aspects of their lives as sexuality and gender identity.

My own experiences as a transsexual teacher who successfully transitioned "on the job" in 1996 perhaps indicate that today there is greater acceptance than ever before for individuals who deviate from the norms of yesterday. I base this on my experiences as a child growing up in post-World War II England, then later as a young adult in Canada, and finally as an older adult when I transitioned.

My earliest memory, at about age 5, is of wanting to be a girl. The culture I was born into made it very clear to me that expressing this desire was absolutely unacceptable. I worried what my parents would do to me if they found out. I quickly learned that while it was somewhat socially acceptable for a girl to be a tomboy, the opposite was certainly not the case. I also learned to keep a "stiff upper lip." I was raised to believe that boys don't cry. It is no wonder that I grew up feeling very ashamed of myself for having such feelings. As a method for coping with these feelings, I believed that one day I would be told by doctors that I was really a girl and was the subject of an experiment to see if it were possible for girls to be raised to believe they were boys.

When I was 11 years old my parents emigrated to Canada, where I entered school and eventually university. I have always been interested in the sciences, especially physics and astronomy. This interest led to academic success and eventually a career in teaching—and it also became another method of coping. By immersing myself in academia, I was able to postpone dealing with my gender confusion, which was getting only more painful. By continually keeping my focus on the "outside" I was able to avoid dealing with my "inside." As I matured I developed yet another coping mechanism: I believed my feelings of wishing to be a woman would disappear when I fell in love.

By the time I reached my late 20s I realized that if I were to fall in love and marry, my feelings of wanting to be a woman would just have to go! How I achieved this I don't know; but by brute mental force I stopped those feelings. I fell in love with a wonderful, caring woman. We were best friends for many years. While she was aware of my feelings of childhood and young adulthood, the two of us believed they were now in my past and we could marry and be a normal, loving couple. Little did we know then that what is recognized today as gender dysphoria and gender identity disorder is a chronic condition that usually intensifies with age. With every hope for the future, we married and spent our first three years as a couple in Singapore, where I taught physics at the United World College of Southeast Asia. Over those three years we explored most of the countries in that part of the world.

In 1983, after completing my three-year contract, we returned to Canada. The Vancouver School Board assigned me to Lord Byng Secondary School, where I taught general science and physics until I retired in 2002. During the late '80s and early '90s, I found it increasingly more difficult to control my ever-intensifying feelings of wanting to be a woman. Fortunately for me, Vancouver had a Gender Identity Clinic. My family physician arranged an appointment for me with one of the clinic's psychiatrists, who recommended that I join what was called the Explorers' Group.

The group consisted of people who, like me, were exploring their own gender issues. In this environment of safety and trust, we were able to explore our innermost feelings. Many of my new friends quickly realized the only way they could achieve the inner peace we all so desperately wished for was to transition. I was a slow learner. I spent several years fighting my inner self. I was afraid of losing everything that was meaningful to me—my wife, my career, and my friends. These fears were not completely unfounded, as I had seen this happen to many of my clinic friends. However, by 1996 I could no longer function. I was three weeks into a new school year when my wife told me she would rather have a live sister than a dead husband. It was then that I realized I had to transition, even if that meant risking everything that was dear to me.

To transition successfully, one needs a plan. At the end of the school year I went to the school administrators and, with them, to the area superintendent, and very openly discussed my gender conflicts. I told them I was suffering from gender dysphoria and that I had a medical condition called gender identity disorder— and to my surprise they were extremely supportive. They told me I was a respected teacher held in high regard by students, parents, and educators alike. They told me that they had never before had to deal with a teacher with my medical condition but that I could count on their support.

So it was no surprise to me that when I applied for sick leave in September I was granted it. Essentially, we agreed that I should take a period of sick leave for my transition and then, when I was ready, I could return to work as a science consultant for the school board until June. Then, in September, I'd go back to active teaching in the classroom. The only thing that the superintendent insisted upon was that I not go back and forth—presenting one day as a man and another as a woman. I assured him that having lived over 50 years as a man and not being comfortable with it, the last thing I would want to do was to go back to being a man.

After four months of transition, I was excited about returning to work. The superintendent and I agreed that it would be best if the staff in the board's office were informed of my medical condition. I have always believed that it is best to be open with people who know you or will interact with you over an extended period of time. By telling the staff, I gave them the opportunity to be comfortable with me and, if they wished, ask questions. I was introduced to everyone in the building. Many of the people I met were colleagues, but many others I had not met before. My first day on the job was wonderful. On my desk in my office was a beautiful bouquet of flowers from my high school principal and a note wishing me success in my new role. Contrary to my fears that I could be placed in some back office counting the proverbial paper clips, I was asked to arrange a district-wide science conference. I was informed that, as part of my new duties, I was to meet with visiting international scientists and science educators.

I knew that the people working in the board offices were required to be civil to me, but I also knew that no one can mandate friendship. So, as I sat in my office wondering whether people would interact with me at a personal level, one of my new colleagues came by and asked if I'd join her for coffee.

During the five months I spent at the board office, I found that I was completely accepted. People asked me to join them for coffee or lunch or for walks in the neighborhood. As people got to know me they would ask me questions. I never talked about my transition unless requested to do so. One of my most memorable experiences occurred when a colleague gave me a lovely aquamarine ring. She told me she did not wear it now, and as she was going through her jewelry box she thought of me. I wear it every day. For me it was, and still is, a symbol of acceptance in my new role.

As June approached I discussed with the superintendent of human resources where I should teach in September. Basically, I had two choices—one was to return to my old school, and the other was to go to a different school in the district. In the end we decided that I would have the best chance of success in my new role if I returned to my old school, as I would not need to prove to that school community that I was a good teacher. We also knew that no matter how passable I was in my new role, eventually everyone would know that I was the transsexual teacher everyone had been talking about a year earlier. It was just a matter of time before the school community would know of my transition and I'd need to deal with possibly adverse reactions of parents or students.

So it was with a great deal of excitement and trepidation that I returned to my old school in September. My excitement was caused by my wish to see my former colleagues and to return once more to teaching young people. My trepidation was due to my concern about the reaction I would receive from my students. Would I be accepted or seen as some kind of weirdo? I realized that even though the board had given me all the support they could, ultimately my success would be governed by the attitude of my students and by my ability to maintain an appropriate learning environment within my classes.

The first day, in retrospect, was an indicator of things to come. I met my homeroom class, introduced myself as Ms. Roberts, took attendance, collected the usual fees, and then, as was school policy, dismissed the students for the day. None of the students made any untoward comments. They reacted to me as hundreds of students had over the years prior. So far, so good.

The following day, I thought, would be the real test, as it was the first day I would meet the students I would actually be teaching. As it happened, the first class I met that day was senior physics. This class would have at least some students from the junior physics classes I had taught for three weeks the previous school year.

Believing as I do in good planning, I had given some thought to how I should greet this class. Obviously, all the students, whether or not they had had me as a teacher in previous years, knew that I was a transsexual teacher returning to the classroom. (You can not keep that a secret!) I believed I had to acknowledge that at least some of these students knew me in my previous role as a man. At the same time, however, I really did not wish to open up discussion on potential issues around my sexuality or gender identity.

My approach was to say, "I am aware that you are aware of my changed circumstances." I told them how much happier I was as a person. I also told them that I was really pleased to be back in the classroom to teach them, that the curriculum was rather lengthy and I thought it best if we got started on the course. It was my hope that this approach would help any of my former students feel comfortable with me. For the students in my junior physics classes who had not had me as a teacher in previous years, I decided to say nothing to them about my changed "circumstances." As I did with my homeroom class, I simply introduced myself as "Ms. Roberts" and approached the class much as I had done with so many before. The school recognized the possibility that some students might have found my transition difficult, and counselors were available to help them. I was told later that not one student took advantage of that opportunity.

The following days were very much like my first teaching day. The students reacted to me just as they had in the past. It soon became apparent to me that for my students only one thing was really important to them—how well I taught. As is normal in a class, some students interact with their teachers in a more personal way. They will tell you a little about themselves—what their hobbies are, what they enjoy, their goals, aspirations, and frustrations.

I found that many of these students during the first part of the year would come up to me and quietly tell me how brave they thought I was. One student told me she thought I was an inspiration. That was one of the most meaningful comments I ever received from a student. It told me that I was accepted, and just as importantly, that I was a role model with whom some students could identify. I don't believe for a moment that this student had her own issues around gender—rather I believe she saw me as a teacher who had significant personal problems and was able to overcome them and become a much happier person. I believe she realized that she, and others like her, could in a similar way resolve their own unique personal issues.

The next major hurdle I felt I had to overcome was the possibility of negative comments at "Parents Walk-through." This occurs toward the end of September and it gives parents the opportunity to meet their children's teachers. The parents follow their child's timetable, meeting each teacher, who in the space of about 10 minutes tells the parents a little about the course and the manner in which students will be evaluated.

I expected each of my classes would be completely full with the 60 parents of the 30 students I had in each of my classes taking advantage of their opportunity to see the transsexual teacher—or so I thought. Instead, the usual half a dozen to a dozen parents visited my classroom and listened to what I had to say and asked me the usual questions about the curriculum or my approach to evaluation. I was on cloud nine! The parents obviously accepted me.

As one mother was leaving my class for the next one, she asked me if I knew a certain student I had taught a few years earlier. I told her that the name was familiar. She explained that he was her oldest son, who was now at university. We talked a little about her son and I asked her how and what he was doing. Then she told me her daughter was in my physics class and how pleased she was that I had returned to continue teaching physics. As she walked out of my classroom she turned to me and said, "You look very pretty." I was overwhelmed! Here was a parent who managed to tell me, without once bringing up the subject of my gender change, that she knew I used to be a man, that I was an excellent teacher, and that she was totally accepting of me as a woman. I floated on the floor for the rest of the evening.

Later that evening I talked to my principal and asked her if she'd had any comments from parents. She told me that only one parent had discussed me with her, and that was to say that "he looks much better as a woman than he did as a man." My principal smiled as she pointed out that all of the parent's pronouns were wrong but her sentiments were good. A little later, as I walked down the hallway, I became aware that my head was held high and that for the very first time in my life I was proud of who I am. For the first time in my life, I was shame-free!

And so the year went on as it started. That year rolled by and then another five. It seemed so little time passed before I was standing in front of the school staff receiving retirement presents and heartwarming comments. When it came time to thank them, I must confess that all my self-control was swept away as I cried and thanked them for the acceptance they had shown me. I left the school and drove home to my "new sister" of six years who loved, supported, and encouraged me as she lost her husband and gained a sister.

This article is dedicated to my "new sister," my best friend and companion, Edith. During many painful years for both of us, she has encouraged and supported me. Just saying "thank you" seems insufficient. Losing one's husband is not really balanced by gaining a sister. I am truly thankful to her for what she gave of herself.

GOWN TO TOWN:
LIFE AFTER BROWN

Tamar Paull
Seventh-grade English teacher
Community Preparatory School
Providence, Rhode Island

The flag was at half-mast when I pulled into the parking lot of my first real job that October morning. Community Prep, a small middle school serving primarily low-income students of color from in and around Providence's inner city, was the perfect place for an idealistic recent college grad to be initiated into the world of education. Not noticing the unusual state of the flag at this early hour, I rushed to my classroom to drink my first cup of coffee and write the night's homework on the board before my seventh graders showed up.

By five minutes to 8 the caffeine had begun its magic and I felt energized and pleased with my plans for the day. It was time to head down to the community room, where I would join the school's 150 students and staff to share announcements, recite a daily pledge promising to take full advantage of every opportunity the day had to offer, and race back upstairs to begin the daunting task of changing young lives. I was fresh out of college, and while I was not exactly certain how to undertake this task, I was quite sure that it could be done.

After a few crucial announcements about the new juice machine and the basketball team's recent victory (undefeated for

178

yet another year!), a fourth grader raised her hand to ask why the flag was broken. I was busy trying to remember which door my class was supposed to use in the event of a fire drill and checking kids off on my attendance sheet just like I had when I'd played teacher in the back of my dad's university classroom, when I heard the principal's explanation. The flag was not broken; it was at half-mast. Apparently a young man had been killed. A body had been found. Something about a scarecrow and iron bars. By the time my principal got to the word "gay," I finally realized what had happened. I felt the familiar hot red discomfort climbing up my neck and cheeks and ran up to my classroom, feeling the coffee rise in my stomach and wishing I hadn't bypassed morning news radio in favor of the oldies. I had exactly one minute to digest the watered-down and patchy version of what would soon enter my vocabulary as "The Matthew Shepard Story" before my students would enter my classroom.

Somehow I stumbled through the morning classes. (Who knows what I taught that first year—something with clearly artic-ulated objectives that I'd be embarrassed to repeat now, I'm sure.) By midday my rage was starting to overwhelm the initial denial: Fresh out of Brown University, I was used to speaking my mind and even being celebrated for such. As a college student, I had come out on a campus and at a time when issues of sexuality were discussed freely and comfortably. Now I found myself working at an inner-city school five miles across the city from Brown, and a world away, with a sizable and vocal population of religiously con-servative families whom I was now obligated to serve and make comfortable.

I stormed into my principal's office and announced that I couldn't stand it any longer: I was just going to come out of the closet. I had to talk to my students honestly about Matthew Shepard's death; I had to make sure they understood, and I couldn't do it without telling them the truth about myself. A carefully closeted gay man, my principal was more than a little concerned by my plan. My boss appealed to my newly developing professional side and convinced the radical recent college grad in me to take a few deep breaths and spend the weekend thinking through my plans.

By Monday morning my need to come out had not diminished. My 22-year-old maturity, however, had prevailed, and I was now able to sit down with my boss and the entire faculty and staff—whom he had invited to an emergency meeting before school—to rationally explain myself. At a vigil I attended that weekend for Matthew Shepard, a local gay activist and gospel singer sang a rendition of a spiritual proclaiming to Matthew that when he reaches heaven's gates he can rest assured that his death will not be in vain. I took these words to heart, and in fact took them as an imperative. In a school of 150 students, some of whom were learning at home and in church that "God hates fags"—as the Reverend Fred Phelps admonished mourners at Shepard's funeral—I knew I had a responsibility to do something. I carefully explained this to my boss and colleagues. I had to come out, I explained to them, so that our students would think twice before becoming the next to tie a gay kid to a fence, beat him, and leave him for dead. This may seem melodramatic now, but the shock of the event and the growing realization that I wasn't at Brown anymore, Toto, was doing strange things to me.

With surprisingly minimal coaxing, my boss did a 180 and quickly took it upon himself to organize the entire faculty around what I would later refer as the "Ms. Paull Comes Out" episode (Ellen DeGeneres having recently paved the way). Our nine homeroom teachers were on board and the plan was set. The next morning at the appointed hour, every homeroom in the school would have an age-appropriate conversation about Shepard's death. Incorporated in that conversation in the most organic and squirm-proof way possible would be the official outing of yours truly. Realizing that 150 eight- to 14-year-olds were about to find out something that I had been told as a student teacher I would have to conceal my entire professional life made me wonder for a moment if there wasn't some other way to ensure that Matthew's death hadn't been in vain. Maybe I could go to another vigil, or write an anonymous letter to the local paper.

But my pride, both gay and stubborn, propelled me forward. If every other teacher in the school could back me and have a conversation with their students that they had certainly never contemplated before, I—a tried and true lesbian feminist with radical roots and a lefty New York Jewish upbringing—was surely brave enough to face a group of 13-year-olds.

So I dove in. I reminded the students about the flag that had been at half-mast the previous week. I asked if they remembered why. They did. I stalled. I gulped, wishing my cheeks didn't turn red when I was nervous. I told them about the vigil I had attended for Matthew over the weekend, stressing the fact that it was at a church and that many people were there. I pandered. I told them about the gospel singer there and how he had sung that Matthew's death should not be in vain. I paused and asked if they knew what "in vain" meant. They didn't, and I was able to hide beneath my English teacher's hat for a blissful moment while I enlightened them. And then I caught the slightly impatient eye of Hazel, a student whose two mothers were friends and mentors to me; she'd been forced into the accomplice role of helping me stay in the closet during the week, though on the weekends she often knew me as her lesbian moms' baby-dyke friend. So I said it. I think I probably looked at Hazel, telling her what she already knew and letting the rest of my students in on what they probably never expected to hear in school. "As a lesbian…" The rest is a blur. I think I may have blacked out. But when I came to, I saw rainbows.

The terror of that initial moment of coming out was matched with an incredible rush of empowerment and possibility. I could now address the name-calling I'd heard in the hallways; I could teach the book about the gay kid who gets teased on the soccer team; I could have eye-opening conversations with my students, who'd hang on my every word. I could hold my girlfriend's hand on the streets of my small city without worrying about the rumors that would fly if I ran into a student.

Of course, once the initial adrenaline rush of self-disclosure wore off, I realized that my moment of bravery was merely the beginning. A few weeks later the family of one of my seventh graders came in for a routine conference. In what appeared to be a rehearsed moment, they asked their daughter to leave the room. The father looked at the mother, who politely asked why I thought that it was in any way appropriate or necessary to inform their child about my sex life. I did my best to explain myself once again, but my 22-year-old skin was wearing thin, and I burst into tears as soon as they left.

That spring, another student announced sadly that she would not be able to participate in the overnight class trip to a farm in western Massachusetts. When I called her mother to convince her that her daughter should attend the trip, her mother awkwardly explained to me that the family did not consider me an appropriate chaperone for an overnight.

The following year, during a unit on civil rights activists of the 1950s and 1960s, a group of four students called me over to their table. They were reading about three teenage boys who were jailed for civil disobedience and wanted to know whether that meant the boys became gay. I was a bit taken aback, but by then I'd learned to find out what kids are really asking before launching into long-winded explanations of what I wanted them to hear. I asked why they were asking, and they explained to me that their parents had told them if you spent a night in jail, you would turn gay. Knowing their parents, I can't say I was entirely surprised by this opinion, but I was surprised by the question that came next. "Ms. Paull, how did you become gay?"

This was it! The eye-opening dialogue I was hoping to engender when I first came out of the closet. I told them that different people have different opinions on the issue, but personally I thought that I had always been a lesbian. So did that mean I knew I was gay from birth, they wanted to know? I explained that I didn't know anyone who thought about whether they liked boys or girls the minute they were born. "I did," proclaimed Nate. "I liked girls the second I was born." High fives went around the table, and I decided to quit while I was ahead.

Seven years later, I am still teaching at the small, inner-city middle school where I began my career. With new students and families each year, I enter every fall with the sinking realization that coming out once was not enough. If I truly stand by my conviction that as an out teacher I can bring more to my students than I could from behind the proverbial closet door, I have to find the strength to out myself year after year. While I have now developed a pretty sizable bag of tricks, lesson plans, and essay assignments that I can recycle and improve upon each year, I am still honing the Ms. Paull Comes Out episode. Each year it seems to take a different form.

For a few years I lived down the street from my school with my partner. She became an active presence at the school, tutoring students and attending performances. Kids enjoyed her, and for a while I enjoyed the relative privilege of being recognized as an acceptable couple. Coming out during those years became as natural as telling the kids about my chihuahua or my older brother in Chicago.

Last year Providence elected an openly gay and Jewish mayor. I decided to come out the day after Election Day by telling my homeroom how nice it was as a Jewish lesbian to feel represented by my city government. Predominantly students of color, they talked about what it would feel like to have a black or Latino president. I was proud of my students for making that connection, relieved to have come out yet another year, and glad to switch the topic from myself to American politics.

Recently I was counseling a student who was entering the foster care system after having been removed from an abusive home. She confided in me that her mother had not only been physically abusing her, as she had told the authorities, but she did something else too. She would dress up "like a man" and flirt with her daughter, asking her out on dates and commenting on her body. My student looked at me through red and tear-filled eyes and told me that she knew this is not what it meant to be a lesbian because she knew

I was a lesbian and would never do something like that to a child. She knew what her mother had done was wrong but that being a lesbian was not wrong.

All these years later, the flag that was at half-mast has been raised. Hanging in our community room among flags of the more than 50 nations representing our student body is now a rainbow flag. The controversy surrounding the school's bold decision to hang that flag has faded into a distant memory. It hangs in the back of the room, and we don't talk about it very often, but I am proud to see it every morning as I recite the school's pledge with the students: "This day has been given to me, fresh and clear. I can use it or throw it away. I promise that I shall use this day to the fullest, realizing it can never come back again." Every day that I have the strength and support to be the only openly lesbian teacher in my school community is a day I am grateful for. Every student who is learning at home that God hates fags and is learning at school that his lesbian teacher cares about him and isn't half bad is a student I am lucky to have.

There are so many things that presented challenges to me as a first-year teacher that I barely think about anymore. I can now confidently average my grades on an Excel spreadsheet, direct large groups of students in Shakespeare productions, and lead parent discussion groups. Seven years after I first came out, the annual coming out "moment" still makes me a bit queasy and sweaty-palmed. Coming out and staying out can sometimes feel like something of a chore that I appreciate most after it's done. But there is nothing as invigorating as bringing my full, true self to work with me every day. Someday, I am confident, coming out and staying out will become as natural and comfortable as writing on the blackboard while balancing a cup of coffee and keeping the eyes in the back of my head focused on a room full of fabulous seventh graders.

NOBODY CAN TELL ME
I SHOULDN'T BE HERE

Mike Russell
English teacher
Benjamin Franklin High School
Philadelphia, Pennsylvania

I grew up in the country in Arkansas; the biggest town within a 75-mile radius had 10,000 people in it. I was baptized in the Church of Christ, which is so Bible-bound it believes that Baptists are liberal sinners who burn in hell because, among other things, they use instrumental music in worship. At the time, I fervently believed in the Church, in the Bible, and in what the authority figures in my life told me.

Every school day, my first-grade teacher led the class in prayer, despite the fact that this was 1978 and doing such a thing had long been declared unconstitutional. This teacher also seemed to delight in being very cruel to many of her students. Back when she taught third grade, she had dragged one poor child into a first-grade room and announced, "This kid's too stupid to learn his lessons. He's going to have to be in first grade for a while." She actually liked me, but nevertheless, I was scared to death of her. For years afterward, if one of my classmates wanted to get a shudder out of us, just saying this teacher's name would work wonders.

The first week of the following year, I was so afraid that second grade would be more of the same that I broke out in hives; it was the only time in my life to date that I've been hospitalized. When I recovered, I found that my new teacher, Beverly Stevens, was one of the sweetest, most caring people imaginable. Whenever I hear someone talk about the difference a teacher can make, I immediately think of her. She single-handedly made me love school again. She was so dedicated that, many years later, when the Jonesboro school shooting happened, I could easily imagine Beverly in the place of that heroic teacher who sacrificed her life to shield a child. She inspired that much confidence. When I got my Masters in Education, I called her and told her she'd been one of my important inspirations.

From puberty, I'd had crushes on some of the boys at school, never the girls. When I realized this I panicked, refusing to accept that I could be one of *those* people, the kind of person about whom my preacher said AIDS "was a good solution to the problem," the kind of person God hated. I withdrew from my peers and gained a lot of weight. I often tried to pretend that puberty had never happened to me; adolescence felt easier to me if I could put the fact of its existence out of my mind. Living out in the country helped. I could escape into a nearby forest, where I'd be the only person for a mile in any direction and I could shut out the pressures of my life.

Although I hoped that nobody ever had any idea about me, I was a bookworm and a dedicated *Doctor Who* fan, both of which made my masculinity highly suspect in the eyes of my peers. That and my weight gain made me an easy target. I was often teased and ridiculed. Though, to be honest, I must admit that I could frequently be just as rude and inconsiderate to my classmates; I was a teenage boy, after all.

In high school, I made some tentative steps toward accepting myself. I never came out to anyone, but I credit my art teacher, Aline McCracken, with showing me that there were other ways to see the world besides fundamentalism. She never preached or put down religion; she led by example, sharing her viewpoints without imposing them.

My parents were and are good, caring people who sacrificed a great deal for my brothers and me. My mother is an English teacher, and she instilled in me a love of learning and books; for example, when I was 4, every night she read *The Hobbit* to me, a little at a time until she covered the entire book. She defied the common stereotype of evangelical Christians being uncurious people yoked to a blind faith. She believed in asking hard questions. Dad always came across as less questioning, but he was still highly intelligent, an accomplished forester who knows more about trees than I'll ever forget. Nevertheless, they let Leviticus determine their opinions about homosexuality.

By the time I was 17, too much of the Bible seemed contradictory and cruel to me. For example, God repeatedly ordered his chosen people to ethnically cleanse other peoples, to kill women, children, and babies. The Old Testament prescribed stoning to death for everything from being gay to talking back to your parents. It began to dawn on me that either the Bible was wrong or I was evil; my upbringing hadn't included a less literal interpretation.

Eventually, I began to feel that the Bible was wrong. Five years after my baptism, Jesus and I got divorced, so to speak. My parents didn't give me the hard time I was expecting them to. My mom said that I couldn't be forced to come to God, that I had to want to do so, and I've always respected her for saying that. I could tell that my dad agreed with her; he had a way of saying things without saying them.

During that time, I also lost a lot of weight, dropping from 250 pounds to 160. I slowly began to feel more comfortable in my own body. I began to accept that I was attracted to men, though I didn't tell anyone until my freshman year at college. But I also never fabricated any girlfriends or went on dates of any kind.

For years after that, despite coming out, I still internalized the idea that being gay meant I couldn't be a part of mainstream society, that I couldn't be a proper role model. In my college years, my attitude was, "Teaching? Are you kidding? That's what my mom does. I'm not anything like her." Of course, part of growing older has been finding out all the ways I'm just like my parents and progressing from finding that notion horrifying to accepting it and, sometimes, celebrating it.

But for years, I thought of myself as a permanent rebel, blasting Public Enemy and Yoko Ono from my dorm, growing half a beard, giving a middle finger to the world in general. This attitude evolved thanks to my first serious relationship, with Stephen Parmer, who dragged me kicking and screaming into believing that I could be as good as anyone else, that I didn't need a chip on my shoulder the size of Montana. He nurtured me as well as he could, until his AIDS-related illnesses grew worse, until I had to switch roles and take care of him, until he finally died in 2002.

It was Stephen who first suggested that I could be a good teacher. I didn't believe him at first, but he kept urging the idea, and I finally went back to school to get my Masters of Education from Temple University. I had also begun to think about how people where I had come from were frequently written off as "white trash." In fact, in the school where I attended kindergarten to ninth grade, English classes taught only grammar until the mid '70s. One teacher forced literature into the school despite being told, "These kids aren't going to amount to anything. They don't need that kind of thing." (She's still at that school and is one of the pillars of the town.)

I saw the same attitude she fought against directed toward kids in Philly. The average person on the street tended to think of Philly public school children as unstable, rude, violent, and stupid. I figured that maybe I could help, because I knew what that kind of societal assumption felt like.

I was a substitute teacher and TSS-wraparound while I pursued my degree. I figured that if I could get through subbing, I could handle being a regular teacher. I applied to teach at public schools in Philadelphia, one of the most troubled districts in the country, a far cry from what I had experienced as a student. Philly schools are frequently chaotic, filled with demoralized staff and students who have had to endure often horrific home lives. Some students really do want to learn, but so much class time is spent on discipline problems that kids' skill levels are often years behind what they should be. I had been told all this before, but nothing prepared me for actually experiencing it.

Kids naturally want to know all about their teachers, even their subs. So I frequently encountered questions about my personal life. Did I want children? Was I married? What was my girlfriend's name? Because most of my assignments were short, sometimes I told the truth and sometimes I changed the subject or otherwise avoided answering. I refused to outright lie and invent a heterosexual life. Sometimes, students took the truth well, thanking me for being honest with them and telling me that their mom, aunt, brother, friend, or other loved one was gay or lesbian.

In general, the girls accepted the truth somewhat more readily; the boys were often nervous, some of them half-jokingly saying, "Don't stare at my ass." A few said I shouldn't have told them, that they certainly wouldn't have admitted to such a thing, even if it were true—a few thought I was kidding. One boy asked me if I was going to be on *Jerry Springer*. A few mouthed the bigotry they had heard at churches and mosques, telling me, "God hates you." I quickly learned not to take that kind of talk personally; my kids simply didn't know any better. Of course, that's easy to say—sometimes I did feel demoralized.

I had one truly bad experience as an art prep sub. Usually, I only answered truthfully to high school students, but this one time I came out to seventh- and eighth-grade students in a middle school. They were completely unable to handle it. This particular school was already out of control; almost all teachers on my floor were first-year teachers. And these students became completely unmanageable, often yelling at me, some calling me "faggot." One girl said, "My mom said you ought to be reported."

One eighth-grade boy came out to me; he was pleasantly surprised that someone working at a school would come out. He also admitted that he was meeting adult men for sex. If I had that time to live over again, I would have cautioned him that such men weren't looking out for what was good for him. But at the time, I felt so drained that I didn't want to start one more argument. This student was very well-behaved, and yet I noticed that his other teachers frequently sent him to the accommodation room. Some teachers didn't bother to disguise their distaste for him. I still feel that I failed him; I just wasn't strong enough then.

A few students were eager for me to teach them how to draw. I gave one girl a few one-on-one lessons during my prep time. I asked her teacher during that period if he minded, and he said, "I don't care if she's in my class or not." His beaten-down, cynical attitude seemed to be typical of that school. The student seemed to appreciate the lesson, though. She almost seemed surprised at having anyone take time out for her.

The next day, after I came out to my students, the principal told me to leave. She claimed that it was because I wasn't adequately controlling my classes, but I knew she was lying. I could have filed a discrimination claim against her, but I just wanted to move on to my next assignment. I was happy to never see that school again.

When I did a semester of student teaching, I really lucked out. My cooperating teacher, Rick Miller, had taught for 31 years and still loved doing it. He hadn't missed a day of work in the past seven years. He had near-total control of the classroom and his students' respect. He had an impressive command of his subject and knew many ways to make it interesting for most of his students. He was a true role model for me, and I will continue to keep him in mind as I progress as a teacher.

Rick, though pro-gay himself, very strongly cautioned me against coming out. He believed that coming out would make my career far more difficult since I would be teaching in a highly homophobic population. He worried that if they knew I was gay, they would just call me a faggot every time I did something they didn't like; I would be known as "that gay teacher." He warned that inner-city culture encourages a rigid, cartoon version of masculinity.

He had good reason to say what he did. From my observations I saw that too many of the student body had never seen their fathers. The boys often learned how to be men from the streets, where anything gay is seen as feminine and weak. And many kids had been sexually assaulted. The mention of anything gay automatically makes some kids remember the awful people who molested them. I didn't know a way around that problem. During that semester, I took Rick's advice, deflecting questions his students had about my personal life.

But staying closeted made me feel like a coward. Rick was right in warning me of the dangers in coming out, but I felt it took too great a toll on my self-respect. Even so, my first semester teaching my own class, I continued to deflect questions about my personal life. However, I'm not the butchest guy in the world, so some students still managed to figure it out on their own, and a few often asked, "Are you gay?"

Stephen grew progressively sicker and died that December; to this day, I feel that he willed himself to live until he saw me started on my career and in a house of my own. He was that selfless. I took a few days off, and when I returned my students naturally demanded to know where I had been. In front of my classes, I said there had been a death in the family. But I did start to tell some individual students the fuller truth. Most of them were sympathetic, wanting to know if I was going to be all right. I had a jeweler interlock our commitment rings and wore them as part of a necklace for a couple of months. Many of my girls thought that was very sweet and sad, and they noticed when I stopped wearing it, one of them saying, "I guess you're not in mourning anymore."

A student offered to set me up with one of her older friends. In a way, her gesture was sweet, except that she was failing my class and had made her offer near the end of the semester, leading me to wonder about her true motives. I declined her offer by saying I wasn't ready to start another relationship yet.

I was out to all the school staff, and they were as supportive as I could possibly have hoped for. My mentor teacher, Barbara White, made me a plaque with a poem of consolation she had composed herself. She and many other colleagues kept checking in on me to make sure that I was holding up all right. They treated me the same way they would have if I had been straight and my wife had died. It was such a profound contrast to the middle school I had subbed in. I felt part of a group. I felt like I belonged.

Whenever I heard my students say something homophobic, I no longer took it personally, but I felt bad for what such an atmosphere was doing to my kids, regardless of their orientation. Very few children felt safe coming out. However, there had been some exceptions. The year before I arrived at this school, a boy had begun to transition to a girl, and she had been accepted for the most part. It helped that the floor coordinator had gone to every room and explained the legal consequences of harassment. But in the minds of many students, that was an exception. In general, being gay was still not OK.

"Faggot" is so commonly used as an all-purpose insult that many students use it when they don't actually mean to be anti-gay. For example, one day a student barged into my room to gossip with a classmate. I calmly told him, "I'm sorry, but you can't stay here."

He waved his hand dismissively and muttered, "You're a faggot, man." One of my students whispered into his ear. He looked horrified and embarrassed and sputtered, "Oh, I'm sorry, I'm sorry, I didn't mean it," and quickly left. I had to struggle to keep from laughing.

In my English 3 class, one of my students, Jamal (not his real name), delighted in being a class clown. He was never malevolent, but he didn't want to do any of the work either. I found out that he had a part-time job designing and writing Web pages, so I allowed him to turn in his Web work for credit. I would show him how to correct his grammar and usage, and he seemed more interested in applying grammar rules to this real-life context. He ended up squeaking through with a D, though he was easily smart enough to have done A work.

Jamal was late turning in one of these special assignments; he said he had finished the work but had forgotten to bring it. So I gave him my e-mail address and told him to send me his work that night. In Philly, we're often discouraged from giving students our contact information, but I wanted Jamal to meet his deadline. What he turned in was easily worthy of an A. Soon afterward, he started Instant Messaging me, asking me how I was doing, talking about how he couldn't identify with the peers he often hung out with in the halls and in the classroom. His admission was a surprise to me; on the surface, he had seemed to fit in well with some of his peers.

Jamal was one of the students I had told about Stephen's death. Soon afterward, he admitted that he thought he was bisexual. He asked me not to tell anyone and said that I was the only person he had ever told. I was so happy to have been there for him that it automatically made all the crap I had been through before worth it. We continued chatting.

He seemed to have a bit of a crush on me. I didn't want to push the issue, especially if my guess was wrong, so I waited to let him bring up what he was feeling. When he admitted to having a mild crush, I thanked him for the compliment but explained that, of course, as a teacher I couldn't—and didn't—return his feelings. Fortunately, he said he understood, and he impressed me with his insight: He said that he was probably just fixating on me because I was the only gay man he knew.

One day after school, I took Jamal to the local LGBT youth center, a very supportive place that made me wish such spaces had existed when I was a teen. Jamal didn't really take to it, but at least he knows where it is should he need to call on it. He still IMs me from time to time to let me know how he's doing.

In the fall semester of 2003, my second year teaching, I came out to all my students on the first day of school. A summer training session I took recommended that teachers spend part of the first day presenting a "Me Bag" containing a few items that said something about who we were as people; we would then assign our students to create their own "Me Bag." I chose a few uncontroversial items: books, an example of my artwork, a young coconut. I also included the interlocking commitment rings and a photo of my boyfriend, Andy. Many students took my revelation well. In particular, the girls were fascinated by Andy's picture and by the rings. But many students were pretty shocked, and some of the boys acted nervous when I walked near them.

Two more students have since come out to me. A few are genuinely curious about what gay people are like, and I answer their questions when I can. By midyear, many who were shocked have gotten used to it and now accept me as their teacher. A few still mutter, "You shouldn't have told us that," and wonder how anyone could possibly be gay.

One of the school counselors advised me to go back into the closet next year, because she believed I was making my job more difficult by being out. But many of my colleagues, including the principal, have been very supportive, and when some students have made antigay comments to me, I've been able to get school staff to take the offending student out until he or she could calm down. I've also learned that many antigay comments aren't about me or gays in general at all. One of my students repeatedly made such hateful remarks as "We need a straight teacher and a black teacher," and would accuse me of staring at him. I eventually found out that this tenth-grader couldn't read and was using insults to keep me from finding out. Once I found out and arranged to get him a one-on-one reading tutor three days a week, his homophobic comments ended.

As a teacher, I have to maintain a tough balance. On the one hand, I recognize how difficult many of my students' lives are. This past spring, one of my students was having a rough time because her 27-year-old drug-dealer boyfriend had been shot dead. Even though she was probably better off without him, she still loved him and spent more time in the counselor's office than in my class. I never was able to reach her. Even one of my colleagues, who has been teaching for decades, admitted, "What some of our kids need, we can't give them." On the other hand, if I just feel sorry for them, I'm not doing them any favors.

But I have no regrets about coming out. I've found that the more myself I am in front of my class, the more effective a teacher I can be.

HAPPY VALENTINE'S DAY

Mary Gay Hutcherson
School social worker
James River High School
Chesterfield County, Virginia

On Valentine's Day, 2000, my partner, Yolanda, and I were married at our MCC in Richmond, Virginia, surrounded by about 300 well-wishers. It was a happy occasion, as all weddings should be, but the big difference was that my coworkers were not included in the celebration of my "big day." I had spent a year planning this fabulous event, but I felt I could not share it with the people with whom I spent so much of my time. I had listened in excruciating silence to others in the teachers' lounge talking about their weddings, their engagements, their significant others, while this biggest event of my life was taking place. It was extraordinarily hard— especially for a 10 on the extrovert scale.

✳

I have served as a school social worker for almost two decades, carefully keeping my personal life and my work life separate for fear of being fired or made ineffective at my job. I wondered if teachers and principals would still refer the cases to me, respect my professional opinion, and treat me with respect if they knew who I really was. The pressure was enormous.

I love my work. I have always felt I was really making a difference in the lives of those more marginal students I serve, and that was my mission as a social worker. It has so perfectly suited me in every way, except its homophobia.

*

The wedding was an epiphany in a special, unexpected way. There were so many good vibrations around it and so many negative ones around keeping it secret at work that I decided I would never hide my true self again. Gradually I began to share my lesbian life with coworkers. I put a picture of my partner and me on my desk; I casually shared the wedding experience and even some pictures with my best work friends.

As a result, I felt different. I felt like I have the right to take up space in this world just like anyone else. Doing this made me feel so much happier at work that many people commented on how upbeat I was. I received support through unexpected avenues. For example, as I shared my Christmas family pictures—of Yoli and me with our dogs—with some friends, the school nurse came in and picked up the pictures. She said nothing, but afterward she came to my office to share that her son is gay and she loves him and his partner very much. I felt so much closer to her, and so much more real, than I had ever felt before during the many years we worked together.

A big factor in becoming more open was that I also realized I was close enough to retirement to retire if it became uncomfortable or if I were fired. But the biggest factor was realizing that I have so much emotional support in the world, and I am so lucky to have found the special person to complete my life, that I can handle whatever repercussions come. Free at last!

I was then approached by another gay teacher telling me that some students wanted to start a gay-straight alliance in my high school. She was nervous for the same reasons I had been but equally respectful of these students' right to do this...so we did it. In the process, I came out to everyone involved. This has been quite liberating, and I haven't had any negative repercussions. I have the support of my principal and my supervisor and the law, to some extent, as the federal Equal Access Act has guaranteed these kids have the opportunity to form clubs like any others that are extracurricular.

So, here I am, 60-something years old, and freer and happier in my work and my personal life than ever before.

GOING BACK TO WHERE I GREW UP GAY

Bethany Petr
Science teacher
Francis Scott Key Middle School (2000-2002)
Paint Branch High School (2002-present)
Silver Spring, Maryland

I work for a school system that "prohibits discrimination on the basis of race, color, national origin, marital status, religion, sex, age, disability, or sexual orientation in employment or in any of its education programs and activities." They offer domestic partner benefits to employees. It's all very promising on a high-falutin' legal level, but "faggot" is still the least-corrected slang thrown at other students in the hallways, and "gay" is used at least a thousand times per day to refer to something that is weak. Students still discuss how "disgusting those fags kissing on MTV" is, and one student will go out of her way to hurt another if it's suggested that the other is a lesbian.

I spent my junior and senior years of high school waiting to go to college so I could find "the gays." I wasn't ashamed of realizing I was a lesbian. I'd already rejected the religious trappings that could have made me feel bad about it. But I believed that you just don't talk about these things. Frankly, as an introvert, you don't talk about much at all. I'd just sit and wait and take solace in the fact that this one really nifty girl that I'd been friends with in middle school had a button on her backpack with a pink triangle on it, and the back of our student newspaper had an ad for SMYAL (the Sexual Minority Youth Assistance League, an LGBT youth support group in D.C). I'd see these things and know that I'd get my chance to be gay soon.

When I graduated from college, I was given an open contract with the school system, and when I finished my last interview, the staffer asked if I'd like to substitute during the last month of the current school year. One of the last assignments I took happened to be at the high school from which I graduated. I was in for the AP bio teacher, so I got to spend a lot of time in the science office with the faculty who'd taught me when I was a student there. The department head, who'd been my AP physics teacher, took the opportunity to share all kinds of dirt with me about the teachers I had known. One, who had an alcohol problem and whose wife left him, spent months sleeping in that very office. Another was discovered to have been writing a column about the gay leather community. This she shared with great horror. "Can you imagine?"

The next fall my first teaching placement was in a troubled middle school. The kids, for the most part, were pretty tough. My colleagues presented a challenge all their own. My coworkers talked about Jesus a lot. They tried on a daily basis to get me to come to church with them. Toward the end of my first year there, I happened to be in the faculty lounge when a couple of teachers were discussing a student, one of our greatest behavioral challenges, who had finally done something that resulted in his removal from our school for the remainder of the year.

"Thank God that faggot isn't going to mess up my class anymore. I'd like to pummel his ugly little face." Other teachers nodded in consent.

Today, I once again work in the high school that I attended as a student. I tell students not to use the word *faggot* because it makes them sound ignorant. Most of them laugh; only a couple continue to use it. (This represents progress, right?) I watchdog homecoming and the prom to make sure neither discriminates against some poor brave gay students. I know most of them will not attend these events. I didn't either.

I don't talk to many people, not to other adults, anyway. It's hard to relate to people who want to talk about their kids, their boyfriends, their husbands, their straight lives. No one asks me about myself. I don't share any details about my life. Only one staff member even knows I have dogs, and that's only because I keep a picture of them on my desk. No one asks if I'm gay. I'm a walking stereotype, yet only a handful of my colleagues are smart enough to see it.

Every year the social committee collects $20 from us. This is to pay for new baby gifts, wedding gifts, anniversary gifts, basically any celebration of meeting societal norms and expectations. Every year I fail to pay by the deadline. Every year some poor fool in charge of collecting the funds hunts me down. Every year I tell myself I'm going to finally step up and say, "Hey—I'm never going to benefit from this fund. I'm not going to get married if the current government has its way; I'm not planning on having a baby, and there's no way I'm going to accidentally become pregnant. Therefore, I'm not giving you my money." Every year I hand over a check for $20. Introverts don't like confrontation.

Recently, in the office, two teachers were discussing just how gay a particular student was. They laughed and joked and degraded him. I shook my head in disapproval and turned to leave, and one of my more savvy colleagues suggested to them that they were ignorant. It's the small things that keep you going.

Toward the end of this year the students were all abuzz because a student teacher in the social studies department had come out to them. It pleased me that this had impressed, rather than distressed, most of them. What bothered me is that one student described to his friends how he'd gone into the social studies office looking for this student teacher and asked Mr. H., a teacher he regards with great respect, "where the faggot was." This teacher, feigning a limp wrist and feminine lisp, responded that he did not know. They spent several minutes bonding over the "silly faggot" together.

Now, that's the kind of faculty that supports the school message of diversity.

I sent my principal an e-mail last year. It said, "Here is a list of all the high schools in this county that have gay-straight alliances. Why don't we have one?" I got no reply.

So why do I stay in this job, despite the stress that makes me spend nights crying? Well, first of all, the kids could use the influence of a cynical, atheist, feminist, radical queer. There's too much of "the right" at play in the school system. Someone should represent a viable alternative. And second, I can talk to them. They still know how to listen. I don't mean listening and following my instructions; I mean listening to me like I might be saying something worth hearing.

I check the back of the student newspaper every month, but I notice that there's no ad for SMYAL these days. I work for a school system that "prohibits discrimination on the basis of race, color, national origin, marital status, religion, sex, age, disability or sexual orientation in employment or in any of its education programs and activities." I wonder why, with all these trappings of progress, things still aren't any better. I wonder what my students see in this high school that gives them hope that they can have their chance to be gay, and everything will turn out just fine. I wonder, and I worry, and then once in a while I remember that there's me.

DID I MAKE A DIFFERENCE?

Steven Click

Elementary teacher

Barrow (1971-1983) and Fairbanks (1983-1997) public school systems

Barrow and Fairbanks, Alaska

As I sit here writing this piece, now in my mid 50s, I look back over the decades of my life and see what has been and not what might have happened.

I am a product of the 1950s, a time, at least in my perspective, when men were the providers and women were slowly changing their roles in the family. I was raised to finish high school, go to college, get married, have a career, and raise a family. I did all that, in that order, and I look back fondly on many great experiences and adventures in my life. That is not to say that I didn't have my down times, my worries, and my innermost thoughts about who I really was and where I fit into the scheme of things.

Growing up in Southern California in a middle-class family where my dad worked in the aerospace industry and my mom worked in the home, I lived a pretty good childhood. Early on I saw that I wasn't interested in "normal boy things" but would rather create crafts (and sell them to the neighbors), take dance lessons (tap as well as ballroom), roller-skate, and play with girls. In Cub Scouts, I was cast (or did I volunteer?) to be a girl in a skit, but I also fell off my bike and lost a front tooth while trying to impress some girls with my riding skills.

I knew that I wasn't interested in "boy things," like sports, surfing, cars, trading baseball cards, or later on, talking about exploits with girls. I knew that I was different than other boys but didn't have a name to put with it. It wasn't until I was almost out of high school that I learned the word *homosexual,* and I knew that I wasn't that kind of person. Though when I finally put two and two together, I figured out that my Uncle Bob and (his partner?) Gordon were "those kind" of men. Yep, I had a gay uncle (and no one in the family *ever* talked about it, according to Mom).

So I hid the fact that I had questions and thoughts as to who I really was because I wanted to be like every other guy, to be a regular young man in high school and community college. I dated, figured out how to undo a bra strap, never hugged another guy friend, and was married at 20. We continued our college education, graduated, earned elementary teaching credentials, and moved to Alaska to become teachers in the fall of 1971. We lived, taught, and started a family in a small Eskimo village on the edge of the Arctic Ocean. And after 12 exciting and comfortable years in the bush, we moved to Fairbanks in 1983. I helped raise two great sons, the younger of whom, like his dad, is gay (and, unlike his dad, has been out since he was 17).

I always worked in an elementary school. I knew I didn't have enough patience for middle-school age students, and I think that the older high school kids intimidated me (at least in my younger years). The dozen years in the native village, where I was in the very small minority of "white" people, taught me more about tolerance and acceptance of everyone, their lifestyles, their culture, and the choices they may make in their lives.

In the late 1970s, just after my youngest was born, I accepted the fact that I was at least bisexual (if not a gay man), but I also promised myself that I would be a live-at-home dad until my son was out of high school. From that point on, I led two lives: one, the public one, of being a teacher, husband, and dad, and the other of being a closeted gay man. I lived with the fear that I would be found out and possibly lose my family as well as my job. It was hard work living two lives (some might say "lies").

My life—which included a successful career in teaching, being an educational employee advocate through NEA, a community-service Kiwanis member, supportive father and family member, and an actor in a local community theater at times—continued until year 26 rolled around and I (along with my wife) was given the opportunity for retirement with a "golden handshake" from my school district. I decided that I wanted to take that opportunity but also knew that for her to make the correct decision for herself, she needed to know some personal information I had never shared. I came out to her one evening about three weeks before she needed to let the district know if she was going to take the "handshake." Needless to say, after 29 years of marriage, she was devastated, hurt, and angry.

Within days, everyone in the district knew that I was gay. I could feel their looks, sense the talk behind my back ("Did your hear? Is it really true?") Not one person asked me about my revelation; I might bring up something in a conversation, but even then there was minimal discussion.

Part of me wanted for everyone to know that they had been teaching with a gay man. I told my principal (and friend) about the situation, and he left it up to me as to whether I would give a small announcement at my last staff meeting. I chose not to say anything, as I wanted my wife to have as easy a time at her school as possible. (The next year, as my "news" spread through the community, two parents had their daughters transferred out of her class for fear of contracting HIV.)

I would guess that all teachers ask themselves throughout their careers, "What influence have I had on my students?" I asked myself that almost every day while I was teaching, and many times since retirement. When I saw a former student years later, I would ask them what their memory was of my class. Most answered that I wore some really wild clothes (Hawaiian at 50 below zero, in the dead of winter, a tuxedo for our Authors Day Celebration) or the cooking that we did in class (escargot when we studied France or dolmas when we learned about Greece). It wasn't until years later that I found out a very important influence I had with at least one student.

Just after moving to Fairbanks, I had the opportunity of working with a most unusual class—one of the "golden" classes of all times. They worked well together, helped one another, were courteous, and basically just wanted to be in school and learn what I was offering. The very quiet leader of the class was a boy who almost always wore a button-down shirt and tie to class (years later, when I asked him about that, he said it was "just a phase"). He earned the lead in the sixth-grade musical and was the peacemaker and the head mediator of the class. I still have the little box with a wizard on the top that he gave me when I was the wizard in a local production of *Once Upon a Mattress*. He was that kind of a kid. He was also one of only two former students who ever asked me to come to a high school graduation.

He and I kept in touch over the years, and I happened to see him the summer after I came out. We had lunch together and I shared my news. He took it quite well, asked some questions; I shared some responses, and after a hug we parted. When I asked him if he or the other kids "knew" or suspected my gay nature back in elementary school, he said that though the term wasn't used, there was some talk. They all knew that I wasn't like the other male teachers—I was more thoughtful, understanding, and not into a macho image.

Later, he e-mailed me asking me some very pointed questions about my "gayness"—When did I suspect? How did I know? How did my sons take the news? Was it normal? I answered, and finally asked him if I was the subject of a paper for one of his college classes. He told me it was something like that but that he couldn't fully explain for a couple more years. Finally, my "gaydar" was activated. It all fell into place: He was reaching out to me because he was questioning his own sexual identity.

I know that I have touched at least one student in a very special way. Of the more than 600 students I've taught, there must have been more than several handfuls of students who are gay, lesbian, bisexual, transgender, or still questioning. I hope that my message of acceptance, tolerance, and equality for all taught them more than their spelling words and times tables.

MS. KEE HAS A WIFE!

Ayana Kee
Elementary school teacher
P.S. 330
Brooklyn, New York

Many people see New York City as a haven of tolerance. But in the five years that I've taught here, I haven't met any female elementary school teachers who were out to their students. I am a second-grade teacher and I am a bisexual, African-American woman. On October 19, 2002, I got married. Since then I've found myself wanting to talk openly about my relationship with my wife. I want my students to know the real me. I'm growing tired of the omissions and the self-censorship. Some days the closet feels cramped.

One Day in May 2003

"Ms. Kee has a wife," said Rashad. I froze.

We were in our classroom getting ready to do math. The children were sitting on our worse-for-wear rug. My back was to them because I was writing the warm-up on the easel.

"Yes, she does. I met her yesterday," he insisted. The sunlight in our classroom suddenly hurt my eyes and the drip, drip of our radiator sounded like metal hitting glass. I finished writing the math warm-up and sat in my chair next to the easel.

I decided not to lie. Ten years of experience has taught me that it is best to be frank with young children. They can detect duplicity as easily as they can smell what's for lunch in our cafeteria. I looked out on the class expectantly. I did not see the shocked stares I expected. I waited for a raised hand and a child to ask the question (or at least for someone to tattle on Rashad). But the children were not looking at me. Four rows of children were sitting cross-legged on the rug, writing the math warm-up in their black and white notebooks.

Correction: Most of the kids were writing, but a few were engaged in the hair-braiding, window-staring, miniscule-scrap-of-paper-turned-into-an-airplane distractions that elementary school teachers see everyday. I shrugged and taught the math lesson.

At lunchtime, I pulled Ms. Johnson aside and related the incident to her. I will never forget the day I came out to Ms. Johnson. We were in the staff lunchroom. (It's really just a small room in the basement, with a full-size refrigerator and a hazardous amount of mold on the ceiling.) Ms. Johnson was carrying on a bawdy conversation with a male teaching assistant. I believe it was about a late-night rendezvous with a lovely lady. I wrote a note mentioning that I had a lovely lady at home and I folded the note twice before sliding it to Ms. Johnson. From that moment on, she was a preaching, teaching mentor for me.

Ms. Johnson had taught almost as long as I'd been alive and was also a pastoral counselor. Perhaps that's how she knew why the kids didn't say anything to me when Rashad spoke about my wife. "It just doesn't fit into their scheme of things, Ayana," she explained. "They ignore what they don't understand."

It fits into Rashad's scheme, though. I first met adorable Rashad, his twin Akeem, his mom Annette, and his mom's partner, Julie, at a Black Pride picnic here in Brooklyn. Annette and Julie have been together a long time, since the boys were toddlers, so the boys have had two moms almost all their lives. My wife got to know them first. Shanté is an artist-activist who is well-known, at least among other young LGBT artists and activists here in New York City. She has been on panels, interviewed for magazines, radio, and television, and filmed in a documentary.

Meanwhile, I've been content to remain in my closet.

I pulled Rashad aside after lunch and asked him to help me keep my private life private. Rashad nodded. He understood the need for privacy. Annette is an out member of the PTA. I found out later that kids teased Rashad because his mom is a lesbian. Perhaps he thought the kids might tease me too. After our little talk, Rashad skipped down the hall to join the rest of the class in the art studio. I stayed on my knees and stared at the wall.

One Day in January 2004

I was teaching the children a fun, Senegalese-inspired dance in preparation for the black history assembly in February. We had rolled up the rug and pushed aside the desks so we could practice in our classroom. I was sitting in my customary chair by the easel and the children were standing in rows.

I took off my wedding ring, put it in my jacket pocket, and buttoned my pocket shut. The ring had hurt my finger as I beat out amateur rhythms on a small drum.

Afua called out from the last row, "Ms. Kee, are you married?"

"Yes," I replied automatically as I tried to remember the next dance step.

"What's your husband's name?" Tony asked from the second row.

I paused. It was a reasonable question. The children had probably met Mrs. Douglas's and Mrs. Friedman's husbands. Mrs. Douglas's husband had been at the school a lot last fall, helping out as his wife's pregnancy progressed. Mrs. Friedman's husband frequently came up to the classroom when he arrived to drive her home at 3:30 P.M. For our writing lessons, teachers were encouraged to talk about their home lives, and most did. Thus, the children were used to hearing all manner of personal details about their teachers. But I wasn't ready to walk the walk.

"That's private," I said.

"Do you have any kids?" Tony tried a different tack.

"Yes. I have 18 children," I replied, smiling. The class exploded into expressions of surprise, disbelief, and wonder.

"And they're all 7 years old," I added.

"I get it," Shamika squealed. "She's talking about us!"

I laughed and the children laughed and then I taught the dance lesson.

Every Day

Many people see New York City as a haven of tolerance. Maybe it is. In the five years that I've taught here, I haven't met any female elementary school teachers who were out to their students. But every day I ask myself: *Is it time for my students to meet the real me?*

SAFE SCHOOLS AND VOICES

Bonnie Beach
Retired teacher
New Trier Township High School
Winnetka, Illinois

It was 2:30 on a beautiful spring afternoon, with a sky that was a knockout blue. I knew the pickets would probably be stationed in front of our school by now, but I didn't know how many there would be or what kind of reception they would get. There was a break in my schedule, and I used the time to go upstairs to the second-floor rotunda, where I would have a panoramic vantage point from which to check things out. I walked up to the rotunda windows and leaned into the overlarge sills. From here I could see it all: the walkways, sidewalks, front lawn, the two-lane street that runs in front of the school, and the quiet, tree-shaded neighborhood that sprawls beyond.

There were the usual gangs of kids spread across the lawn, twos and threes sitting on the concrete walls that served also as benches, and individuals coming and going, as the last period of the day was about to begin. Across the street a man braced against the rear fender of a late-model car caught my eye. He had a large, old-fashioned video camera sitting on his shoulder. The camera was pointed at the near side of the street. I let my gaze follow back along the path of the camera and found a scruffy-looking middle-aged man who held a picket sign in one hand and a handful of flyers in the other. A small group of students standing at the junction between our walkway and the public sidewalk were focused intently on the picket. As I watched, the man approached the group of curious students and extended a flyer toward one of them. Two other men wielding picket signs stood under a tree across the street, talking to each other.

"Three pickets," I thought to myself. "For all the threats this guy made, I would have expected a small army."

He had called me several times. At first he had asked respectfully if he could come and present "the other side" of homosexuality to our health classes. I explained to him that we only invited guest speakers who were connected to our own community, and pointed out that he and the organization he represented were based some 40 miles to the southwest of where our school was located.

"This is a public school," I explained further. "Students are obligated by law to be here. We believe that education is best delivered in a climate where students feel safe and respected. From what you've told me, your message runs counter to what we are trying to teach here. The safety and respect for all of our students, including those who are LGBT, questioning, or those students who have family members or friends who are gay or lesbian, is very important to us. Therefore, you are not welcome here and will not be invited to speak to our classes."

It was then that he told me he was going to contact the principal. I told him that was certainly his right and gave him the phone number. Apparently he got much the same message from our principal and followed up with a letter in which there was the threat of some kind of picketing action. He had called the police, the news media, and our school administration to advise them of today's visit.

I focused on the signs the men were carrying.

HOMOSEXUALITY...AN ABOMINATION AGAINST GOD!
UNFAIR! EDUCATION IS ABOUT TRUTH
STUDENTS NEED TO HEAR THE OTHER SIDE
HOMOSEXUALITY IS SINFUL AND UNNATURAL
STUDENTS MUST KNOW THE TRUTH

Outside, there were several hundred students standing on our walkway or lawns, calling across the street to the two pickets stationed there. A group of 25 or 30 had formed a semicircle in front of the man on the near side of the street. In that group, I recognized several students from my health class. The man with the video camera was frantically panning across the scene. Several students yelled out loudly. The sounds of their voices but not the words drifted up to me through the open rotunda windows. By this time, more students were in possession of flyers. Many looked at them, pointed, talked among themselves, and either dropped them, returned them to the near-side picket, or tossed them into one of our large, outdoor trash barrels.

I saw our principal, Wes Baumann, walk out from under the front portico. Moving toward the nearest group of students, he stopped to talk. There was some laughter and I saw him point his thumb over his shoulder. The group turned and made for the front door. Wes continued to walk among the students, stopping to talk to groups or individuals, motioning for several students to pick up some of the flyers now scattered and blowing over the front lawn.

At the far end of his circuit, Wes turned toward the front door. He stood for a moment listening and looking, then walked quietly back inside.

"You would be proud of what these kids are saying to those men," said Wes, appearing at the window beside me a few minutes later as we continued to watch the action outside. "Most of the kids are disgusted with the fact that those people are out there. They asked if I could just call the police and make them leave. I explained that as long as the pickets stayed off school property, they were perfectly legal. I wonder what that guy with the video camera is doing?"

"Maybe he's making a documentary. Maybe he's just trying to intimidate us. Who knows? What else are the kids saying?"

"A number of students are refuting the statements on the signs and the flyers. I heard kids saying 'We talk about this in our health class. We have heard gay speakers.' One girl told the picketers, 'Gay is OK. My brother is gay.' Another student said, 'We talk about sexual orientation. We do it respectfully. We don't need you.' Their responses are thoughtful and they are asking the picketers good questions. You know what? It's obvious that we've done a lot of good work here already. These fellows chose the wrong school to target."

Wes turned and walked up the hall toward his office. I turned back to the scene on the lawn. Busses were beginning to circle the block and pull up in a long line in front of school. The cameraman was moving around across the street, trying to film between the noisy yellow behemoths. I thought back over my long career at New Trier, this suburban Chicago-area high school. I thought about how this news, so empty of threat now, would once have chilled me. I lost myself to remembering how much had changed.

✳

In 1967 there were few nondiscrimination clauses in employment contracts. There were no harassment prevention policies, and as far as I could see there were no out homosexual teachers in any school I had ever attended, although two of my high school teachers had come out to me when I was in college and had given me advice about being a teacher and a homosexual. "If you are ever threatened," they advised me, "don't run and don't hide. Confront the situation. Count on the good reputation you are making as a principled and skillful teacher to carry you through."

I put their advice to use when the subject of homosexuality and Bonnie Beach raised its scary head during my third year of teaching. I had found a note on the gym floor after one of my classes. I assumed the note had been passed between two female students. The note read, "Beach is a lesbian and you love her. I'm going to tell your parents." I was terrified. My first reaction was to tear the note to shreds and flush it down the nearest toilet. Instead, with a great deal of apprehension, I took the note to our dean of students. He read it. He asked me if I had any idea about which student had written the note, and when I replied, honestly, that I did not, he crumpled it and tossed it into his wastebasket. We talked about other teaching matters, how I liked the Midwest, and after 10 or 15 minutes of small talk he bid me goodbye by saying, "Forget this. Kids say a lot of things about teachers. It's not important."

My overwhelming emotion was relief. The dean had supported me. And he hadn't asked if I was, in fact, a lesbian.

Years passed, and they were good ones for me. I became a successful teacher, coach, and adviser. As a single woman in her 30s whose roommates had all been women, I believed that most of my colleagues assumed I was a lesbian. Being out only by assumption offered me protection from the open disapproval of others and offered others the comfort of not having to "see" and deal with who I really was.

It also allowed me to avoid taking positions on issues that touched too close to home, if I so chose. There were times when a parent intimated his or her discomfort with having a daughter who was involved in athletics, "because, you know, it's not the best thing for a young girl…" In those days I was not eager to follow with "Why is that?" We both understood the inference that many female athletes were lesbians. Worse yet, were those few parents who let me know in ways subtle and not so subtle that they thought I was a lesbian. I didn't pursue that line of thinking either. By and large I continued on in my profession, assuming I was safe in the protection of my dimly lit closet. At the time, it seemed a reasonable trade-off for the life I was living.

The day that every closeted educator dreads came for me during the winter of 1990—a time when I was feeling most gratified with my career and my personal life. I was finishing my last year as president of the teacher's association and my first year as department chair. I had found the love of my life, and we had just moved in together. One afternoon an administrator who was also a good friend came into my office at the close of the school day. She shut my door and pulled a chair over to my desk.

"Bonnie, I've come to tell you what the administrators have

been discussing for the last two hours. A parent called the principal today and said, 'Bonnie Beach is a lesbian. She is involved with a female teacher.' I thought you should know. The rest of the administration and I thought it best for one of us to talk to you about the phone call and our conversation. I volunteered."

I sat stunned. I thought to myself, *Well, here it is. I can lie and deny what the parent said, or I can tell the truth. This kind colleague who has come to talk with me will accept whatever I choose to tell her. If I lie, my partner and I will be at the mercy of anyone who wants to blackmail, intimidate, or terrorize us for the rest of our working lives. That is not the way we want to live. If I tell the truth, we will be free from this moment on.* I was very nervous, but sure of what I was about to do.

I said that what the parent had reported was true, and if it cast the school or my department in a negative light I was willing to resign—as department chair, or as an employee of the district. My friend shook her head and assured me that was not the reason for the visit.

"Both you and Pam are wonderful teachers and you both have earned a great deal of respect at New Trier," she said. "This is just gossip, but malicious gossip just the same. We thought you should know about the phone call and our conversation."

"Do you think it would help if I talked personally with the other administrators and told them what I have just said to you?"

"I think," said my friend, "that if you could do that it would be a fine idea. I don't think it's necessary, but I certainly think it would be the courageous thing to do."

"OK," I replied. After she left I sat quietly for a minute. The sense of my newfound freedom surged inside me. For the first time I was unfettered by my secret, and I felt light, and happy, and scared all at the same time. Then, with some trepidation, I set out for the second floor and the corridor of offices housing our administrators.

Forty-five minutes and five offices later, I opened the door leading to the office of the then-assistant principal, Wes Baumann. I gave him what was now a very well rehearsed speech about my sexual orientation.

"I guess I've known for a long time that you were a homosexual…a lesbian," he said, clearly uncomfortable with the word. "All my life I've believed that homosexuality is wrong. But I just can't believe that anymore. I'm so sorry for what you're going through, but I'm glad for the opportunity to tell you how I feel. I have tremendous respect for you as a colleague and a friend. Whatever I can do to help you, I will."

As I left Wes's office, I literally ran into the principal. His office had been closed and locked, so I thought he was gone. Now we were standing in the hallway, face to face. This was the conversation I most dreaded. This man was legendary for his aversion to controversy and confrontation. I was feeling as though I had already caused him enough distress today. I delivered a shortened version of my speech.

"This," he said, "will blow over. Hold your head high. Go on about your business, and people will soon find something else to talk about. Have a good weekend, and don't worry."

I walked back down to my office shaking my head. What an amazing day this had turned out to be.

*

Outside there was a loud noise and commotion. I was yanked from my reverie and wondered how long I had been standing there lost in memory. Some students were yelling, wadding up leaflets, and throwing them at the picketers. The 3:20 bell rang and behind me in the hallway I heard classroom doors opening as students filled the hallways. Athletic teams began to load onto busses. Students scurried down the walkways and out onto the sidewalks.

On his way to an after-school meeting, Wes stopped to check the front lawn once again. He shook his head and muttered, "Amazing. Just amazing. I just can't get over our kids. If we could get all of our teachers and adult staff to take the same kind of responsibility for the climate here we'd be a much better—a much safer school." Without waiting for a reply he patted my shoulder and strode off to his meeting.

This story is dedicated to the people who live in the center of my heart: With love and appreciation to my editor and partner, Pam Liebing. Great thanks and admiration for Hank Bangser, superintendent, New Trier Township High School, and Wes Baumann, retired Principal, New Trier Township High School. Allies of great courage and kind hearts—my companions along the way: Jan Borja, Julie Ann Carroll, Steve and Jo Ham, Michael O'Hare, Darrelyn Marx, Matt Stuczynski, and Bob Ward.

Part Four
Change Agent

THE IMPORTANCE OF DISCOMFORT

Richard Ognibene
Chemistry and physics teacher
Fairport High School
Fairport, New York

"So, Mr. O., what are you doing for Thanksgiving?" she asked innocently on a November Tuesday in 1994. It was the end of sixth-period physics class and the students were huddled around the door waiting for the bell to ring. As is my custom, I asked various students about their Thanksgiving plans. When Priya returned the question, I answered with words that would forever change my life: "David and I are going to my parents' house for dinner."

Like an E.F. Hutton commercial, the room suddenly became very silent as another student asked the obvious follow-up question, "Who is David?" "He's the man I've been dating for the last year," I replied. The bell rang, and as the students filed out the door my stomach churned like Mt. Vesuvius. I was sure I'd be summoned immediately to the principal's office. Yet, amidst the fear and panic, other feelings started bubbling up inside me: relief, freedom, pride, honesty, and excitement. I had finally done it. I had come out to my students. I had not consciously planned on coming out that day. I was just tired: tired of the lies and half-truths, tired of keeping my school life and my home life in separate compartments, tired of contributing to my own oppression.

I have been teaching science since 1986, in three high schools and one community college. I've been out to my colleagues since 1987 and out to my students since 1995. I now have the best job on the planet, teaching at Fairport High School. If you entered our school today you would see a few rainbow stickers on cars in our staff parking lot, you would see signs for our gay-straight alliance, and you would see a principal who routinely chastises students for using homophobic language. You would see a district-wide tolerance-and-diversity program called Brotherhood-Sisterhood Week. You would see a few brave gay or lesbian couples holding hands in the hallway. And you would see me, an openly gay science teacher who can safely bring his partner to school events.

You might assume that life has always been this good for me and my school, but in fact it has taken many steps to get to this point. Each of those steps seemed impossible at the time. Each step was filled with stress and discomfort. If I have learned anything from my journey, it is that old prejudices do not die easily. As Elisabeth Kubler-Ross noted, there is always denial, anger, and bargaining before acceptance. Far too many gay teachers spend their whole lives in the closet because they want to avoid discomfort for themselves or for others; ironically, this tactic just continues the cycle of homophobia, because society needs to go through the discomfort to get to acceptance. The discomfort is part of the process.

Step 1: Coming out to myself and my family

My journey as a gay man started in the fall of 1985. I was a graduate student at the University of Rochester. I had finally come to terms with the fact that I was attracted to other men, but I didn't know what to do about it. While reading a student newspaper I stumbled across an ad for the gay-lesbian student group. On a crisp fall evening I walked across the campus to Meliora Hall to attend the meeting; as I approached the building I got scared that someone might recognize me, so I made a U-turn and sprinted back to the chemistry building.

The next week I actually made it to the meeting and met my first gay friends; that night I sat on my balcony, had two glasses of cheap wine, and wondered if my friends and family would still love me. By Thanksgiving I had been dating a fellow graduate student for a month, and I felt ready to come out to my family. I told my siblings, Beth and Chris, late Thanksgiving night; neither of them were particularly surprised. The next day, with my heart racing and voice cracking, I told mom and dad. My parents cried a little, worried about AIDS a lot, and told me that they loved me. For about a year there was some tangible discomfort. Over time, through efforts on all sides, the discomfort disappeared and I was finally able to live honestly with the people I loved most. My family is the rock upon which I have built my life; the reason we are so close is that we were all willing to go through the initial period of discomfort.

Step 2: Surviving in rural America

My journey as a teacher started in September of 1986. I got hired to teach seventh- and eighth-grade science in a rural town 40 miles outside of Rochester. I grew up in suburbia surrounded by highly educated, liberal adults. I had never experienced conservative small-town America. Needless to say, I learned as much as my students did that first year. Initially, my sexual orientation was not an issue; between teaching science, coaching soccer, and attending graduate school, there was little time for dating.

In October of 1987 I attended my first March on Washington. The event transformed my life; being among thousands of gays and lesbians was empowering. I was no longer the oddball—I fit in. The freedom I felt in Washington over the long weekend was astonishing. For three magical days I could be unabashedly gay and proud. I decided that I wanted to live this way all the time.

When I returned to school, I spent the next week coming out to colleagues, one at a time, in excruciating detail. They were uniformly kind, though each gave me some version of the following advice: "It's OK with me, but I wouldn't let too many others know. And heaven forbid the kids should find out." One teacher specifically said, "I don't tell the kids who I have sex with and neither should you." Intellectually I never bought that argument, but I was too young to combat it. Now when people present that argument, I ask them if they wear a wedding ring or have a photo of their spouse on their desk or brag about their children. When they reply yes, I mention that *all* of those simple acts are ways of letting the kids know that you are heterosexual. I also note that sexual orientation is much more than the mechanics of intimacy; it is a spectrum of emotions, feelings, and people in our lives that make us who we are. And if your students can know who you are, why can't my students have that same right?

I survived, but I spent a lot of time each spring looking for a job in a community where I could live a more fully integrated life.

Step 3: Finding the right job and educating the staff

In 1992 I got my lucky break when I was hired by Fairport High School. I had no intention of storming the Bastille for gay rights during my first few years, but several opportunities quickly arose. During my first year at FHS, the Multicultural Diversity Club (MDC) put on a "Diversity Forum" in our auditorium. The speakers included an African-American man, a Latina woman, a woman in a wheelchair, a gay man, and a lesbian. Students walked up the aisles to a microphone at the front of the auditorium to ask questions. As I quietly observed the program, I realized that 90% of the questions were directed at the gay panelists. Clearly the students were thirsting for more information on this topic, information that was noticeably lacking in their curricula.

The following year some of my colleagues wanted to do an inservice training about the elevated suicide risks for gay adolescents and they asked me—untenured me—to be part of it. I thought about it for a few days and realized that I might not have this opportunity again; I said yes.

We wanted the forum to be a faculty meeting so that *everyone* would be there; we had no desire to do an optional workshop where we would be preaching to the converted. Our principal said yes, then no, then yes, then no, then yes...you get the point. There were many heated meetings and much discomfort, but the day of the workshop finally came.

For 45 minutes you could have heard a pin drop. My part of the program was to speak about my personal experiences as a gay student and as a gay teacher. I started full of fear, but my rhythm and confidence picked up as I went along.

Looking back, I realize what a big effect that meeting had on our school culture. The 20% of our staff that was comfortable with gay issues were excited, the 20% that was uncomfortable with gay issues were angry, and the 60% in the middle were exposed to issues that they had never thought of before. It's these people in the middle who eventually became our allies and helped transform the school culture. I still remember a colleague telling me that her brother was dying of AIDS and that our presentation helped her family.

The most surprising part of the presentation was the response of some of my gay and lesbian colleagues. They were uncomfortable because I had exposed the elephant under the rug. Many had been closeted throughout their careers and here was me saying, "I'm gay, I'm a teacher and it's OK to be both." I just kept repeating my mantra: "The discomfort is part of the process."

Step 4: Educating students

Even after coming out, one still has to address homophobia. Once, during chemistry class, I heard a student tell this horribly offensive joke: "What do you call a fag in a wheelchair?" "Roll-AIDS." I was so distraught by that joke and by the prevalence of homophobic put-downs used by adolescents that I wrote an article for our student newspaper in which I effectively came out to the entire school.

Once again there was some discomfort, not to mention a few parent phone calls to one of our assistant principals. The silver lining was the overwhelming support shown by my colleagues and my administrators—support that was at least partially related to the aforementioned faculty training.

Once I came out, I had the energy and courage to be a more creative teacher. The students felt closer to me and became more interested in my subject matter. I remember chaperoning the 1995 Senior Ball. Toward the end of the night, the DJ played "YMCA" by the Village People. I was standing by my date, David, along with the other chaperones. A senior couple, Amy and Jay, approached us and asked us to join them in a dance. We walked out as a couple and joined their circle and had the most spectacular dance I have ever experienced. The memories of all my awful high school and college dances faded away as I danced for the first time with male partner at a school event.

In June I was chosen by the senior class to be their graduation speaker. I addressed the 500 graduates (and 5,000 family members) in the perfect end to a perfect year.

Step 5: Forming a gay-straight alliance

In 1998 two seniors approached me about forming a gay student group. I was a little timid at first, as no nearby schools had a similar group; however, the students' courage inspired me to move forward. Our principal was very supportive but said we'd first have to get clearance from the superintendent. The superintendent was very supportive too, but he needed to make sure the board of education was comfortable with the concept.

It took months of meetings and negotiations to clarify what the group was and what the group was not. The administrators' big fear was that the alliance would be perceived as a club where kids talk about sex.

After a whole lot of stress, the group had its first meeting in March of 1998, but I was not allowed to be adviser. People were worried that the group might be challenged and that I could get hurt in the exchange. I was angry, but in retrospect I know that my district was trying to protect me.

In October of 1999 I officially became cofacilitator of our GSA, which we call the Fairport Rainbow Alliance. The first year we put up signs in the hallway, some of which were defaced. Now we put signs in each homeroom and they last the entire year.

Over the years we've gone from a small group of tentative, quiet kids to a raucous group of proudly out teens. (Even so, we talk about mundane stuff like homework and jobs and family much more than we talk about relationships.) In 2003 we participated in our first Day of Silence, with 50 people participating. I was a little worried about the day, not knowing how students and teachers would respond. But it went off without a hitch. However, discomfort is still part of the process.

Step 6 : Educating staff in other buildings

As a result of my experiences with the Rainbow Alliance, I realized that kids are coming out and dealing with sexual orientation issues at younger ages than ever before. A friend who is a talented elementary teacher suggested we develop a program to broach the issue with elementary and middle-school faculty.

We make a dynamic duo as she is a straight female elementary teacher and I am a gay male secondary teacher. Together we prepared a 20-minute program that included a clip from the video "It's Elementary." We then shared stories about gay kids being harassed by peers and how the harassment is often ignored by teachers.

Over five months we went to six schools. Though we believed our presentation was quite mild, we made some staff very uncomfortable, and multiple times, colleagues told us to soften our presentation.

I can honestly say that these presentations caused me more discomfort than anything I've ever done; they also provided some great results. We gave many teachers the courage to address homophobic bullying and to teach diversity lessons. What once seemed unthinkable suddenly became possible. The discomfort was part of the process.

Step 7: Celebrate progress and plan for the future

At the opening 2001 faculty meeting it was announced that my partner, Matt Fleig, and I had a civil union ceremony in Vermont.

When people cheered I realized just how far my school had come. During the last few years I have helped teachers at other schools start their own GSAs. I have seen a lesbian couple attend our junior prom. I have received e-mails and visits from college students who have recently come out. Seeing the progress makes the struggle worthwhile.

This profession has come so far in the last decade. And yet we have miles to go before we sleep. We need every high school in America to have a GSA. We need curricula that make gays and lesbians visible. Most of all, we need more gay and lesbian teachers, at all grade levels, to come out of the closet. Ambrose Redmoon said, "Courage is not the absence of fear, but rather the judgment that something else is more important than fear." The lives of our gay and lesbian youth must become more important than fear.

Discomfort is part of the process. My challenge to all my gay and lesbian colleagues is this: Put yourself and your school through a little discomfort!

THE HUNTINGTON HIGH PROJECT:
A TEACHER STORY OF SOCIAL ACTION

Irene "Toodie" Ray
Teacher (AP composition, creative writing, TV broadcasting)
Huntington High School
Huntington, West Virginia

It wears a person out. Teaching from a closet is a ridiculous notion; way too much of the best stuff gets buried in there. My dream has always been to teach or work with gay youth. This would, of course, be in an environment where I could be totally out as a lesbian, somewhere my sexual orientation was not an issue. Therefore I could be completely the authentic teacher-person I am.

I've been so tired of semiplaying the "don't ask, don't tell" game. How could I possibly teach kids to be proud of who they are from some dark box? How could I model to gay and straight students that we are all much more alike than we are different? How would they see that I was like their own mothers—always worried about my children (who, by the way, were their classmates and peers), enforcing curfews, expecting high GPAs, attending their activities—*and* I was a lesbian? So I just gave it up; I stopped playing the game. I finally came out at school, especially to students. Too many of them needed me to.

In the state of West Virginia, teachers sign a morals clause; sexual orientation is nowhere near being protected by state law. I can be fired without any reason. Before I came out, I expected that

I'd have to leave the area because even the small-scale feats I'd been doing came with a price: the constant fear that I could lose my job.

Now, despite these very real concerns, an incredible amount has happened at our school, beginning with the formation of a gay-straight alliance and snowballing to a performance about our students' reactions to viewing NBC's *The Matthew Shepard Story*. Suddenly, leaving Huntington High School in West Virginia does not seem as necessary. If one day that morals clause rears its ugly head, and the board of education decides this lesbian teacher does not belong in her classroom, I will go out with much noise.

There were several incidents and situations that led up to the establishment of our GSA and prepared the soil for the school assembly that was the product of Layne Amerikaner's senior project. The first—and most influential for Layne—was also the most positive. A gay student, Justen Deal, sought "refuge" at Huntington High in the winter semester of 2001. He left his home school after years of constant bullying became dangerous. Here he met and became close with Layne and her circle of friends.

The second incident took place in the fall of the next school year, when a despicable crime was committed in our small city. Five young males followed a 28-year-old man from a gay club to a bank parking lot near his apartment, where they savagely beat him, so badly that his friends could not readily identify him. Two of the accused were HHS students. This incident and the way it was handled during the next year and a half caused, to put it mildly, a rift in our school.

This was an especially sensitive subject because one of the students, who had (allegedly) beaten the young man with the butt of a pistol, continued to attended class for the rest of the 2001–2002 school year as he would the next, later wearing an ankle band as part of his "home confinement." He boasted about the gruesome details of the gay-bashing as if he were a hero ridding Huntington's streets of homosexuals. The other student, a star athlete and favored "son," was not charged at all.

Awareness of the mistreatment of gays began to grow among our student body, and just before the holiday break of 2001 Layne and three other students asked me if I would advise a gay-straight alliance for our school. Thirty to 35 students attended the first meeting of Huntington High's GSA in February of 2002.

Later that same school year another school, Boyd County High in bordering Kentucky, also formed a GSA. This school is 20 minutes away by Interstate—but apparently a universe away in mentality—from HHS. Their voyage was not smooth sailing: More than 500 students walked out of school to protest the club's meeting on campus. Local churches organized 2,000 citizens to protest the existence of the club. The situation for the Boyd County GSA grew ugly; sometimes they felt helpless and hopeless—like the whole world was against them.

So our GSA invited them to Huntington for pizza and camaraderie. After the pizza party, I felt grateful for how wonderful my faculty and student body seemed compared to the other school's. I wrote a letter to the population of HHS telling them how heart-wrenching the stories from Boyd County were and how happy I was to be at HHS, where people were more tolerant, open minded, and compassionate—more "21st-century human beings." The letter was printed in the school newspaper. This action had a reciprocal effect—the more thankful I was for their wonderful attitudes, the more wonderful their attitudes became.

A few weeks later the hate group led by the Reverend Fred Phelps, attracted by the Boyd County struggle, descended upon the tristate area to spread their religious message of hate through picket lines and heinous antigay language. In reaction, an antihate rally was held, and my students and I were invited to speak. Huntington High's GSA organized our own "Go Love" rally held in front of City Hall. Both events were successful beyond my expectations. We got heavy and very positive press and support. Parents and community members as well as a few faculty members joined our rally that weekend.

Later, the experiences of Huntington High's GSA and Boyd County's GSA were contrasted in a *New York Times* article. Few people, even those who had earlier participated in the protests in Kentucky, wanted to be associated or identified with the hateful and ignorant homophobic rhetoric that had attracted national news coverage mostly due to the Phelps group. In that light, even the mildest opposition to a handful of high school students and their fearless adviser trying to spread tolerance and acceptance seemed ridiculous. Many people had to question their own homophobic attitudes. Some people recognized that hate is hate in its most extreme form and in its mildest form. These events set the stage for Layne Amerikaner's senior honors project.

Members of Huntington High's Honors Program who stick it out until their senior year must complete an exit project. The project has to be something real, something useful and beneficial to the student and to a community. It requires research of some kind, presentations with visual aides, and documentation, like these projects usually do. But the process must include personal growth, and the final product must reflect a stretch on the part of the student.

When Layne first asked me to mentor her project, she knew she wanted to do something about hate crimes. By the end of her junior year, in June of 2002, she had narrowed her topic down to "something about Matthew Shepard" and using some sort of performance as part of the project. In early 2003 she nailed down exactly what she was going to do: show the NBC movie, *The Matthew Shepard Story*, at school, have students complete a survey about their reactions to the film, and use their comments to create a reader's theater, monologue-like performance. Of course she wanted to perform it for the school. But I knew that completing the project, even without getting class time for the performance, would mean persuading some people at our school to take a few giant steps.

Layne's proposal was approved by Sandy Linn, sponsor of the Honors Program, and then by principal Todd Alexander, who didn't bat an eyelash. First Layne wrote an e-mail asking teachers to take part in her project, and we sent it to the whole faculty via my school e-mail account. While we waited for teachers to respond, she wrote the survey and arranged for the movie to be broadcast over the school's Smart System. A total of 11 teachers agreed to participate in the project by allowing their classes to watch the movie and then complete the survey. However, many more classes than those 11 watched the movie without using the survey. We had made extra copies of the movie, so that if the scheduled broadcast time wasn't right for some teachers, they could play it any time they wanted. As word got out, more and more students were sent to my room for copies of the movie, and students in other classes talked their teachers into tuning in to the scheduled broadcast. *The Matthew Shepard Story* was the buzz of the school, the topic of discussion in classrooms, at lunch tables, in hallways all over the school, and even at dinner tables in homes for almost a week after the official broadcast for Layne's project.

The surveys came in, just under 200 of them. Most of the reactions, on the surveys as in discussions and conversations, were positive or at least curious, or shocked and angered that such a thing had happened. Only a few—at least that I heard of—expressed outloud antigay sentiments. A handful of kids had real epiphanies: One or two wrote to Layne about how much the movie had affected them, how it had changed their minds about gay people, how after seeing the movie they could no longer understand why they had hated gay people. Others wrote or talked about their own or a friend's or family member's sexual orientation. I answered more questions about homosexuality, hate crimes, the Matthew Shepard incident, and sexuality in general in the three or four days following the movie than I have in the last several years.

The next step was the most challenging for Layne: what to do with those surveys. It is difficult to say how many hours she spent poring over them, trying to find patterns so that she could somehow organize them into a script. She said that even after they were typed up, she could remember the handwriting the comments had been written in.

Layne's mother is an expert in qualitative research, so no doubt she was able to advise Layne in this next step of her project. Layne finally came up with five categories that she would represent as "characters":

1. Saddened (disheartened by the whole thing; that it can and did happen)
2. Angry (outraged at the two boys who committed the crime, mad at the whole world for being such a rotten place where such things happen)
3. Hateful (hostile, mostly toward gay people)
4. Indifferent (didn't affect me, so I don't care)
5. Unjust (can't believe things like this happen; it isn't right or fair)

Next Layne cast the show. Luckily, she had talented and willing friends. Four of the five students cast had at least some sort of acting experience; all very much wanted to take part in the project. Only one of the cast members was openly gay. As part of the play, Layne decided to read the questions on the survey, and then have the characters respond with answers. Most of the lines were exactly as the students had written them; only a few had been revised for clarity. The script consisted of questions from the survey and her arrangement of the responses.

In addition to writing the script and finding students willing to perform the controversial material in front of several hundred of their peers, Layne got a date for two back-to-back performances approved. We spent three weeks in intense rehearsal, and the show began to come together. Layne and I put together a video that included a beautiful black-and-white photograph of Matthew Shepard, Layne's title and acknowledgments, and the cast list, with soft music in the background. It also included the beginning of the movie, the eerie, slow-motion, sound-distorted scene in which Matthew is beaten with a pistol, tied to a fence, and left to die. We hoped it would provide a powerful intro when projected on the huge screen in our school's auditorium. Once again we e-mailed teachers, this time inviting them to bring their classes to the performance of *The Huntington High Project: A School's Reaction to The Matthew Shepard Story.* All 11 of those classes who had originally participated in Layne's project replied that they were coming as well as several more.

On the evening of final dress rehearsal, one of our two technicians was 30 minutes late; "Hateful" was tired and sounded sleepy but not at all hostile; "Unjust" forgot part of her costume. I told Layne all was perfect; everyone who's done any theater at all knows that a bad dress rehearsal means a wonderful opening. The next morning the cast waited backstage as I prepared to herd the 200 students and teachers we expected to the front and center seats— but they kept coming and coming. Many more teachers than we expected brought their classes to see both performances. We almost filled our auditorium both times.

I was shocked by some of the teachers who attended. Some of them had been accused by students of making homophobic remarks or allowing verbal gay bashing in their classrooms. Students had told me stories of bigotry of various forms—sexism, racism, classism—and now these people were bringing their classes to a performance speaking out against gay bashing and homophobia. I was overwhelmed by what was happening at my school.

Then the house lights dimmed and faded to black, leaving us in nearly pitch-darkness, the only light reflected by the giant white movie screen. The cast took their places. Our video was indeed powerful. It faded; the readers began.

Layne: "What was your initial reaction to seeing what happened to Matthew Shepard at the beginning of the movie?"
Saddened: "Terrible…that doesn't even describe it."
Angry: "Disgusting!"
Hateful: "I said, 'Ha ha, the stupid fag was killed.'"
Indifferent: "I don't really care."
Unjust: "Horrifying."

My kids—well, Layne and *her* kids—were indescribable... extraordinary...glorious...splendid! At times you could practically hear those seeds—the ones Layne had been planting—germinating among 500 high school students; at other moments, showers of tears fell.

Afterward, Sandy Linn (the sponsor of the Honors program), Layne, and I heard compliment after compliment. A number of people said what I too had thought: "You should take that around to other high schools." And it's true; the script is good enough, powerful enough to travel.

It hasn't finished its mission. This little girl from Huntington, West Virginia, this little Layne Amerikaner, with a mind like a river and a heart as big as the moon, made a difference in the lives of many people—a few we know about, but likely many we don't. Where the soil was tilled, she planted seeds, and then she handed beautiful blossoms to her classmates and teachers.

At Huntington High's graduation that year, I heard one of the better student-written graduation speeches of my teaching career; I cried as he talked. Trey Curtis, senior class president of Huntington High's class of 2003, spoke of how important it is to make a difference, to embrace, accept, and create change. He illustrated his point with the National Merit Finalists, the star athletes and musicians, debate winners, the friendships, all the good times, scholarship winners, the experience of losing a beloved classmate during the school year, award winners...and finally he spoke of Layne Amerikaner, who with her senior project had made a real difference in his mind and in the minds of hundreds of people. He called her a hero.

It's funny to me still that the seven of us—Sandy Linn, Nicole Gray, Katherine Mohn, Emanuel Gunn, Philip Pham, Colin Reynolds, Layne Amerikaner, and I—who worked so hard to make *The Huntington High Project: A School's Reaction to The Matthew Shepard Story* come together seem more or less to have just taken this all in stride, like it was something we do every day. We didn't notify the local press; we didn't have enough time to answer all of the audience's questions or discuss the performance with them; we didn't even have a party to celebrate. I am not positive that those six other people all know, all understand what a spectacular, intelligent, brave, important humanitarian thing they did. I hope they have said their own private "hip-hip-hoorays." I hope they know that they have changed potentially hundreds of people they don't even know in ways they will never know, and those people will change others, and so on and so on… It's mind-boggling. All of it began with people willing to take risks.

And Sandy and I are the only ones more than 18 years old. Layne Amerikaner and the other kids are just getting started; they won't be able to stop, not after such a big taste at such an early age. I am honored to have worked with human beings with such courage, humanity, compassion, and grace.

DANCING WITH THE ISSUES

Clarence Brooks
Dance instructor (sixth, seventh, eighth grades)
Bak Middle School of the Arts
West Palm Beach, Florida

A Gay Teacher

When I was asked if I would consider submitting stories about my teaching experiences for possible inclusion in this new book, I was fascinated by the thought of how much has changed in the decade that's passed since the last edition. As a gay African-American male teaching in the South, I can give witness to this. As my stories will show, I am simultaneously a product and an agent of this growth and these changes.

It was the summer of 1998. I was preparing to return home to Seattle from a trip abroad. As a favor to a friend, a teacher at Bak Middle School of the Arts, I agreed to stop over in West Palm Beach, Florida, to interview for a position at the school where she taught. In all honesty, having just ended an 18-year career as a professional dancer, I was not interested in teaching middle school–age youth. But I was duly amazed at the diversity, focus, and talent of the students I taught in the master class.

As my day of interviews came to a close, the principal, assistant principal, and department chair collectively told me that the position was mine if I wanted it. Their only request was that I give them an answer soon, so that if I chose not to accept the offer they'd have enough time to continue interviewing for the position

240

before school started: I felt that that was only fair. But I had another problem. I was worried about being a gay teacher in a public school.

That same year, the Oklahoma legislature was contemplating passing a law that would have made it illegal for lesbian, gay, bisexual, and transgender people to hold teaching positions in that state. I did not relish the thought of packing up all of my belongings, leaving my home and friends in Seattle, traveling across the entire country, and starting a new life, only to get booted out of a job because I was gay. After all, Florida was the birthplace of Anita Bryant's infamous "Save the Children" campaign. To my reasoning, it was quite possible that Florida could follow Oklahoma's lead should this unjust and discriminatory legislation pass.

After several days of mental anguish and mind wrenching, I called the principal and asked her point-blank if she had a problem with me being a gay teacher. I explained to her that I had been out of the closet for roughly eight years and under no circumstances was I about to go back in. I felt that I was out from under the proverbial cloak of shame that denoted the gay closet, and I was out for good. At that time, however, I hadn't even contemplated being out to students. I was mistakenly living under the internalized homophobic impression that my gay sexual orientation (unlike that of my heterosexual colleagues who speak openly about their families) had no place in the workplace and certainly not in the schoolyard.

In my explanation, I told the principal that I would never come out and say, "Hi, I'm Mr. Brooks, and I'm your new gay teacher." But I also assured her that under no circumstances would I conceal my gay identity from a student, parent, or colleague if asked.

I explained to her that I had faced both overt and covert racist bigotry before. Life had taught me that I would face, at best, a modicum of homophobia. If I had my druthers, I would much rather know up front that someone harbored hate toward me rather than risk getting stabbed me in the back by someone I thought was liberal-minded.

I wanted her to save me the time, the energy, the money, and the trouble of making another cross-country move. If she had, or could foretell, any problems with having a gay teacher on faculty, I wanted to know before and not after I had uprooted myself.

I am now enjoying my sixth year as an openly gay teacher in the nation's 14th largest school district, Palm Beach County.

The Faggot Ballet Teacher

In the first months at Bak, during a mandatory lunch duty, I witnessed an eighth-grade male student spill his entire lunch on the cafeteria floor. When I saw that he made no effort to pick up any of the mess, I approached him and asked him to get the broom from the cafeteria manager. Oddly, he ignored me and then turned his back to me.

Since our student body was by and large very well mannered, focused, and disciplined, this behavior seemed out of the ordinary. After my third, more forceful request, he physically challenged my authority by standing up—towering over me—and looking down at me. At this point, I threatened him with a visit to the assistant principal and a referral. After a brief pause, he backed down and retrieved a broom.

I was shaken by the experience. Why had he ignored my request to clean up his mess? Why had he physically challenged me? Was it an issue of race? As he left, I saw that he had been seated with quite a diverse group of his peers. Clearly, race was the not the issue.

When he returned with the broom the answer became all too clear. As he cleaned his mess I heard him say, "I didn't know if I was supposed to back down from the faggot ballet teacher or not."

I was shaken. For the rest of the day that statement echoed through my head.

The pain came with the realization that I had not come out to any students. This young man and his classmates had determined that I was a "faggot" anyway: I was a male teaching dance, therefore I had to be gay. But that was not the end of the internal fight going on in my head. Because I was perceived as a "faggot," I could be ignored, or even worse, physically and verbally challenged. The fact

that I was a teacher and that I was an adult was of little consequence to this young man.

Now I was shocked. He had absolutely no respect for me as a
teacher, as an adult, or even as a fellow human being. If he and his
peers had no respect for these identities, how would a student who
was perceived to be LGBT fare?

It took me a few days to recover. But I did so with full dignity
and grace, determined to make changes. I was not going to let this
ever happen to me again. I also decided to champion the cause of
protection for real or perceived LGBT youth. I joined my local
GLSEN chapter and Equality Florida, began collaborating with
PFLAG, and started my volunteer relationship with Compass,
Palm Beach County's LGBT community services center.

Failing School District

In the fall of 1998, GLSEN National surveyed the largest school
districts in the nation to analyze LGBT youth attitudes about their
school environment. Palm Beach County, *my* district, received a
failing grade.

I had been teaching only a few months when the results of this
survey were made public. Here was the opportunity for change
that I was seeking. I vowed to improve this grade.

I drafted a letter and sent it out to the superintendent of schools
and all seven members of the district. Introducing myself as a new
gay African-American employee, I invited them to call upon me as
a resource available to them to earn a passing grade and make our
schools a safer place regardless of real or perceived sexual orientation, gender identity, or gender expression.

The one response I received from the school board was a message from my principal. She received a call from one school board
member asking for a definition of the term "heterosexism" that I
had used in my letter. That was the extent of their reaching out to
me as a resource or agent of change. My principal merely asked
that I keep her informed about any other such actions I was
planning so that she would not be surprised in the future.

Teaching the Children of Homophobes

It was 2001, and the School District of Palm Beach County had just refused to add "sexual orientation" to the discrimination policy, although they had agreed to add this language to the harassment policy. GLSEN Palm Beach had won a partial victory on behalf of all public school children regardless of real or perceived sexual orientation, gender identity, and gender expression.

The final public discussion prior to the vote was quite contentious. Homophobic individuals and organizations came in by the busload to voice their antigay bigotry. I was not present at the meeting, but the following day as I walked into my musical theater class, I heard the bigoted echoes of this homophobia.

One of my students, in a voice intentionally above a whisper, echoed her parent's homophobic sentiments. Ostensibly, she was talking to a girlfriend, but it was obvious that I was the intended audience of this hate.

In true Christian character, I turned the other cheek. I taught class, being sure to give her the same kind of constructive criticisms I offer to all of my students. I was the teacher and she was the student. She and her homophobic parents depended on me to help educate my misguided charge. As I taught, I steadied myself by humming Rogers and Hammerstein's immortal lyrics from *South Pacific*:

> "You have to be taught to hate and fear before you are 6, or 7, or 8.
> You have to be carefully taught."

"That's So Gay"

With the school board's decision to add "sexual orientation" to the harassment policy, I decided to conduct an unscientific survey of homophobic comments that could be defined as harassment. I found three four-minute windows of time per week to research this topic.

At various times before, during, and after school, I would stand quietly and inconspicuously in a crowded and well-traveled corridor as the unsuspecting student body passed me by. Just as a wildlife conservationist would camouflage himself to observe animals in the wild, I was careful not to draw attention to myself as I unceremoniously tallied how many times I heard homophobic comments such as "faggot," "that's so gay," and other such terminology.

I was surprised by my findings. Over a period of four weeks, I heard these terms spoken roughly 17 times per week. Considering the fact that Bak is a magnet school of the arts, with diversity and individuality as the bedrock of the school culture, this was an astounding discovery.

Today when I hear such derogatory comments, I am quick to address them directly and to make it a teachable moment. My general lesson is to make the student(s) aware that the remarks—no matter how innocently they were intended—are indeed derogatory and hurtful to me and to countless others within earshot who are or who have LGBT family members, relatives, and friends.

After asking the students' art major, I name a few famous LGBT individuals whose record of achievement in that field has left an indelible mark on our lives, culture, and history. Before telling them that school board policy prohibits such abuse, I assist the student(s) in finding other more appropriate words for what they are trying to express. I also ask for their assistance in ridding our campus of such demeaning phrases by enlisting them to educate their peers.

Coming Out in the Schoolyard

October 11 is National Coming Out Day. Just as I had come out to my family and friends several years ago, I determined that I was going to come out in an "appropriate" and absolute manner. "Appropriate" would, of course, be self-defined. After all, being both an artist and a teacher requires thinking out-of-the-box.

One of my prime methods of LGBT activism was to write editorials in response to articles I had read. One such article I read was in *Dance Magazine,* an international dance publication. The article, written by a retired ballerina turned clinical psychologist and advice columnist, dealt positively with the fact that many local dance studios had LGBT youth participating in their programs and needed to be aware of this population. The article listed GLSEN and PFLAG (among others) as resources that directors and faculty of dance studios should contact as resources for more information about issues that concern LGBT youth.

For two decades, I had read this and other national and international dance periodicals. Never had I come across an article written with such openness, respect, and advocacy for LGBT youth. I wrote the author to thank her. She in turn asked if I would agree to have our subsequent e-mail exchanges copied into an editorial for a future edition. I drafted my part of our correspondences acknowledging the fact that I was a gay, African-American dance instructor, listing my full name and place of employment. I knew full well that most of my past and present students, as well as most of the local dance studios, would see this editorial.

The reaction was something I could not have planned. Some enterprising student brought a copy to school, enlarged it, and then distributed copies around campus. I had honestly forgotten about the editorial until one of my assistant principals called me into his office to tell me that he was dealing with a "situation." Evidently, one student had called home to tell his or her homophobic parent. This parent called the area superintendent to alert her to the fact that an "openly homosexual person" was teaching at their school.

Her response was purportedly that I, as an American citizen with the right to free speech, was entitled to write the article. I had done so during my own time and without the use of school facilities or supplies. Although my union, the Classroom Teachers Association, has coverage for LGBT teachers, I was so glad that I had previously come out to the entire school board.

I received no personal flack for coming out in *Dance Magazine*. The students who were caught making copies were reprimanded for using school property for noncurricular activities. Unfortunately, the topic of sexual orientation was skirted. No matter. Even though I did not have a public forum to discuss this "situation," the article and I were now the talk of the campus. In fact, three non-LGBT parents thanked me for writing the editorial. When I walked the hallways, students turned to watch me pass proudly and gracefully by. Students were quick to learn not to say "that's so gay" within earshot of me.

Being a Mentor

My campus has roughly 1,350 students, so the number of students who greet me by name on a daily basis amazes me. I often tell people that I have nearly 200 children, the number of students in the dance department. But six years of teaching have taught me that I "teach" anyone who knows my name or reputation.

A few years ago one of my colleagues took a call intended for me from a recently graduated high school student. During their brief conversation, this young lady explained that although she was never a student at Bak and had never met me in person, she was calling from college to thank me for being out and openly gay.

She wanted to thank me for being there, somewhere out there, visible. This message touched my straight colleague as deeply as it touched me. I never learned this young lady's name, but she taught me the good that it does to publicly acknowledge all diversity, my own as well as others. By my interpretation, the mere fact that I was another gay person in a universe of heterosexist hegemony kept her sane. My being openly out let her know that there were others like her out there in the world, living gracefully and contributing proudly.

Each and every group has its distinguishing characteristics and histories, but the coming-out process is something that distinguishes the LGBT experience from other oppressed populations. At times these histories and characteristics run parallel to that of other minority groups.

I am visibly an African-American. I cannot hide my skin color. My homosexuality might not be so visible; I might have the option to remain in my closet and pretend to be straight. Nevertheless, I can state from my experience as a double minority that neither identity has more baggage than the other. Unfortunately, all oppressions are equal, and they cause harm to everyone—the intended victims, the bystanders, and yes, the perpetrators.

I believe we should openly acknowledge our identity or identities. If we lived in a perfect society, a society that accepted, tolerated, and respected everyone regardless of real or perceived characteristics, I might feel differently. But we do not live in such a utopian or democratic world; we are still building toward it. Until that time when we reach this goal, it is important to note the vast contributions that LGBT individuals, among others, have contributed to our universe.

SOMETIMES YOU HAVE TO RISK THE DARKNESS TO SEE THE LIGHT

Laura Persichilli
English teacher
Smithtown High School
Smithtown, New York

"Watch out, man, that's the lesbian teacher," the small teenage boy said with trepidation. I turned and looked at the table of rambunctious boys and considered approaching them to question the comment. They settled down, trying not to look me in the eye.

As I watched my class of 11th graders sitting quietly in the library receiving a lesson, I pondered how to react to these unknown boys. I decided that, although the comment had unnerved and angered me at first, it wasn't really negative—it was simply the truth.

Later that day, after the hallways cleared and the buses were dismissed, I thought back to a time when I wasn't so comfortable in my own skin. Years before, while teaching English in another Long Island public high school, I was careful, cautious, fearful. I never even considered coming out because of the possible repercussions. Would I be harassed by students, parents, school administration, my own colleagues? Would I lose my job? There were clearly too many risks, and I was not about to challenge the heterosexism that has kept so many gay teachers in a closet nailed shut by homophobia.

So on I went, teaching and living a lie. Then one day it fell apart, and I learned a lesson that has changed me forever.

It was September of 1997, and my new class of 10th graders was entering my classroom. They were quiet and nervous—it was the first day of school, and they were new to the building. Each of them sat down and waited for me to speak, except for one. She bounded into the room, getting everyone's attention. She was loud, rude, abrasive.

I knew she would immediately try to undermine my authority. I began to address this new group of students, and much to my surprise, after only a few minutes, she settled down and seemed to be listening. I wondered what I had said that got her attention.

As time passed, Crystal continued to make her presence known as she entered the room. She insulted her classmates on a daily basis, although most were too afraid of her to say anything. There were times that I expected a fight to break out, but the verbal confrontations never came to blows. Students feared her or pitied her, but they all quickly learned to ignore her. Still, as soon as I began to speak, Crystal would stop the antics.

At the end of the first grading period, Crystal announced to the class that this was the first time that she had ever passed English. "You rock, Ms. P.!" she said with a smile. Of course, she followed that up with a five-minute tirade about how every other teacher in the district was an "incompetent asshole."

All I could say was, "I'm proud of you, Crystal, but please don't speak that way about others." I wanted to reward her success, but it was so difficult to compliment such rude behavior. I worried that the rest of my class would think me weak. I changed the subject, but Crystal's face was still swollen with pride, perhaps for the first time in her academic life.

The year went on without incident in my class, but I soon discovered that Crystal was not doing as well in her other classes. Other teachers constantly sent her to the assistant principal. She wasn't well liked by anyone, but as the school's star soccer player she knew when to draw the line and the administration knew how far to go with disciplinary measures. It made me sad, but I decided that my incredibly unique teaching style must be the reason for her success. The year ended, and Crystal passed English. She thanked me, gave me a high five, and left for summer vacation.

The next school year began and I moved on to a new group of eager tenth graders. As I stood outside my classroom door during the change of classes, I often spotted Crystal creating a scene. She was wilder than ever, but she always stopped to wave to me in the midst of her chaotic behavior. Her teachers dreaded every minute they spent with her and often asked me how I could even speak to her. I ignored them. I began to worry about her. She seemed unusually thin and less muscular than I remembered. Her soccer jersey hung loosely from her frail body. Something wasn't right.

As time passed, I busied myself with new ways to teach *Lord of the Flies* and *Of Mice and Men.* I spent endless hours grading essays and torturing myself with the paperwork that makes you wonder why you went into teaching. But as soon as I stood before my classes, I remembered how important my work was. Absorbed in complimenting myself for my service to such a noble profession, I forgot about Crystal, and it was weeks before I noticed her absence. When I questioned her English teacher, I learned that Crystal was in a drug rehabilitation program. While most of the school was relieved over her absence, I was shocked and saddened by the news. I naively assumed that an athlete like Crystal would never get mixed up in drugs.

It was about six weeks later when I realized how my "gaydar" had failed me. Although closeted myself while at school, I always had a sense of which students I believed might be gay. Many of them struggled in school and had problems at home, but I wasn't about to put my career on the line by broaching the subject with them. Crystal was not on that list. She spoke often of her "boyfriend" who lived in Florida. I never thought to question if he really existed. Why would she lie? It's funny how your own twisted sense of reality can keep you from seeing things clearly. After all, I was not exactly the model of truth.

Crystal returned to school with a new look. Her long curly hair was now shaved so short that you could see her scalp. Her designer flared jeans and short, tight T-shirts were replaced with baggy khakis and men's button-down shirts. She passed me in the hall several times but didn't seem to notice me. She was louder than ever. She would shout random comments down the hall at no one in particular. I wanted to stop her so many times and ask how she was doing since her return from rehab, but my sudden fear of her newfound expression of sexual orientation kept me from looking her in the eye. What if she always knew about me?

Talk of Crystal's return subsided rather quickly. My colleagues speculated about the drug use, but no one mentioned the fact that she might be a lesbian. That was the one comfort of heterosexism—everyone must be straight, so there was no need to discuss otherwise. As wrong as it was, it worked for me.

Spring arrived, adolescent hormones raged, and I continued to consider myself teacher extraordinaire. Then tragedy struck, shattering my tremendously undeserved ego trip. The principal called an emergency faculty meeting after school. We were informed that Crystal had died the night before from a drug overdose. She had been missing for a few days and was found at the home of a friend that she met at the rehab program. They were shooting heroin, and the police suspected that it might be suicide. The friend was being questioned.

I sat there for what seemed like hours after the meeting ended. I was dizzy, nauseous, and unable to get out of my chair. Somehow, I got myself down the hall to the English office, where there was always someone who had the inside story because they played tennis or golf with the principal. My breathing was just returning to normal when I heard one of my colleagues, for whom I'd had great respect, say with disgust, "I heard she was a lesbian. No wonder she killed herself."

The rest of my story is simple. In June I left teaching and moved to California. I felt as though I had betrayed Crystal and all those other gay students who might have benefited from my honesty. It took about six months for me to realize that I had run away like a wild rabbit being chased by the neighborhood dog. The long months of tears, depression, and reflection led me right back to the scene of the crime. I returned to Long Island and landed a job teaching English in Smithtown. I knew that the classroom was where I belonged.

Within three months of landing my brand-new nontenured teaching position, I went head-first into a battle with the district to start a gay-straight alliance. I was responding to a request by students who seemed to recognize immediately that I was gay. While I was still testing the waters and not quite ready to wave my rainbow flag, I knew that I had been given the gift of a fresh start, and I wasn't about to blow it this time.

These amazingly courageous students spoke to me about the uncorrected physical and verbal harassment suffered by gay students. They had researched other GSAs across the nation and were determined to make their school a safer place. They were smart, savvy, and willing to launch an attack on the opposition. I never flinched. I never thought about losing my job. I simply did what I knew in my heart was the right thing to do.

It took nearly one year to get the GSA approved. We argued with the high school administration, we went head-to-head with the superintendent, we went to Board of Education meetings and pleaded, and we discovered that heterosexism and homophobia is alive and thriving beyond what any of us had imagined. We solicited the help of incredible organizations such as Long Island Gay and Lesbian Youth (LIGALY), Parents, Families, and Friends of Lesbians and Gays (PFLAG), and the Gay, Lesbian, and Straight Education Network (GLSEN). We learned important lessons about politics, and were shocked and appalled by the true colors of many individuals. However, we also were warmed by the support of those who were brave enough to risk criticism from others.

Now tenured, I am about to enter my fourth year of teaching in Smithtown. Our GSA has had two successful, albeit not entirely easy, years of service to the school community. We have displayed rainbow-splashed posters, administered a school climate survey, conducted workshops for both students and faculty on antigay remarks, handed out "safe space" stickers to teachers and staff, and commemorated both National Coming Out Day and the Day of Silence. We are still learning, exploring, and testing the waters. We are risk-takers and initiators of long-needed change. We are, despite the beliefs of many, both gay and straight, standing together in a united front against discrimination and in search of equality.

I still think about Crystal and the lessons that she will never know that she taught me. I don't live my life with regret now. I live it with a sense of empowerment and wonder.

"Watch out, man, that's the lesbian teacher."
You bet.

ONE MORE PERSON TO LOVE THEM

Mike Record
Language arts department chair
Broward County Public Schools
Fort Lauderdale, Florida

They insist it's a choice we make. They insist we can simply choose another way to be. But those of us who have tried to hide who we are and those of us who have lied to ourselves and others know you can't deny your true nature. For a few years when I was younger I lived a lie and forced myself down a different path. But the sense of misery at an unfulfilled destiny led me to admit the truth: No matter how hard I try to redirect my natural urges, I was born to be a teacher.

Being gay and therefore "one teacher in 10" has, for me, meant being an advocate for lesbian, gay, bisexual, and transgender students. To the consternation of my straight colleagues, being an advocate for LGBT students has also meant being a role model. These teachers think that they don't announce their sexual orientation to the class—so why should anyone? Heterosexual privilege has a significant power to blind people to the reality in front of them. They don't understand in how many ways they announce their sexual orientation to the class every day.

I made a decision in college that I wasn't going to work anywhere that didn't tolerate my living honestly. If that meant I wasn't going to teach, then I wouldn't teach. That might be why

I gave up Future Educators of America as a sophomore in college to take a leadership role in the gay and lesbian student union.

But, when I graduated in 1994, the classroom called me back, and I become a seventh-grade teacher. I am surprised to report that it turned out that being gay and being a teacher has not been difficult to reconcile in the nation's fifth-largest school district. Quite honestly, when I started out, it didn't occur to me that my two identities would need to be reconciled, but they did. As I talked to veteran teachers, I started hearing stories of those who avoided talking about their personal lives, used false pronouns, or lied outright to prevent colleagues finding out they were gay. "It's about classroom management," someone told me once. "I can't be an effective disciplinarian if kids don't respect me because rumors are flying around the school. And if anyone at school knows, everyone at school knows." I wasn't going to hide like that, but I desperately wanted to be an outstanding teacher. I had a problem that needed a solution.

In search of the "solution" to my "problem," I stalked the teacher supply store obsessively and searched the Education section of the local bookstore daily. That's when I found *One Teacher in 10*. Back in those days, the idea of a gay teacher was not as common as it is today. For me, then, *One Teacher in 10* had come out just in time. I devoured it.

The last page of *One Teacher in 10* listed information about contacting local chapters of GLSEN. GLSEN, I thought, would be a way to meet a husband. The Gay, Lesbian, and Straight Education Network sounded to me like a party circuit for single teachers. So I enthusiastically headed into gay Fort Lauderdale. As a first-year teacher, I would be the belle of the ball.

GLSEN, it turned out, was some kind of advocacy thing; no husband material in the room that night. As I ruminated on my disappointment, I was distracted by someone talking about the position of LGBT students in the local school system. It had never even occurred to me that there was such a thing as a gay student.

How could it not have? Seventh grade suddenly deluged my

consciousness. I was no longer at the Floridian Restaurant; I was at Coral Springs Middle School and later Taravella High School— hating myself and terrified that someone would find out what I really was. My entire adolescence was nothing more than a morass of sorrow at the realization that the horrible word "faggot" symbolized both the verbal violence I received and the strange set of feelings I encountered the first time my gym class met in a locker room. Where I went to school, kids got beaten up for having the wrong brand of jeans, let alone the wrong sexual orientation. How could GLSEN not be about the students?

Over the next five years, I gave an extraordinary amount of time to GLSEN. I cannot describe my experience with this movement as anything other than life-changing. What it turned out to be about, more than anything, was giving people a sense of their own power—which is at worst a cliché and at best a mantra.

The first test of my mettle as a GLSEN member was the *Miami Herald* reporter who interviewed me at a joint meeting of GLSEN and the Gay and Lesbian Youth Group of Fort Lauderdale—one of the first functions I attended as a middle school teacher. Not only were there newspaper reporters there, but two school board members had shown up at GLSEN's invitation to hear the youth talk about what their school days were like.

Their stories were sad. They fell into one of three categories: (1) hiding who I am; (2) honest about who I am and tormented by peers; and (3) I dropped out months ago.

When the *Miami Herald* asked me if I was willing to be credited with the quotes I gave during the interview, what choice did I have? In the face of all this inequity and suffering, was I going to perpetuate the problem by hiding? Newspapers throughout the next four years identified me as Mike Record, an openly gay middle school teacher. As much as I regretted the pigeonholing, the appendage to my name has been something of a blessing in disguise. When I interrupt the use of the word "faggot" in my class, I invariably have a student comment, "Oh, yeah, you were the one in the paper for being gay." Suddenly I am out without having to come out. Then I have to talk about the fact that my identity, and the work I do in the community in the name of fairness, should not be the reason they stop using the word "faggot." They should stop using the word "faggot" because it's not a nice word. It's wrong to put someone down because of who they are.

As simple as that assertion is, many people just don't get it. In my own community, there is a contingent of people who will go on record as saying that LGBT kids *should* be harassed and discriminated against. To interrupt the harassment and discrimination, these folks argue, would be to validate a lifestyle that is dangerous and unacceptable. GLSEN Greater Fort Lauderdale made a teacher training video with the Broward County Public Schools' Office of Diversity and Cultural Outreach. The simple message of the video was that every student deserves a safe and welcoming classroom, regardless of sexual orientation or gender identity. However, one school board member told us that teachers called his office and complained that they were asked to watch it. They found it inconsistent with their religious practices.

Sadly, much of the opposition to the safe schools work GLSEN does is based on so-called religious principle. During a GLSEN issue campaign, our most vociferous opponent was Reclaiming America for Christ. This organization works to train local Christian activists to win school board seats and inject "Christian" principles into public education. It always shocked me that the general public was not alarmed that, despite everything we know about multiculturalism, this group was seeking to undo the separation of church and state.

GLSEN has brought me face-to-face with people at their worst, but it has also exposed me to people at their best. One of the most rewarding experiences in my life was sitting in the office of State Senator Skip Campbell with three Broward County youth. We had traveled eight hours in a cramped rental car to lobby for the Dignity for All Students Act—which would make all Florida schools responsible for protecting all students from bullying and harassment. It would mandate that schools track incidents and create policies that ensure the appropriate response when an incident occurs. Of Florida's 64 school districts, only four currently have a policy that extends protections to all students, including LGBT kids.

Three students and I formed a lobbying team and headed into the capitol building. Joey, David, and Crystal were juniors and seniors in Broward high schools. They witnessed on a daily basis how pervasive antigay slurs are and they wanted to do something about it. This is what brought them to GLSEN Greater Fort Lauderdale. These young people were intimidated to be in the state capitol, in the office of a legislator, but they did it because there was a problem in their schools no one was doing anything about. It was during that visit that Senator Campbell agreed to be the bill's first sponsor. Suddenly, how a bill becomes a law was no longer a *Schoolhouse Rock* cartoon; it had come to life in front of us.

I'm proud of the work I have done on behalf of GLSEN. Everything I have done on GLSEN's behalf has made schools safer places, increased the number of students to whom educational opportunities were available, helped my colleagues be better teachers, or reminded citizens in our democracy about their own power to change whatever is wrong. I am not going to hide these activities. My school district has a character-education curriculum. They probably didn't know what they bargained for when they decided to teach traits like citizenship, honesty, and tolerance in *my* district.

Most good teachers get letters from students telling them about the impact they've had. The most powerful notes I've received from students have been related to my taking a stand on antigay bias. To these students, it is inevitable that antigay bullying will occur in classrooms. It is inevitable that teachers either let it go on or suffer rumors that they themselves are gay. Further, in these students' minds, any open challenge about a teacher's sexual orientation will be met with the "That has nothing to do with why we're here today, so let's get back to learning English" speech. To witness a teacher look a student in the eye and with an unwavering voice say, "Yes, actually, I am gay, and I'm probably not the only gay person you know," is shocking to them. But the shock wears away as they listen to the rest of the speech. "Everyone in our class is welcome here. I am going to make this classroom a safe place for each of you, no matter what makes you different. That's why we don't use put-downs in this class."

As I look back on my own journey, I realize now that I was lucky enough to have a mentor whose career has paralleled mine in such a way that I have been able to learn from her in high school, college, and graduate school. One day, after she got her doctorate and I was starting graduate school, I asked her for advice about being a classroom teacher. She said that things had changed so much in the short time she had been out of the classroom that she felt ill-equipped to advise me. After a moment, though, she corrected herself. "Love them. That's the one thing I can tell you that will help you in every situation. Nowadays, one more person to love them—in some cases the only person to love them—is the difference between them making it through school or not."

This felt right when I heard it. I come with a love of language, literature, and learning in general. My goal is to pass that on to my students. So love is already there. Slowly, we are getting to where we need to be. While it's easy to lose hope, the situation is clearly better now than it was when *One Teacher in 10* was published, not only for us as a nation but also for the tentative young teacher who first picked that book up 10 years ago. Someday, when bureaucrats say "Leave no child behind," they're actually going to mean it. That's the day I'm working toward.

THE BEST WAY OUT
WAS THROUGH

Sheridan Gold
Special day-class teacher, alternative education
Marin County Community School
San Rafael, California

Sometimes when you are holding a secret, you use so much energy trying to hide the secret that the hiding keeps you prisoner in your own mind. You can't say certain things, you always have to censor what you do say, and you are always going back and forth in deciding what to say, depending on who you are talking to.

When I first started teaching, this is how it was with my students. My students were in alternative education, i.e. expelled youth and kids locked up in Juvenile Hall. Just as the community was extremely intolerant toward these kids, so were my students intolerant of anyone who was different from them. They were the most homophobic students I had ever run into.

Every morning I would hand out newspapers, and we would discuss the current events of the day. However, every morning before I handed out newspapers, I would scan them to see if there were any articles about gays in the military, gay marriage, or even gay-bashings. If there were any of these stories, I'd choose not to pass out the newspapers, and we'd go to the next activity. This way I could have some kind of control over the conversations—and to my delight, no student ever questioned why we weren't reading the newspaper on any given day.

The years passed by and I was somewhat comfortable in the closet. The kids got the message that I was not open to discussing anything gay-related, and the subject rarely came up as a class discussion. However, there'd always be the whispering, the gossip about their lesbian teacher, and the questions followed by laughter about such things as the meaning of the rainbow or what my husband's name was. "What does the rainbow mean, Ms. G.?" "I don't know, other than what comes out in nature after the rain," I would reply, my heart racing and my breath becoming shorter. "Are you married, Ms. G.?" "No," I would reply sternly, even though I was in a 20-year relationship. My stern reply gave them the message I was absolutely not into sharing my personal life with them.

Then Matthew Shepard was murdered and my life changed forever. I was stunned. I knew I could no longer be comfortable in my silence. My students needed to see a real live lesbian, somebody who was happy and healthy.

It wasn't easy, coming out. I didn't accomplish it in the snap of a finger. What my students thought of me was terribly important: I wanted to be accepted and liked and respected. But what kept playing over and over and over in my mind was that if Matthew Shepard could go through what he went through, I certainly could come out and say, "Here I am, I am gay, and I am happy."

During the time of Matthew's murder, I had been teaching for five years. I was in a Masters program creating an in-service to help make schools safer for LGBTQ youth. The tragedy reminded my professors and me just how important that in-service was. Matthew's murder brought home the importance of my work to a much higher level— not only for potential victims but especially for potential gay-bashers. Matthew's murderers were recently out of high school. I taught high school, and my colleagues taught high school, and we were all responsible in some way for the choices our students made. It was our responsibility to create a safe learning environment, free of name-calling and violence. If I could impact these teachers to stop the homophobic slurs, the bullying, the laughter, the gossip, perhaps I could turn all the horror into something positive.

I started my in-service with an original monologue about my life growing up as a youngster surrounded by homophobia. I start out as a very joyous, smart, and lively girl and end up a taunted, terrorized dropout. There's not a dry eye in the audience at the end of the 20-minute performance. It's my hook, and the teachers grab on. From there, the teachers are open to receiving statistical information about gay youth and those perceived to be gay and they are stunned at what they hear. We all leave the four-hour in-service changed people.

Although in seeing the impact of this work on other teachers I grew stronger, I was still guarded. On the first day of school in my ninth year of teaching, one of my students asked me a question that set me free.

"Hello everyone," I said. "Welcome to the first day of school."

Before I could continue, a returning student raised his hand and asked, "Ms. G., aren't you going to tell everyone your secret?"

"What secret?" I asked innocently, knowing full well where my student was going with his question.

"You know, Ms. G.," he continued, "your secret."

"Oh!" I exclaimed. "You mean when I was a kid I had a pet rat I let out every Saturday morning and let her run under my covers and snuggle up while I read?" The students shrieked and squirmed.

"No, Ms. G. Your secret. You know, your secret?"

"Oh," I exclaimed. "You mean that I am Jewish?"

"No, Ms. G.," he said as a smile spread slowly across his face. "That you are gay."

I looked at my student and said with a laugh, "That's no secret. Everybody knows I'm gay. Do you have any concerns about that or is there anything else I can help you with?" He became mute and shook his head. We moved seamlessly along to the next subject.

I am out of my prison of silence.

A MILESTONE FOR LIBERATION

Takashi Sugiyama
Home economics and health teacher
M Private High School
Saitama Prefecture, Japan

It has already been five years since I quit teaching at a private high school in Saitama, Japan. As I reflect on that experience, I see how my journey to that school—and to where I am now—began long ago.

My High School Days

I realized my gayness when I was 17 years old, a second-year high school student. I noticed that I was attracted to a boy, T., and my gaze followed him everywhere. The main topic that boys talked about at school was girls; for example, a guy had dated someone, or a guy had sex with someone—"someone" who was, of course, a girl. That was always the worst moment for me. T. was heterosexual and liked to talk about girls. I liked him very much. He didn't have the same kind of feelings as me, however, and neither did many other boys. The rigid rule of sexual love being only between a man and a woman was oppressive. I feared that my sense of feeling would be buried or destroyed by this strong heterosexual environment. I thought I'd never be able to reveal my feelings.

I was quite shocked when I discovered my sexuality. Although I had been aware that I was different from other boys around me, I didn't realize I was gay because I hadn't learned anything about different sexualities at school and I had no information about gays and homosexuality. I was alone. At middle school and high school, students and teachers told me, "You're like a woman." In high school I was called *okama*, or "homo." It hurt, but I couldn't talk back to them.

Some of the teachers and students in my high school class also made fun of gays. A boy said, "I met a male molester on the train last week." I couldn't stand the idea that people thought all gays were like that molester. I could not accept myself as gay. I sought out "normal" gay people, but I could not find ordinary gay people in this heterosexual society.

All I learned at school was that being gay was wrong or sick. Eventually, however, I started asking myself questions about why people use talk of homosexuality only to amuse others and why we don't learn about sexuality, including gay issues, formally at school.

After Finishing High School

I entered a university in Tokyo, majoring in education. It was my dream to become a teacher. I also hoped my gayness would be cured. Just after I started university, I joined a *konpa*, a group of male students from one university who meet a group of female students from a different university with the goal of meeting a romantic friend or lover. However, the more I participated in it, the more consciously I knew that I differed from the others. I felt oppressed. Moreover, realizing that I was gay influenced me enormously in my dream of becoming a teacher because I had the idea that a teacher must be flawless, and thus heterosexual. I thought I would not be morally qualified to be a teacher if I could not change my gayness.

I had nobody to talk it over with. I was frightened. I stopped attending classes and shut myself up in my house. I felt like I couldn't go anywhere.

Finally, I approached a gay organization. It became one of the most important things in my life. I made friends with other gay people of my age. I learned that being gay is normal. I was very happy, especially when I found a boyfriend. Finally, I had a positive image of myself and gained self-confidence.

Encounters With Sei-Kyo-Kyo and Naohide Yamamoto

I sought out an educational program that would have parameters to protest homophobia and could teach about all kinds of sexuality. Almost every school uses a guidebook created by MEXT (the Ministry of Education, Culture, Sports, Science, and Technology) for sex education. It doesn't touch on homosexuality at all. Then I heard about a group of teachers who belonged to Sei-Kyo-Kyo, a private organization that supports research and education on human sexuality and gender bias. They were educating students about homosexuality. Founded in 1982, Sei-Kyo-Kyo provides workshops and teaching materials that help teachers to help students make choices about their sexuality and social lives that are informed by scientific fact and human rights. Since 2001 it has published research articles, lesson plans, and other resources for educators in its journal, *Sexuality.*

I met Naohide Yamamoto, the president of Sei-Kyo-Kyo, in 1995 when the Fuchu Youth House incident became a court case. Young members of Occur, a national gay rights organization, were refused the use of a public educational institution, and in response Occur sued the Tokyo Metropolitan Government. Mr. Yamamoto testified before the court for the justification of gay rights. He pointed out that it is necessary to include gay issues in education and that the decision of the Tokyo Metropolitan Board of Education lacked credibility from the viewpoint of human rights; Occur won the case.

Mr. Yamamoto was an inspiration to me. When he asked me to be a board member of Sei-Kyo-Kyo, I was hesitant because I was still a university student, but I did become a member and engaged in educational research. I visited many schools and met various teachers who actively carried out education on gay issues. Moreover, I met a group of gay and lesbian teachers who have included gay sexuality in their curricula. It was the first such group established in Japan.

I think gay teachers should come out in order to point out problems in education and to introduce different viewpoints about sexual diversity that are missing in sexuality education. But because of persistent heterosexism and homophobic conditions in Japan, nobody wants to come out as a gay teacher. Even teachers in the Sei-Kyo-Kyo circle did not want to reveal their names because of the fear of revealing their gayness publicly.

With Mr. Yamamoto's support, I came out at Sei-Kyo-Kyo and became the chair of gay and lesbian issues. It was Mr. Yamamoto who introduced a teaching job to me in the 1997 academic year. One day he said, "Sugiyama-san, why don't you teach at J High School? That will make your dream come true, won't it?" I went to the school and took an exam and had an interview. Later I learned that my sexuality became a topic of discussion. Some teachers supported me, saying, "It's no problem that he's gay. We should evaluate his personality, his teaching skills, and his ideas for the position." I also knew that Yamamoto recommended me strongly, saying that I am a good person and that I have a firm viewpoint on sexuality education.

I got the job.

A Rookie High School Teacher

From April 1998 until March 1999 I taught home economics and health at M High School and was an assistant classroom teacher for second-year students. This high school was exceptional in many ways, and working there changed my expectations as a teacher. Unlike most Japanese public schools, students at M High School called their teachers "Mr." or "Ms." with their surnames instead of the traditional and much more formal way of referring to teachers as *sensei* with their surnames. In many schools, students rise and bow at the beginning of classes following a teacher's or head student's call; this emphasizes the authority of teachers and the hierarchy at school. M High School didn't use this ritual, which indicates clearly that both teachers and students were considered equal human beings.

But there was a downside to the informal atmosphere. During the cleanup period, no students showed up, so the classroom teacher and I always had to clean our classroom. (In the Japanese school system, except at university, students are expected to clean the entire school.) Many students said they were free to decide whether or not they would attend homeroom sessions and their classes. Although there were 40 students registered for the class, at first there were typically only five or six students in the morning homeroom session and only two or three students in the math class. If 20 students attended a class, it was evaluated as "excellent." Over time, I came to have 30 students consistently in my classes.

In my school, teachers were able to make lesson plans freely on their own. I was able to cover more topics in my sex education lessons in one year than most teachers cover in 10. In Japanese public schools it is usually very difficult for teachers to include their own ideas in sex education courses due to governmental guidelines, which they are expected to follow. I organized my lessons around three key points: "The Structure of Human Bodies," "What Is Love?," and "Society and Sexual Diversity." In the second section I introduced gay issues. I used a love letter—written by a boy who fell in love with a same-sex classmate—as an introduction, and I asked the question, "Who you think wrote this letter?" I continued, "I know him. He's a teacher now."

"I don't know who he is," a student said.

"This person is *me*."

I had come out. I felt all of my students looking at me. I then talked about the difficulty of being gay. I hoped that they would understand being gay as a familiar and normal existence.

I was glad about my coming-out. Students gradually accepted the fact that I was gay and naturally connected with me. I was very happy that I could talk freely with students about myself and even about my then-boyfriend, who lived in Osaka. I told them that the long-distance relationship was hard. When I went to the Kansai area once a month to prepare my application for graduate school, some students said, "Sugiyama-san, you'll get to see your boyfriend, won't you?"

After my coming-out, a student handed me a letter and said, "Sugiyama-san, please read this," and ran away. It was filled with her struggles, experiences, and sufferings as a lesbian. I could feel her pain through her writing. Some other students secretly came to my office to talk with me. I helped them as much as I could, and I became more confident about myself.

Closeted Teachers

My position as a gay teacher who came out publicly is an extreme rarity in Japan. I soon noticed there were three other gay teachers at the school. One of them revealed his orientation to me; eventually two others revealed came out to me secretly, or we ran into one another in Tokyo's Shinjuku Ni-chome district, where many gay bars are located. We started getting together secretly and going to Shinjuku Ni-chome to socialize.

However, none of the three ever came out at school. In fact, they sometimes tried to avoid meeting me at school because they feared people would suspect they were gay if they were seen being friendly to me.

One evening one of the closeted teachers called me on my cell phone and said, "Sugiyama-san, I'm at a gay bar in Shinjuku Ni-chome, and I ran into one of your students here. He's sitting with an *oji-san*." (*Oji-san* literally means an uncle or a middle-age man, but in the right context it is widely understood to be a man who sexually exploits teenagers.) He continued, "We pretended that we didn't know each other."

I talked with the closeted teachers about this student, who was in my homeroom. I was shocked that he'd elected to go to a gay bar with an *oji-san*. I was even more shocked when one of the teachers said, "We have to do it," by which he meant that a young gay person must be invited by an *oji-san* to experience gay sex for the first time.

I was very angry with their attitude. Did they take it for granted that a young gay man's first sexual experience would be that he gets molested by an older man, and that we as gay people have no other choices? Why would a gay teacher say something like that without thinking about his student's feelings? Then I remembered that a researcher had said that closeted gay teachers intentionally keep their distance from gay students.

After that I gradually distanced myself from the closeted teachers. I realized that gay teachers would not necessarily be on my side. It was extremely difficult for me to share my thoughts and work with them for the good of our students. They did not face their own situations, were narrow-minded, and were not working to establish better conditions for gay youth. A year later I resigned from the school to enter graduate school.

Despite these bizarre experiences I generally built very good relationships with teachers, students, and parents. I hid nothing and faced the students seriously and honestly, and I think this won their hearts. I also think my course made an impression on students. It was very significant for me to have examined human sexuality by supervising classes and conducting lessons. Teaching school as a gay person was a great encouragement for me.

Where I Am Now

Through my experiences, accepting myself as gay, establishing friendships with other gay youth, having a boyfriend, and teaching sex education at school, I arrived at a positive gay lifestyle. Gay issues are not visible in sex education in Japan. Education is based on heterosexuality. Although many people say, "We are very tolerant of homosexuality in Japan," in practice homosexuality is thoroughly ignored rather than tolerated. Gay issues are not clearly included in governmental education guidelines, so most schools and teachers do not render them seriously as a topic in their courses. Students, however, learn about gay issues outside of classes through friends, teachers, and the media, which usually contains negative and humiliating portrayals.

I am confident in stating my position in favor of inclusive sex education, especially because I do not want other gay students to experience adolescent loneliness in high school as I did. Nowadays, I work for Sei-Kyo-Kyo as chairman of the gay and lesbian issues section, basically as a volunteer. I give lectures at schools or at meetings and write essays for books and magazines, as well as modeling lessons for curricula. In Japan, sex education that includes gay sexuality is gradually spreading. For example, gay issues were introduced in a home economics textbook for high schools in 2003.

I sometimes wonder what the three closeted teachers I worked with are doing now. I look forward to a time when they can act naturally and live ordinarily as gay teachers in public. That day will be a milestone for liberation in the country's educational system.

The author truly appreciates the advice from Keiko Ofuji in writing this essay.

IT'S BETTER TO LEAD
THAN TO FOLLOW

Bart Birdsall
Media specialist
Greco Middle School
Temple Terrace, Florida

If someone had told me six years ago that I would become one of the "leaders" in the Tampa Bay LGBT community, I probably would have laughed in that person's face. I've always viewed myself as a follower.

As the "baby" in my family, I have always had people taking care of me. My earliest memory is of my sister holding my hand on the way to first grade. I followed. I did not lead.

In the 1980s and '90s I was busy partying both in Europe and the United States at schools and universities. Surrounded by liberal Europeans and out to my family and friends, I felt no reason to fight for my rights. "Being gay is not my whole life," I once told a friend.

I was content to let others lead the way. I followed.

Then my sister died, and the bottom fell out of my life. I wanted to die. Needing a change in life, I discontinued my literature and language studies and enrolled in my school's college of education.

Suddenly, after years of being out to everyone, I found myself going back into the closet. *How "out" can I be as a teacher?* I asked myself. Professors, other students, and, later, GLSEN Tampa members could not help me with that answer.

I realized I had to create my own answer to that question. I decided even having to keep my mouth shut about my life was unjust. Having to keep quiet made me angry. I suppose this realization was the first time discrimination slapped me in the face.

Step by step, I came back out. I told teachers at my school. I became cochair of GLSEN Tampa and joined the Safe Schools Coalition of Hillsborough County. At the request of the Safe Schools Coalition, I called school board members to set up appointments to discuss the harassment of and discrimination against LGBT youth. I can still remember my nervousness at calling my "bosses" and asking for an appointment. Eventually, I met with every school board member. We took students with us to tell their stories. Each meeting made me braver. When I found the administration prevented a student from forming a GSA, I spoke with the assistant principal in charge of clubs. When I could not get her to agree to allow the GSA, I went above her head to the assistant superintendent. As a result of meeting with the assistant principal, the school allowed the GSA to form.

In addition, the principal placed me on the school district's Antibullying Committee. On the committee I have lobbied hard for and achieved the inclusion of "sexual orientation" and "gender identity" as protected classes in the sexual harassment policy.

After much difficulty, I will perform a teacher training on LGBT issue in the upcoming school year. Throughout my activist work in the schools, I have made a couple of enemies but many more friends. I realized that helping make schools safer for LGBT youth would empower both students and teachers of the future to take a stand. I didn't want even one more person feeling it was necessary to "shut up" about his or her life.

I selfishly went into this volunteer work to find answers, to find job protection for myself. I looked for a leader to give me answers, but I had to find my own: not to be afraid, to do the right thing, and to do what I believe in.

On a personal note, I grew up believing that when people found out who the true Bart was, they would reject me, hate me, and be disgusted. Since I've come out and become an activist, I have found more people liking—even loving—me than ever before. And when I see the courage of LGBT youth starting gay-straight alliances at their schools, I think, "This is why I continue to work on this issue!" To see the youth starting to take over the leadership is thrilling.

What is strange is feeling that leading is even better than following. Following is full of questions and fear. Leading is full of answers and empowerment.

WHERE I'M FROM

Jan M. Goodman
Teacher
King Middle School
Berkeley, California

I'm not from TV
Where families stay together,
Mothers kiss their children goodbye
And give them a lunch as they go to school
I am from my secret place
Where mothers hurt you and then they leave
Without worrying about your school lunch, or a kiss.

I'm not from the world of Christmas
Where families wake up to rooms of presents
And sing carols at midnight mass.
I am from my hidden Jewish self
Whose traditions died with my grandparents
Until I cooked matzo ball soup at age 25.

I am not from the world of fairy tales
Where princesses wait for princes
Or transform frogs into handsome husbands.
I am from real life
Where classmates tease and hurt
And there are many ways to live and love.

I am not from ancestors who "founded" this country.
I am from dislocation,
From grandparents who escaped persecution in Europe
To seek American streets lined with gold
And made a life for themselves, despite anti-Semitism.
I am from sights, tastes, and advice
"Always wear clean underwear in case you're in an accident"
"Girls can't play baseball"
"Be who you are" but "Do you have to dress *that* way?"

I am from fitting in and being shut out
From schools where teachers and students looked like me,
and spoke my language
But did not understand my pain
Where there was always enough food, but few vacations
Where policemen pulled over the cars of darker-skinned people
And let me pass by
Yet people yelled "*dyke*" when I held my lover's hand.

I am from a world of contradictions
Where I must sort through confusion
To finally arrive at
Where
I
Am
From

I wrote "Where I'm From" during the second week of my English–American history class at King Middle School in Berkeley, California. To begin the school year, the eighth graders and I explored our racial, cultural, and family identities through brainstorming, discussion, and writing of "Where I'm From" poems (an exercise from *Reading, Writing and Rising Up: Teaching About Social Justice and the Power of the Written Word* by Linda Christensen). Mine was carefully crafted to express the fact that lesbianism was central to my view of myself but not the totality of my existence. I needed my students to know that I too have struggled through pain and confusion to become the person I am today. By coming out as a lesbian, a Jew, an abused child, and an antiracist white woman, I gave my students permission to be who they are, acknowledge privilege, and receive respect for all parts of themselves. This set the tone for the entire school year.

Next year will be my 30th as an educator. I've worked as a teacher from preschool to adult education, an elementary school principal, a consultant, mentor, curriculum developer, researcher, and writer, in progressive and conservative communities, on the east and west coasts of the United States, in the public and private sectors. In every setting, my lesbian identity and pride has been an integral part of my public persona.

As I look back on three decades, there have been challenging, frightening, heartbreaking, humorous, and joyous moments. It's never been easy. I came out and began my teaching career in the early 1970s, when lesbians were invisible in society and a shameful element of the feminist movement. My family and friends needed considerable education to become, ultimately, supportive. There were times when I was the only lesbian administrator in a conservative school district or the only gay teacher in a school. In defense I developed what I call the "Supreme Court Syndrome." I reasoned that I would have to be twice as good as a heterosexual teacher (or administrator) in order to protect myself from anyone who would attempt to challenge my competency on the basis of my sexual orientation. If I were an exemplary teacher, then I could survive any challenge to my right to teach, even up to the highest court.

The "Supreme Court Syndrome" has given me the strength to fight back in a myriad of situations where I've been targeted by homophobia. Despite the challenges, I don't regret a single time that I came out to students, teachers, parents, guardians, community members, or the media. I don't see myself as a heroine; I just did what I had to do when it had to be done. I took advantage of teachable moments and created them when they didn't exist. I refused to cut out a part of my heart-soul-identity and store it in a closet. In doing this, I became a role model and supportive resource for children of all sexual orientations, kids from gay-parented families, LGBT staff members, and other people whose lives I touched, professionally and personally. As I reflect on this three-decade journey as an educator, there are many lessons to share.

Lesson 1: Take risks to move out of your comfort zone. Understandably, the biggest factor that keeps us from coming out is fear, both real and imagined. Every time I identify as a lesbian, I open myself up to struggle and possible repercussions. However, most often, I have found unexpected support.

I remember my first year as a principal in a conservative school district south of Oakland, California. As I set up my office, I unpacked the photograph of my lover and moved it to several places in the room, eventually choosing to display it strategically on my desk, facing me. Visitors would have to go behind my chair to see it. On Mondays, when discussions among the staff inevitably centered on husbands, wives, or church sermons, I was unusually reticent. After I had gained the respect of the community, I opened up to colleagues, many staff members, and some parents—and I put the photograph in a more prominent place. Later that year the school secretary told me, "I never knew a lesbian until you came to school. I always thought lesbians were sinful people, but you are wonderful. Now I'm confused, but I think that's a good thing." In June, I was interviewed by a television reporter during the Gay Freedom Day Parade. The caption read JAN GOODMAN, LESBIAN EDU-CATOR. The next morning, the custodian greeted me, "Hey! I saw you on channel 4 last night. I was real proud of you!" I can still remember the unexpected hug that followed.

During my first year as principal in Berkeley, I arrived at school one morning and was greeted by two concerned staff members. "We need you to see some disturbing graffiti," they said. "We'll go with you." As we approached the back of the school, I looked at the wall facing the playground and saw, spray-painted in large, black letters, THE PRINCIPAL IS A FAG! I first felt a great deal of fear for my own safety. The elementary school students and teachers would arrive in 15 minutes; I had to think quickly to decide how to deal with the situation.

I was extremely vulnerable and uncomfortable. My first instinct was to remove the problem, to protect myself. I spoke with the custodian, who sympathetically awaited my instructions. "Please find some paint to cover the words," I said, but then hesitated. "On second thought, cover the wall with butcher paper. This is a hate crime, and I'm going to report it." I wrote a note to the teachers about the graffiti so they would know why the wall was covered. Then, I went into my office and dialed the Berkeley Police Department. Later in the day, when the students were all in their classrooms, the police arrived to photograph the message. Throughout the day, I was approached by supportive and nurturing staff members, parents, and guardians, and I received many warm embraces. I had moved out of my comfort zone to confront homophobia head-on, and this felt good to me.

Lesson 2: Remember that you are not alone. It is incredibly alienating to feel that that burden of reeducation is solely on our shoulders; however, that is rarely the case. There are many heterosexual people who are anxious to support LGBTQ colleagues but don't know what to do; they need our assistance to figure out what steps to take. As an out lesbian, I open myself up to new allies in the fight against homophobia.

In my first year at middle school, I planned a social living class with Patty, a teacher who was also new at King. We agreed to include a range of social justice issues and created a one-week model on same-gender relationships. Although the topic was relatively unfamiliar to Patty, she was eager to be a model of a heterosexual woman who confronted antigay stereotypes even though these misconceptions were not directed at her. Patty's willingness to take on the curriculum defied the common middle school stereotype that anyone who talks respectfully about LGBT people must be gay herself.

Presently, I work closely with Victoria, an eighth grade humanities teacher. Married, with a daughter in our school, Victoria is my number 1 ally at King and a good friend. Last year, our school had a Day of Silence, when all LGBT people and allies did not speak. Rather than remain silent, Victoria came into my classroom and told my students why it is important for her, and all heterosexuals, to stand in solidarity with gay people in our struggles for equality. She also gave the same message to all of her classes. When we designed a project on "Unsung Heroes," Victoria helped find LGBT people to include in the students' research choices; she also consistently shares current events that connect to gay issues and writings by LGBT youth.

Lesson 3: Take advantage of teachable moments. There are countless times when I reflect back on a situation and think, "If only I'd..." These teachable moments are opportunities to confront and address homophobia, make a commitment to recognize and respond to it, and then share my strategies with colleagues. As a preschool teacher, I discovered that homophobia is learned at an early age. One day, I was approached by a group of 3- and 4-year-olds, who appealed to me, "Jan, please help us! We're playing Sleeping Beauty, and we don't have anyone to be the prince and wake her up. We asked every single boy at school and they all said no! Can you be the Prince?"

"I can't be the prince," I replied. "I'm a woman and a prince is a man. But I can be the princess and wake up Sleeping Beauty!"

"*No way!*" the girls insisted. "A princess can't kiss Sleeping Beauty. Now, what are we going to do?" The girls huddled in a corner of the room to solve the problem. After a few moments, they came to me and said, "We decided that it's OK for you to wake up Sleeping Beauty. It doesn't have to be a prince!"

Teachable moments occur every day, during class discussions, staff meetings, parent or guardian conferences, in hallways, PE locker rooms, on the playground, with our children, and in the community. Whenever I hear a student use the word *faggot,* I now find it easy to intervene and say, "That offends me." The other day I approached a group of students who were shouting "That's so gay!" to one another. Their response was, "It's not an insult." I then asked them to name a time when they said "That's so gay" to describe something positive that had happened. "I can't think of one," the students replied, and then added, "Oh…now I get it. Sorry." Teachable moments occur every day; don't pass them up.

Lesson 4: It's about safety, not morality. Keep in mind that students of all sexual orientations can not learn in school environments where homophobia, racism, or other forms of oppression are tolerated. Every educator would agree that safe schools respect the rights of all students. Contrary to the beliefs of fundamentalists, the issue only becomes a "moral" one when schools fail to protect students who are misunderstood, ostracized, and harassed by others. It is a moral issue when an at-risk population is systematically excluded from representation and resources in the educational system.

To emphasize the issue of safety, I worked with the Associate Superintendent for Curriculum and Instruction to bring the exhibit "Love Makes A Family" to our school district. The exhibit (available from Family Diversity Projects, www.familydiv.org) features photographs of families with LGBT parents and interviews with the members of each family, at elementary and adult reading levels. For a month, the photographs were set up in various schools throughout the district, and principals were asked to send all classes to tour the exhibit. I conducted a workshop for principal-teacher teams from each school to help them respond sensitively to the exhibit. There was some resistance: Not all classes attended; a teacher brought her kindergartners to the exhibit but did not mention the word *gay;* some teachers refused to take their students; homophobic responses to the exhibit were not always confronted. However, thousands of students in grades K–12 learned that there are many ways to live and love, and children from gay-parented families found validation in the photos and stories. If that's not safety, what is?

Lesson 5: When you're out, you can become a resource and role model for others. As a visible lesbian in the school system, I have become an unofficial contact person for students, teachers, administrators, and parents who are dealing with sexual orientation issues within and beyond the classroom. In our middle school, students are more likely to take the risk to come out as gay, lesbian, bisexual, or transgender because they know that there are positive, supportive role models on-site; I am honored to be one of them.

I often get calls from teachers who have come out, or administrators who want to support a gay teacher, parent, or guardian but are unsure of what steps to take. In our district, principals may face resistance from a small but vocal group of parents who request a class change for their child after a teacher comes out. I help administrators recognize their responsibility to enforce our district's nondiscrimination policy—which includes sexual orientation—and our commitment to include LGBT issues as part of the curriculum. Therefore, any classroom in Berkeley should address these issues, so moving a child from one class to another will not make a difference. These interventions are never a burden; they are a step to change the cycle of oppression that makes schools unsafe for all students, and in some cases they save lives.

Lesson 6: Turn anger into action. In a homophobic world I am assaulted by negative messages that injure a core element of my identity. I have been told that LGBT people are unfit to teach children, that family diversity discussions should not include gay-parented families, that homosexuality is a moral issue and should be omitted from the sex education curriculum. This makes me justifiably angry, but if I let my anger disempower me, I become immobilized.

During my early years as a principal, I worked with a teacher who had applied for my job and resented the fact that she did not get it. She became increasingly confrontational at staff meetings and consistently challenged my authority. When I responded calmly and continued to treat her with respect, she planned the ultimate act of revenge. During the spring Open House, she circulated a false rumor among staff and parents that I was having an affair with a female teacher at the school. When this divisive lie reached my office by the end of the evening, I was enraged. For a moment I was consumed by anger, unable to fight back.

After quite a while I calmed down and found my pride; it had been obscured by the rage and hurt. I called Essie, a heterosexual ally and principal who was friends with my accuser; she agreed to advise the teacher to stop the rumor. "I'll talk to her, and don't you worry, she will stop," she reassured me, but that wasn't enough.

Although I trusted Essie to keep her word, I made an appointment with Ron, the personnel director, the following morning. "I need you to know that last night, Mrs. C. told a number of parents and staff that I am a 'lesbian agitator from San Francisco' and am having an affair with a female teacher on our staff."

Ron delicately inquired, "Is it true?"

"That is not the point," I replied. "But I will answer your question. The rumor is only partly true. I am a lesbian—many people in the school already know that I am gay—and I am active politically in the gay community. However, I am not an agitator, I do not live in San Francisco, and I am not having an affair with a staff member. With all due respect, what are you going to do about it?"

"As long as you're not having an affair," he said, "there's nothing to worry about."

I felt my anger rise again, and struggled to remain calm. "Ron," I emphasized, "First of all, it is your responsibility to stop sexual harassment in this district. This teacher's goal is to jeopardize my job as principal. I need you to know that if you don't intervene and Mrs. C. succeeds, I will not be fired or told to discretely leave the district; I will publicly and loudly fight for my right to stay. I also want to point out that just a few years ago, the male principal of Elm School married a female teacher who worked for him at his site for many years. Was that a problem for the district?"

Ron looked at me, recognizing the district's double standard and his responsibility as a personnel director. "OK, Jan. You're right," he conceded. "I'll take care of this." As I rose to leave the office, Ron awkwardly put his hand on my shoulder and said, "I've never had a—a—situation like this before, but I'll deal with it."

I'm not sure what occurred, but the rumors stopped and Mrs. C. discreetly retired that summer. My anger had turned into action; the district was forced to look at inequities in its policies; and I emerged from the situation with a newfound pride.

Lesson 7: Some battles are not worth fighting. It's important to choose your issues; otherwise you will burn out as an activist. When I was a principal in Berkeley, our PTA sponsored a workshop about how to address sexual orientation issues at the elementary school level. The library was overflowing with concerned staff members, parents, and guardians, including several deeply religious teachers who attended church in the school community. Most everyone wanted to find strategies to confront homophobia or create an inclusive curriculum. At the end of the workshop, I expressed how wonderful it felt, as a principal and as a lesbian, to see so many staff and community members at the event. The night was a high point in my career; unfortunately, it was followed by a low point.

On the day after the workshop, it was time for my weekly lunch date with a struggling student. He came to my office and said that his grandma told him that he couldn't have lunch with me anymore because I was gay, and that the preacher at church says that being gay is a sin. That same day, his grandma put a beautiful card in my mailbox with a message that God could show me the right way. In it were a variety of Bible quotes about homosexual sex. I was deeply saddened, particularly because the child would lose a source of significant support. At the same time, I realized that there was nothing that I could say or do to change his grandma's opinion of me. I had to let go of it. The lesson: It is important to save your energy for the fights that can be won.

Lesson 8: Struggle against all forms of oppression in schools. In many ways, my oppression as a lesbian has given me the strength and empathy to fight against all forms of injustice in schools. In my commitment to make schools safe for students, staff, and community members of all sexual orientations, I find it impossible to ignore that many students and adults, including those who are LGBT, are marginalized, disrespected, misunderstood, and disempowered, mirroring the inequities in our larger society. From the first week's "Where I'm From" poem to the last day of school, my students know that I will work for fairness and equity for all people, including children. I consciously teach my students that LGBT people have made significant contributions to U.S. history, and at the same time that our country was built on the backs of enslaved Africans, dislocated indigenous people, and poor immigrants from Europe and Latin America. When we study the First Amendment as part of a unit on the U.S. Constitution, we read a news article about Karl Debro, a heterosexual teacher who taught about homophobia, was reprimanded by his school district, and won over $1 million in a lawsuit. During the same unit, we look at racial profiling in light of the 14th Amendment and hypothesize as to why no one on Death Row is affluent. My students see me as a teacher, also a lesbian, who looks at all inequities in our society and believes, as we say in our Passover seder, "No one is free if any person is oppressed." Because of this belief, I gain many allies, both teenagers and adults.

Lesson 9: If you respect students, they will be more likely to respect you. Although it is often a challenge, I work hard to create a democratic classroom, where all students have a voice and there is room for discussion and disagreement. I am open to respectful criticism, rarely raise my voice, use inclusive language, and am an advocate for students' rights. I let students know who I am and how I feel. In short, my students know that I respect them, and usually this is what I ultimately receive in return.

During the middle school social living class, half of the curriculum focused on sex education. The question was not whether I would come out to the 90 students during the unit, it was how and when. The issue was particularly compelling because so many teenagers struggle with sexual identity during middle school, when homophobia is at its peak. Patty and I had planned a week to focus on lesbian, gay, bisexual, and transgender identities. We had several videos, some readings from gay youth, and a culminating panel from the local Gay and Lesbian Speakers' Bureau.

After a brief introduction to the unit, I asked my students, "How many of you know someone who is lesbian, gay, bisexual, or transgender?" About half to two thirds of the students raised their hands. "Actually, all of you know someone who is gay," I said calmly. "Your social living teacher is a lesbian." In two of the three classes, students responded with silence, surprise, and some respectful questions. However, my second period's spirited response remains vivid in my mind.

"You're a lesbo," one young man shouted as he fell off his chair. "You don't look like a lesbo. You don't act like a lesbo." A number of students erupted with laughter.

"The word is 'lesbian,'" I corrected, in a friendly and calm manner. "And how does a lesbian look or act?"

"Well, you're nice," he replied, "and you don't dress like a—"

Tameka, a leader in the class, waved her hand in the air. "I got something to say. I don't think it's our business to know if you're a lesbian. That's a private thing. Besides, it's against the Bible. It's unnatural. It's not normal."

"You're right that it's not the norm," I responded. "About 10% of the population is gay or lesbian. That's one out of every 10 people. So…in a class of 30 students, three could grow up to be gay." When a chorus of "Not me" followed, I remained focused.

"You each have to decide whether you will treat 10% of the population with respect, or whether you'll prejudge them in a negative way," I continued. "I'm telling you that I'm a lesbian because I know we care about one another. I also know how important it is for you to feel safe in the world, and I want you to think about whether or not you make the world safer for others."

When the gay speakers arrived at the end of the week, I warned them that my second period class might be disrespectful. However,

I discovered that my coming-out had challenged my students to examine their personal beliefs and actions. As two men and two women sat down, Tameka approached me. "This is your day," she said. "You just sit down in the back of the room and listen to the speakers. I'll take care of the class." Tameka sat in the director's chair with the class participation clipboard and warned the students, "These people deserve your respect. That means no talking during the presentation and no fooling around either," she added, snatching an umbrella that was waved in the air. "If you do, I'm sending you out."

With Tameka in charge, I relaxed and studied my transformed class. They listened respectfully. Their questions were thoughtful and empathetic. "Did you know you were gay in middle school? How did the kids treat you?" "Were you ever physically hurt? Did anyone defend you?" The panel was impressed. So was I.

Lesson 10: Keep up the struggle. In a few weeks, the school year will begin again. My lover will meet her fourth- and fifth-grade students and plan an appropriate time to share her family with them. Our son will start high school and will figure out whether it is safe to let new friends know that his moms are lesbians. Our daughter will leave for college, her first year on her own. My eighth-grade class will write "Where I'm From" poems, and I'll share mine.

As I open the classroom door for my 30th year, I will join LGBTQ educators and our allies as we work to transform a world full of injustice. The task is formidable. It takes courage, perseverance, and commitment. It is impossible to estimate how many attitudes we will change, how many lives we will save. But I know that schools will be safer and more respectful places because of our influence. And isn't that what education is about?

LIVING WITH THE POSSIBILITIES

Ruth Kupfer
English and reading teacher
Lincoln High School
Lincoln, Nebraska

Ten years ago when I wrote the essay "You Can't Tell Him I'm Not" for *One Teacher in 10,* I was excited to have the opportunity to tell a story about a pivotal moment in my teaching life. I had been propelled into disclosing my sexual orientation to my school's administrators when I reported that a student was sexually harassing me. As I wrote about that upsetting treatment and the way it affected me in my classroom, I began to realize that I was also empowered by the outcome of the experience. Finding the courage to speak up in that situation opened the door to a new sense of freedom and purpose in my career as a public school teacher.

Even so, I had a difficult decision to make when it came time for me to decide whether to use my real name or a pseudonym on my submission to *One Teacher in 10.* On one hand, it *was* a story about coming out to my administrators. But my ultimate decision to use a pen name came out of the fear that, without job protection language written into my teaching contract, it was still a possibility that someone would want to rid my district of a teacher who spoke out about her sexual orientation.

In the decade that has passed since then, I have moved from being guarded and apprehensive, weighing my every word and action, to the way I find myself now—unflappable and eminently mindful of my responsibilities to my students and to myself as a lesbian teacher. Finally—now that I am 50!—my lesbian identity is synthesized into the whole of who I am, and I feel completely at ease in the classroom and in my school every day, whether references to sexual orientation arise or not. I wouldn't think of using a pen name for any of my writings now.

The next time I outed myself came when I made two presentations at the National Council of Teachers of English (NCTE) national convention. Each was about what it has meant to me to be a lesbian teacher. These speeches came about as an outgrowth of my Masters work in curriculum and instruction, for which my final project was to write about the intersection of my teacher and lesbian identities. I chose this project deliberately in order to continue the personal development I started when I wrote for *One Teacher in 10*.

Through writing my narrative project and making those presentations at NCTE, I explored the juncture of my professional and sexual identities from several angles. I investigated what it means for me to work with students who are straight as well as those who are questioning or openly gay or lesbian, and in the process I examined the implications of my position as a teacher who was working through the stages of a personal lesbian identity. Taking that story to a national audience at the conventions and in publication represented a risk I was ready to take on a journey from which turning back was no longer an option.

As it has turned out, that journey contained a series of experiences and circumstances that have brought me to this self-assured stage in my identity. Of these, one notable factor in my growth has been the climate at my school—one in which difference is valued and nurtured. If these qualities were not prevalent in my work setting, I am sure that it would be much more difficult to feel as safe as I do about being openly lesbian.

My school is a public high school serving close to 2,000 students in Lincoln, Nebraska's capital city, and the kids who attend it represent all racial and socioeconomic groups. We also have many students who have emigrated from other countries and are English-language learners, and like many schools our kids often identify with various social subgroups, like the goths or jocks or preps. There seems to be a place for everyone to fit in there, no matter what their background is or how they identify themselves. Our school's educational goals include preparing students to live and work with others who are different and teaching them to value those differences. These expectations help create an environment in which a person's sexual orientation is one of many characteristics that define her or him.

I would like to say that everyone at my school—staff and students—is gay-positive, but I can't. There are still some staff members who believe that anything having to do with lesbian, gay, bisexual, and transgender concerns—whether curriculum or policy-related—represents an immoral influence that doesn't belong in public schools. A couple of years ago a teacher at my school wrote a letter to our principal protesting the school's sanctioning of the now-traditional Pride Prom event in the spring. Pride Prom is a yearly highlight of the activities of the Gay-Bisexual-Transgender-Straight Alliance (GLBTSA) groups in each of the six high schools in Lincoln. They come together at a dance at which everyone can feel welcomed, regardless of how they identify or who they bring as a date. One of the posters advertising the event contained a picture of two men in tuxedos, one behind the other with his arms around his partner, and the teacher wrote in his letter that he felt this was an inappropriate image to have posted in our hallways. He continued, saying that the Pride Prom was a dangerous event because it sanctioned same-sex sexual activity, and that in doing so it would promote the spread of HIV. To reinforce his point, he attached statistics from an Internet site about the numbers of HIV infections and deaths from AIDS.

The other club sponsors and I also received copies of the letter, and when I read mine I was furious. It took me about 10 seconds to stomp to the principal's office to demand that he let that teacher

know in no uncertain terms that Pride Prom would go on as scheduled and that his notions about HIV and AIDS—as well as LGBT
youth—were riddled with dangerous misconceptions. The principal
listened carefully to my concerns; we talked about the best approach
to the teacher's homophobic response; and he incorporated my suggestions into the conversation he had with the letter-writer. Not one
poster came down, and the dance was a roaring success.

Our GLBTSA was founded in 1992—the first to be formed in
the Lincoln area. Since then it has evolved into a club that from
year to year has 70-plus members. It has enabled LGBT and
straight ally students to develop powerful voices that are heard all
over the school. With projects ranging from bringing panels of the
AIDS Project Names Quilt to school to working against the passage
of the state law restricting marriage laws, students have been able
to create a compelling understanding about what it means to be
gay and what the civil rights of LGBT people are. As a result, no
one who goes to our school believes for long that no one they
know is lesbian or gay, and an expectation that their lesbian and
gay friends be treated with respect soon becomes clear among
most of the school's social groups.

As one of the cosponsors of the GLBTSA, I have had the opportunity to engage in amazing conversations with students as they
develop the language and the insight they need to become leaders
in the young queer movement. Having grown up in an era in which
they were able to easily see real lesbians and gay men on TV, read
readily available queer-themed novels, and study gay and lesbian
history in school, they have been able to express their own orientations in ways that are much more authentic and healthy than my
generation was allowed. Interestingly, they have been as much my
role models as I have been theirs: They give me a sense of how to be
adventurous and inquisitive, and I show them that lesbians do grow
up and become vocal, productive community members.

Of course, those changes in the larger cultural climate in the last
40 years have played a part in creating a more comfortable personal

space for me as well. Today I find myself talking with my straight colleagues about queer TV programming and queer rights issues as well as about the joys of life with my partner, Mary, and our typical trials with being homeowners—conversations that make me feel accepted as an equal, and that were unimaginable when I started teaching in 1976. Just a couple of weeks ago, a straight teacher in my department, my friend Joanna, told us to watch a new show she loved, which features five gay men who improve a straight man's appearance and apartment. We took her advice, and *Queer Eye for the Straight Guy* quickly became one of our favorites.

This collegial acceptance has been crucial for me in sustaining my confidence as a teacher-leader. The backing of ally teachers was manifest this past year when a concern was raised about the use of the term "queer" in the title of our GLBTSA's newsletter, which the club members named "Queer Times." The newsletter is delivered via the mailboxes of teachers who are expected to distribute them to club members in their classes, and a couple of teachers peeked at the contents and discovered this title. They refused to distribute the newsletters and raised strong concerns about the term with our principal, who in turn brought the issue to the Principal's Advisory Council.

Another GLBTSA sponsor and I were invited to that meeting to address questions about the use of the term *queer,* and we explained how it has been transformed from its pejorative connotation to one that is inclusive of the wide range of diversity present within the LGBT community. We gave examples of ways the term is used by universities to name courses, by journalists in mainstream publications, and especially by those who are part of the young LGBT movement to express the limitless arena of self-expression they explore.

One teacher in the meeting suggested that students would not be able to discern the difference between derogatory and positive uses of *queer.* Two of my straight colleagues in the English department spoke up to say that they were confident that their standards for behavior would enable students to distinguish the difference, and they defended the club members' use of the word. That these individuals didn't defer to me or the other sponsor (a gay man) to address the concern meant not only that they had done their homework thinking about LGBT issues, but it also suggested that they saw these issues as ones about which they *should* educate themselves.

Even more crucial than the support of straight colleagues is the bonds I have created with other queer teachers. The strongest of these has been with my friend David who teaches at another high school in Lincoln and sponsors the GLBTSA there. The conversations we have about the pitfalls as well as rewards of being queer teachers help me create ways to perceive and approach my work as well as inspire my courage. But more important, they remind me that this is a journey that I undertake together with many other creative and loving people.

These valuable bonds have led me into yet another stage in my identity development, one in which my focus is on actively helping others better understand their responsibilities to LGBT students. So for the past few years David and I have been making presentations to other educators about the importance of making schools safe for LGBT students. Together we have assembled information that we use for these workshops, including facts about the status of LGBT youth in schools, legal responsibilities of educators to ensure a safe environment, and ways that classrooms and hallways can be made welcoming to LGBT students. We also tell pieces of our own stories: David recounts growing up with teasing and harassment from classmates; I tell about how the invisibility of LGBT people and issues during the late 1950s and '60s prevented me from understanding and expressing my sexual orientation.

The comments that workshop participants make during and after our presentations make me feel that the workshops we are leading are enabling other educators to recognize ways in which they can support LGBT students and parents—and to think hard about their personal beliefs and classroom practices. Additionally, I know it is good for me to keep telling my own stories about growing up lesbian and being a lesbian teacher, because it reminds me of the ways my growth has been fostered.

It has been essential for me to have family members who support and push me. My longtime partner, Mary, continually weighs risks with me and urges me to embark on the paths that need to be traveled for the sake of LGBT kids, even if doing so could be somehow perilous. Our goddaughter is a young Latina college student with whom we talk at length about the racism and discrimination present in her experiences. Her unflinching ability to speak up to those who are biased toward her is a constant inspiration for me. Both women provide me with perspectives that help me to understand what I need to do and how I should do it, as well as always assuring me a safe and loving home in which I can revitalize my energies for this work.

When I think about the life I've been able to build as an openly lesbian teacher here in Lincoln, Nebraska—a city of only 250,000 people in the Midwest—I become amazed. But then I remind myself that it's all the result of intensive efforts—my own and those of valued friends and family—and that if it's possible to be an activist lesbian teacher here, it's possible all over this country. I just took that first step, and kept moving, and found that the rewards always overshadowed the risks.

ABOUT THE CONTRIBUTORS

Tarah Ausburn currently teaches high school English at South Pointe Charter High School in Phoenix, Arizona. She spends her free time dodging her students who have snuck into the city's queer nightlife, frolicking in an estrogen-laced household of four womyn and their cats, and creating slogans that could one day be another bumper sticker for her car.

Bonnie Beach was a teacher, coach, and department head at New Trier Township High School for 35 years. She is retired and—with her partner, Pam—does consultation work in educational diversity. They live in Estes Park, Colorado.

Bart Birdsall has been a middle school teacher for seven years. For five years he taught language arts and reading. Currently he is a media specialist. He lives with his partner, Tim Garren, in Tampa, Florida.

Clarence Brooks, after 18 years as a professional dancer, is enjoying his sixth year as a dance instructor at Bak Middle School of the Arts in West Palm Beach, Florida, where he teaches ballet, modern, and jazz dance to sixth-, seventh-, and eighth-graders.

Steven Click retired from teaching in 1997 and moved to the central coast of California to live with his architect partner, Dana. Steve is working on his artistic talents, volunteers in a few LGBTQ groups, and is sometimes a "guest teacher" (substitute) in the local schools.

Kathleen Crawford has taught both middle and high school in a variety of content areas for over 19 years, in public and Catholic schools. She is currently teaching math at Highland Middle School, with an eye on future writing, consulting, and training opportunities. Kat and her partner, Cindi, live in Louisville, Kentucky, with three teenagers, Ellie, Anna, and Joe.

Brian Davis has survived nine years as a middle school teacher. He enjoys blending language arts and social studies into a seamless whole for eighth graders in San Francisco, where he lives with his husband (the law be damned!) and two overweight cats. He is actively involved in Marriage Equality California (MECA) and urges his students to get involved in whatever issue they care about and to fight hard until they win.

Mike Fishback teaches language arts and social studies at the Park School of Baltimore and cosponsors its middle-school gay-straight alliance. He is a 2001 graduate of Yale University, where he majored in political science.

Joel M. Freedman (jmfreedman145@yahoo.com) currently coordinates drama and teaches English literature and composition classes at King/Drew Magnet High School in Los Angeles. A former actor and director, he has been married 20 years to Mike Player, the founder of the improv sketch comedy group the Gay Mafia.

Michael Fridgen, a graduate of the University of Minnesota, Duluth, is the music specialist at Pinecrest Elementary in Hastings, Minnesota. After school he operates a small studio of private voice and piano students.

Randall Furash-Stewart has been in love with teaching ever since his first job when he was 15 as a peer health educator at the Washington, DC nonprofit Advocates for Youth. He graduated from Hampshire College in Amherst, Massachusetts.

Sheridan Gold has been teaching at-risk youth for the last 12 years. She also presents workshops to educators about breaking teacher silence around homophobia. She recently married her partner of 26 years, Dianna; they live in Sonoma County, California.

Jan M. Goodman has worked as an educator for 30 years, most recently at King Middle School in Berkeley, California. In addition to teaching, she coordinates beginning and veteran teacher support for Berkeley Unified and works for the Berkeley Federation of Teachers. She is the founder of the Lesbian, Gay, Bisexual, Transgender, and Allied Issues in Education Network for the Association for Supervision and Curriculum Development (ASCD). Jan lives in Oakland, California with her partner, Maggie, and their two children, Ali and Niki.

Julia Haines, MM, CMT, educator, music therapist, multi-instrumentalist, and composer, has designed and implemented music therapy programs over the past 20 years. She works at Stratford Friends School, a Quaker school for students with learning differences, and shares her life with her beloved, Rosanne, in Philadelphia, Pennsylvania.

Mary Gay Hutcherson, LCSW, has been a school social worker for 18 years. She is currently retired and living with her partner, Yolanda Farnum, and their four Pomeranians in Chesterfield, Virginia, where they are activists for gay rights and social justice. She is the organizer of Virginia Rainbow Rivers and the editor of Richmond Lesbian Feminists Newsletter Online, and she was the leader of the Marriage Equality Action that received press coverage nationwide.

Chip James has been a school social worker for 15 years. He is a consultant for CANDLE (Community Awareness Network for a Drug-free Life and Environment) and the American Psychological Association, providing professional development on LGBTQ youth issues. He is cofacilitator for TRUST, a psychoeducational support group for LGBTQ teens, and he has a psychotherapy practice in Nyack, New York, where he lives.

Elizabeth Katz teaches in the English department at Phillips Exeter Academy in Exeter, New Hampshire, where she lives in a dorm and is an adviser to the gay-straight alliance. She has been teaching for three years and has worked with GSAs since she was in high school.

Ayana Kee loves teaching, writing, and dancing. She received her BA from Duke University in 1994 and her MS from the University of Oregon in 1998. Ayana began teaching in elementary schools in 1994. In addition, she enjoys working with other teachers and is an instructor for education courses at a local college. She lives with her wife, Shanti Smalls, in Brooklyn, New York.

Judee King was a second-generation San Franciscan who credited her love of writing to growing up in this enchanting city of Golden Gates and cable cars that climb to the stars. Judee worked in the field of education for 26 years—doing everything from facilitating programs for at-risk teens to directing after-school programs—until she succumbed to breast cancer in 2004. She is survived by her loving girlfriend, Dani.

Ruth Kupfer has taught English and reading in public secondary schools for 28 years. She is also currently serving as a cosponsor of the Gay-Lesbian-Bisexual-Transgender-Straight Alliance, which is in its 12th year at her high school. Ruth and her partner, Mary, make their home in Lincoln, Nebraska.

Anafaith Lubliner has been a theater and music teacher for four years. She is also an an actress, writer, vocalist-songwriter, and wild improvisational singer who takes any word from the audience and creates a song on the spot. She lives with her gorgeous drummer-juggler partner, Katrine Spang-Hanssen, in San Francisco. For more information about her music and antics go to anafaith.com.

Cindy Lutenbacher has been a teacher for 18 years. She is currently an assistant professor of English at Morehouse College, where she has taught since 1990. She lives in Atlanta, Georgia, with her two daughters.

Patricia Lyons has been a teacher of religion and ethics for five years. She lives with her partner, Karen, in Alexandria, Virginia.

Jannette Manuel has been a teacher for four years. She is currently teaching family and consumer science courses in the Seattle School District in Seattle, Washington. She is originally from the Philippines and has lived in Seattle for 15 years.

Patricia Nicolari is currently an administrator for the Ansonia High School Alternative Education Program in Ansonia, Connecticut; previously she taught health and physical education in grades K–12 over the past 22 years. She has been on the GLSEN CT Board for the past six years and is actively involved in professional development for faculty in Connecticut schools regarding LGBT issues. She was named 2004 Teacher of the Year in Ansonia.

Richard Ognibene has been a teacher for 18 years. He currently teaches chemistry and physics for Fairport High School. He lives with his partner, Matt Fleig, in Rochester, New York.

Tamar Paull comes from a long line of wonderful teachers. She discovered the treasure of Community Prep School as a student teacher eight years ago and has been teaching English there ever since. She lives in Providence, Rhode Island.

Laura Persichilli has been teaching English for nine years, currently at Smithtown High School in Smithtown, New York. She is president of the Long Island Gay-Straight Educators Association and a member of the Long Island Coalition for Same-Sex Marriage. Laura lives in Riverhead, New York, with her partner.

Bethany Petr has been a teacher for four years. She is a science and computer science teacher in Montgomery County. She lives with her partner, Emily, in Columbia, Maryland.

Irene "Toodie" Ray has taught in public schools for more than 20 years; she is also a codirector of Marshall University's site of the National Writing Project. She has two grown children, Ian and Morgan, and lives with her partner of 10 years, Donna.

Michael J. Record is a native of Fort Lauderdale. For six years, he has taught seventh-grade language arts for Broward County Public Schools, the nation's fifth-largest school system.

Gayle Roberts is an MTF transsexual who transitioned "on the job" in 1996. She was a high school physics and general science teacher for 33 years and a science department head for the past 12 years. She taught in Vancouver, Canada, and at the United World College of Southeast Asia in Singapore. She holds a B.Sc., an M.Sc., and a diploma in teaching. Gayle retired in June 2002 and now lives with her "new sister," Edith, and her mother-in-law just outside Vancouver.

Mike Russell has been a teacher for two years. His students have informed him that he is "so hype" for not dismissing them from the classroom before the scheduled time. In Philadelphia, Pennsylvania, he is currently working on a novel tentatively titled *Storming Arkansas,* is painting his walls to resemble the time tunnels in *Doctor Who,* and is vainly ordering his three spoiled Siamese cats to stop throwing up on the carpet. Against all known laws of the universe, his wonderful man, Andy Matthews, continues to put up with him.

Takashi Sugiyama is a Ph.D. candidate at Yokohama National University and a researcher and lecturer for Sei-Kyo-Kyo, the Council for Education and Study on Human Sexuality in Japan. He taught at a private high school in Saitama Prefecture and was the principle editor of a book titled *Homosexuality and Other Sexuality: How to Teach About Human Rights and Living Together* (Kodomo-no-mirai Publishing, 2002).

Malana Summers has been a middle-school instructor for 24 years. She currently teaches eighth-grade language arts and social science. She lives in Atwater, California, with her partner, Kim, and Tweety, a precocious cockatiel.

Steve Trujillo is a 27-year veteran of public school teaching and counseling. A native Californian, he has been writing for years of the incredible journey of California public education and its metamorphosis.

Roberto Wheaton has been teaching for 20 years and is currently teaching high school science in Southern California, working on his graduate degree, and running marathons.

Josephine Allison Wilson is in her third part-time year of her Ph.D. in gender at the London School of Economics (LSE) Gender Institute. Prior to that, she completed a Masters degree in (just to be original) gender and a Bachelors degree in psychology and philosophy at the LSE. She is also a dancer, drummer, and story-teller who performs regularly in London, where she lives.

Dan Woog is the openly gay head soccer coach at Staples High School in Westport, Connecticut. He is also a writer. His most recent book is *Jocks 2: Coming Out to Play*.

ABOUT THE EDITOR

Kevin Jennings is the founder and executive director of GLSEN (www.GLSEN.org), the Gay, Lesbian, and Straight Education Network, a national education organization working to make schools places where young people learn to value and respect everyone, regardless of sexual orientation or gender identity. The second edition of *One Teacher in Ten* is his fifth book. He lives in New York with his partner, Jeffrey Davis.